ALPHABETICAL LISTING OF PHILOSOPHERS A

Abelard, Peter	1079–1142
Al-Ghazali	1058–1111
Anaxagoras	500–428 B.C.
Anaximander	c. 610–545 B.C.
Anaximenes	c. 580–500 B.C.
Anselm, Saint	1033–1109
Aquinas, Saint Thomas	1225–1274
Aristotle	384–322 B.C.
Augustine, Saint	354–430
Austin, John	1911–1960
Averroës	1126–1198
Avicenna	980–1037
Ayer, A. J.	1910–1989
Bacon, Francis	1561–1626
Beauvoir, Simone de	1908–1986
Bentham, Jeremy	1748–1832
Bergson, Henri	1859–1941
Berkeley, George	1685–1753
Boethius	c. 480–524
Carnap, Rudolph	1891–1970
Comte, Auguste	1798–1857
Copernicus, Nicholas	1473–1543
Darwin, Charles	1809–1882
Democritus	c. 460–360 B.C.
Derrida, Jacques	1930–
Descartes, René	1596–1650
Dewey, John	1859–1952
Dostoevsky, Fyodor	1821–1881
Eckhart, Meister	c. 1260–1327
Einstein, Albert	1879–1955
Empedocles	c. 495–435 B.C.
Engels, Friedrich	1820–1895
Epictetus	c. 50–138
Epicurus	341–270 B.C.
Erasmus, Desiderius	1466–1536
Erigena, John Scotus	c. 810–877
Foucault, Michel	1926–1984
Freud, Sigmund	1856–1939
Galileo	1564–1642
Gorgias	c. 483–375 B.C.
Hegel, Georg W. F.	1770–1831
Heidegger, Martin	1889–1976

Heraclitus	c. 540–480 B.C.
Hobbes, Thomas	1588–1679
Hume, David	1711–1776
Husserl, Edmund	1859–1938
James, William	1842–1910
Kant, Immanuel	1724–1804
Kierkegaard, Søren	1813–1855
Leibniz, Gottfried	1646–1716
Locke, John	1632–1704
Luther, Martin	1483–1546
Maimonides, Moses	1135–1204
Marx, Karl	1818–1883
Mill, John Stuart	1806–1873
Newton, Sir Isaac	1642–1727
Nietzsche, Friedrich	1844–1900
Ockham, William of	c. 1280–1349
Parmenides	c. 515–450 B.C.
Pascal, Blaise	1623–1662
Peirce, Charles S.	1839–1914
Plato	c. 428–348 B.C.
Plotinus	205–270
Protagoras	c. 490–420 B.C.
Pyrrho	c. 360–270 B.C.
Pythagoras	c. 570–495 B.C.
Quine, Willard V. O.	1908–2000
Rorty, Richard	1931–
Rousseau, Jean Jacques	1712–1778
Russell, Bertrand	1872–1970
Ryle, Gilbert	1900–1976
Sartre, Jean-Paul	1905–1980
Schopenhauer, Arthur	1788–1860
Scotus, John Duns	c. 1266–1308
Socrates	c. 470–399 B.C.
Spinoza, Benedict (Baruch)	1632–1677
Thales	624–545 B.C.
Voltaire	1694–1778
Whitehead, Alfred North	1861–1947
Wittgenstein, Ludwig	1889–1951
Xenophanes	c. 570–478 B.C.
Zeno the Eleatic	c. 490–430 B.C.
Zeno the Stoic	c. 336–264 B.C.

CHRONOLOGICAL LIST OF PHILOSOPHERS

THE ANCIENT PERIOD

Thales	c. 624–545	B.C.
Anaximander	c. 610–545	B.C.
Anaximenes	c. 580–500	B.C.
Pythagoras	c. 570–495	B.C.
Xenophanes	c. 570–478	B.C.
Heraclitus	c. 540–480	B.C.
Parmenides	c. 515–450	B.C.
Anaxagoras	500–428	B.C.
Empedocles	c. 495–435	B.C.
Zeno the Eleatic	c. 490–430	B.C.
Protagoras	c. 490–420	B.C.
Gorgias	c. 483–375	B.C.
Socrates	c. 470–399	B.C.
Democritus	c. 460–360	B.C.
Plato	c. 428–348	B.C.
Aristotle	384–322	B.C.
Pyrrho	c. 360–270	B.C.
Epicurus	341–270	B.C.
Zeno the Stoic	c. 336–264	B.C.
Epictetus	c. 50–138	
Plotinus	205–270	

THE MIDDLE AGES

Augustine, Saint	354–430
Boethius	c. 480–524
Erigena, John Scotus	c. 810–877
Anselm, Saint	1033–1109
Avicenna	980–1037
Al-Ghazali	1058–1111
Abelard, Peter	1079–1142
Averroës	1126–1198
Maimonides, Moses	1135–1204
Aquinas, Saint Thomas	1225–1274
Eckhart, Meister	c. 1260–1327
Scotus, John Duns	c. 1266–1308
Ockham, William of	c. 1280–1349

THE MODERN PERIOD

Erasmus, Desiderius	1466–1536
Copernicus, Nicholas	1473–1543
Luther, Martin	1483–1546
Bacon, Francis	1561–1626
Galileo	1564–1642
Hobbes, Thomas	1588–1679
Descartes, René	1596–1650
Pascal, Blaise	1623–1662
Spinoza, Benedict (Baruch)	1632–1677
Locke, John	1632–1704
Newton, Sir Isaac	1642–1727
Leibniz, Gottfried	1646–1716
Berkeley, George	1685–1753
Voltaire	1694–1778
Hume, David	1711–1776
Rousseau, Jean Jacques	1712–1778
Kant, Immanuel	1724–1804
Bentham, Jeremy	1748–1832
Hegel, Georg W. F.	1770–1831
Schopenhauer, Arthur	1788–1860
Comte, Auguste	1798–1857
Mill, John Stuart	1806–1873
Darwin, Charles	1809–1882
Kierkegaard, Søren	1813–1855
Marx, Karl	1818–1883
Engels, Friedrich	1820–1895
Dostoevsky, Fyodor	1821–1881
Nietzsche, Friedrich	1844–1900

THE CONTEMPORARY PERIOD

Peirce, Charles S.	1839–1914
James, William	1842–1910
Freud, Sigmund	1856–1939
Husserl, Edmund	1859–1938
Bergson, Henri	1859–1941
Dewey, John	1859–1952
Whitehead, Alfred North	1861–1947
Russell, Bertrand	1872–1970
Einstein, Albert	1879–1955
Wittgenstein, Ludwig	1889–1951
Heidegger, Martin	1889–1976
Carnap, Rudolph	1891–1970
Ryle, Gilbert	1900–1976
Sartre, Jean-Paul	1905–1980
Beauvoir, Simone de	1908–1986
Quine, Willard V. O.	1908–2000
Ayer, A. J.	1910–1989
Austin, John	1911–1960
Foucault, Michel	1926–1984
Derrida, Jacques	1930–
Rorty, Richard	1931–

THE VOYAGE OF DISCOVERY
A HISTORICAL INTRODUCTION TO PHILOSOPHY

THE ANCIENT VOYAGE
The Greeks and Romans

SECOND EDITION

William F. Lawhead
University of Mississippi

WADSWORTH

THOMSON LEARNING™

Australia • Canada • Mexico • Singapore • Spain
United Kingdom • United States

WADSWORTH
THOMSON LEARNING

Publisher: Eve Howard
Philosophy Editor: Peter Adams
Assistant Editor: Kara Kindstrom
Editorial Assistant: Chalida Anusasananan
Marketing Manager: Dave Garrison
Marketing Assistant: Adam Hofmann
Print/Media Buyer: Barbara Britton
Permissions Editor: Joohee Lee

Production Service: The Book Company
Text Designer: Wendy LaChance
Photo Researcher: Myrna Engler
Copy Editor: Jane Loftus
Cover Designer: Yvo Riezebos
Cover Image: Shinichi Eguchi/Photonica
Compositor: Thompson Type
Cover and Text Printer: R. R. Donnelley, Crawfordsville

Printed in the United States of America
1 2 3 4 5 6 7 05 04 03 02

For permission to use material from this text, contact us by:
Web: http://www.thomsonrights.com
Fax: 1-800-730-2215
Phone: 1-800-730-2214

Wadsworth/Thomson Learning
10 Davis Drive
Belmont, CA 94002-3098
USA

For more information about our products, contact us:
Thomson Learning Academic Resource Center
1-800-423-0563
http://www.wadsworth.com

International Headquarters
Thomson Learning
International Division
290 Harbor Drive, 2nd Floor
Stamford, CT 06902-7477
USA

UK/Europe/Middle East/South Africa
Thomson Learning
Berkshire House
168-173 High Holborn
London WC1V 7AA
United Kingdom

Asia
Thomson Learning
60 Albert Street, #15-01
Albert Complex
Singapore 189969

Canada
Nelson Thomson Learning
1120 Birchmount Road
Toronto, Ontario M1K 5G4
Canada

Library of Congress Cataloging-in-Publication Data
Lawhead, William F.
 The ancient voyage / William F. Lawhead.
  p. cm.
 Includes bibliographical references and index.
 ISBN 0-534-56125-X
  1. Philosophy, Ancient—History.   I. Title.

B171 .L39 2001
180—dc21   2001045346

CONTENTS

THE VOYAGE OF DISCOVERY

This current volume belongs to a four-part paperback series that includes *The Ancient Voyage, The Medieval Voyage, The Modern Voyage,* and *The Contemporary Voyage.* Each of these four volumes focuses on one particular period in the history of philosophy and represents one of the parts of the complete one-volume work *The Voyage of Discovery: A Historical Introduction to Philosophy* 2nd ed. It is hoped that publishing the book in multiple formats will make it more flexible and will increase its usefulness for instructors. Those who are teaching a particular historical period can use the appropriate paperback volume or volumes for that time period. This makes it cost effective to use my historical discussions with a collection of primary source readings. On the other hand, some will prefer to use the complete one-volume work for an introduction to philosophy course that covers significant thinkers from the Greeks to the contemporary period. Others (like me) teach a topically organized introduction course and follow that with one or two courses that survey the history of philosophy, using the complete *The Voyage of Discovery.*

This book has grown out of my thirty years of teaching the history of Western philosophy. I love to teach this subject. I have found that the history of philosophy develops students' critical thinking skills. After journeying with the course for awhile and following the point and counterpoint movements of the great historical debates, students begin to show a flare for detecting the assumptions, strengths, problems, and implications of a thinker's position. Furthermore, the history of philosophy provides students with an arsenal of essential terms, distinctions, categories, and critical questions for making sense out of the barrage of ideas they encounter in history, literature, psychology, politics, and even on television.

One reward of teaching philosophy is to see students develop new confidence in themselves on finding a kindred spirit in one or more of the great minds of history, who agree with their own assessment of what is fallacious or sound. By ex-

posing students to unfamiliar viewpoints that are outrageous, fascinating, perplexing, hopeful, dangerous, gripping, troubling, and exhilarating, the history of philosophy helps them gain a renewed sense of childlike wonder, teaching them to look at the world with new eyes. Finally, throughout the history of philosophy, students often find ideas that are liberating and challenging, leading them down exciting paths that were not even on their conceptual maps when they started the course. I hope that this book will be an effective navigator's guide to such intellectual journeys.

GOALS THAT GUIDED THE WRITING OF THIS BOOK

After many years of teaching a course, a professor begins to get a sense of the "ideal" textbook. For me, an effective history of philosophy text should achieve the following goals:

1. Make the ideas of the philosophers as clear and accessible as possible to the average person. A student-friendly philosophy text will not read like an encyclopedia article, which contains dense but terse summaries of factual information.

2. Provide strategies for sorting out the overwhelming mass of contradictory ideas encountered in the history of philosophy.

3. Find the correct balance between the competing concerns of (a) technical accuracy versus accessibility and (b) breadth of scope versus depth of exposition.

4. Communicate the fact that philosophy is more than simply a collection of opinions on basic issues. Understanding a philosopher's arguments is just as important as the philosopher's conclusions.

5. Encourage the reader to evaluate the ideas discussed. The history of philosophy should be more than the intellectual equivalent of a wine-tasting party, where various philosophers are "sampled" simply to enjoy their distinct flavors.

Although that is certainly one of the delights of studying philosophy and should be encouraged, assessing the strengths and weaknesses of a philosopher's ideas is equally important.

6. Make clear the continuity of the centuries-long philosophical conversation. A course in the history of philosophy should not be like a display of different philosophical exhibits in glass cases. For me, the guiding image is philosophy as a big party where new conversations are continually starting up, while the themes of previous conversations are picked up and carried in different directions as new participants join the dialogue.

DISTINCTIVE FEATURES OF THIS TEXT

• *A consistent structure is used.* For consistency and ease of comparison, the majority of chapters follow the same basic pattern:

1. The life and times of the philosopher

2. The major philosophical task that the philosopher tried to accomplish

3. Theory of knowledge

4. Metaphysics

5. Moral and political philosophy (when relevant)

6. Philosophy of religion (when relevant)

7. Evaluation and significance

• *Analysis of philosophical arguments is provided.* To emphasize that philosophy is a process and not just a set of results, I discuss the intellectual problems that motivated a philosopher's position and the reasons provided in its support. The book analyzes a number of explicitly outlined arguments of various philosophers, providing models of philosophical argumentation and analysis. In addition, I informally discuss numerous other arguments throughout the book.

• *The evaluation of ideas is stressed.* Most of the chapters end with a short evaluation of the philosophy discussed. These evaluations, however, are not presented as decisive "refutations" of the philosopher, which would relieve the reader of any

need to think further. Instead, the evaluations have been posed in terms of problems needing to be addressed and questions requiring an answer. Whenever possible, I have made this section a part of the historical dialogue by expressing the appraisals given by the philosopher's contemporaries and successors.

• *The significance of the ideas is emphasized.* The conclusion of each chapter also indicates the immediate and long-term significance of the philosopher's ideas and prepares the reader for the next turn in the historical dialogue. It makes clear the ways in which philosophical ideas can lead robust lives that continue far beyond their author's time.

• *The continuity between historical periods is emphasized.* Because each of the four paperback volumes represent a slice from the whole of Western philosophy, a special introductory chapter has been written that is specific to each of these four volumes. This chapter will situate the time period of that particular volume in terms of the philosophies that preceded it so that there will be no loss of continuity. Since *The Ancient Voyage* covers the beginnings of Western philosophy, the introductory chapter for that volume discusses the importance of studying the ancient Greeks. The introduction to *The Medieval Voyage* shows how that historical period arose out of the philosophies of the Greeks. In the introduction to *The Modern Voyage,* the shift from medieval thought is outlined in terms of four contrasts between the medieval and the modern outlook. Finally, *The Contemporary Voyage* begins with a brief overview of Immanuel Kant's philosophy and the various responses to it in the nineteenth century in order to set the stage for twentieth-century philosophy.

• *The philosophers are related to their cultural contexts.* In addition to these introductory chapters that emphasize the continuity with the thought that preceded the philosophies in each paperback volume, each major historical period covered by a particular paperback (Greek, early Christian to medieval, Renaissance and Reformation, Enlightenment, the nineteenth century, and the twentieth century) is introduced with a brief chapter discussing the intellectual-social milieu that provides the setting for the philosophies of that era. The questions addressed are: What were the dominant concerns and assumptions that animated each period in history? How did the different philosophers respond to the currents of thought of their time? and How did they influence their culture?

• *Diagrams*. Diagrams and tables provide visual representations of the elements of various philosophers' ideas.

• *Glossary*. A glossary is provided in which key terms used throughout the book are clearly and thoroughly defined. Words appearing in boldface in the text may be found in the glossary.

• *Questions for review and reflection*. At the end of each chapter are two lists of questions. The questions for understanding are more factual and enable the readers to review their understanding of the important ideas and terms. The questions for reflection require the readers to engage in philosophy by making their own evaluations of the philosopher's ideas, as well as working out their implications.

• *Instructor's manual*. In addition to the usual sections containing test questions and essay questions, this manual provides suggested topics for research papers, tips for introducing and motivating interest in each philosopher, chapter-by-chapter topics for discussion, and the contemporary implications of each philosopher's ideas.

SUGGESTED WAYS TO USE THIS BOOK

This book may be used with students who are already familiar with the leading issues and positions in philosophy and who now need to place these ideas in their historical context. However, since it does not assume any previous acquaintance with the subject, it may also be used to introduce students to philosophy for the first time, through the story of its history. I have tried to make clear that philosophy is an ongoing conversation, in which philosophers respond to the insights and shortcomings of their predecessors. Nevertheless, the chapters are self-contained enough that the instructor may put together a course that uses

selected chapters. For example, the chapter on Aquinas could be used as representative of medieval philosophy and Descartes used to represent the modern rationalists (skipping Spinoza and Leibniz). In the case of chapters that discuss a number of philosophers, only certain sections could be assigned. For example, to get a quick but partial glimpse of the wide range covered by analytic philosophy, the students could read only the sections on the early and later Wittgenstein. Although skipping over key thinkers is not ideal, teaching is a continual battle between time constraints and the desire to cover as much material in as much depth as possible.

The *Instructor's Manual* contains objective and essay questions that may be used in making up tests. In addition, Part 1 contains more reflective questions for discussion and essay assignments. I would encourage the instructor to make use of these questions in class in order to emphasize that philosophy is not a list of "who said what" but that it also involves the evaluation and application of the great ideas. Furthermore, because the students will have some of these topics and others posed as questions for reflection at the end of each chapter, they can be asked to have thought about their response to these questions prior to their discussion in class.

ABOUT THIS SECOND EDITION

I am gratified by the responses to the first edition of *The Voyage of Discovery* that I have received from professors using the book, from students who have been introduced to philosophy and its history through it, as well as from interested readers around the world who read it for personal enrichment. This second edition continues to have the distinctive features that so many enjoyed in the first edition and that have been highlighted in the previous sections of this preface. The subtitle has been changed to "A Historical Introduction to Philosophy" to communicate the fact that the book is intended to be used to introduce readers to philosophy for the first time as well as providing a comprehensive survey of Western philosophy. Besides some changes that have been made to aid in clarity and ease of reading, this current edition ends each chapter with questions to aid the reader in studying the material and in engaging in philosophical reflection on the ideas. Some of these questions have been taken from the essay and discussion questions in the *Instructor's Manual*. Nevertheless, over fifty percent of the essay questions in the *Instructor's Manual* remain unique to it. This edition is now available in two formats. As before, there is the one-volume edition that covers philosophy from the early Greeks to the contemporary period. New to the second edition is an alternative format that divides the book into four paperback volumes, corresponding to the four parts of the book. This makes it much more economical for the instructor to use parts of the book for courses that emphasize only particular time periods.

I hope that everyone who uses this book will find it both profitable and interesting. I encourage both professors and students to share with me their experience with the book as well as suggestions for improvement. Write to me at: Department of Philosophy, University of Mississippi, University, MS, 38677-1848. You may also send me e-mail at: wlawhead@olemiss.edu.

ACKNOWLEDGMENTS

From the initial, tentative outline of this book to the final chapter revisions, the manuscript has been extensively reviewed both by instructors who measured its suitability for the classroom and by scholars who reviewed its historical accuracy. Their comments have made it a much better book than the original manuscript. I take full responsibility, of course, for any remaining shortcomings. I am indebted to the following reviewers of this second edition: Jim Friel, State University New York—Farmingdale; John Longenay, University of Wisconsin—Riverside; Scott Lowe, Bloomsburg University; Michael Potts, Methodist College; and Blanche Premo-Hopkins, University of South Carolina—Aiken.

I also want to thank the reviewers of the first edition for their contributions: William Brown, Bryan College; Jill Buroker, California State University at San Bernardino; Bessie Chronaki, Central Piedmont Community College; Vincent Colapietro, Fordham University; Teresa Contrell, University of Louisville; Ronald Cox, San Antonio College; Timothy Davis, Essex Community College; Michelle Grier, University of San Diego; Eugene Lockwood, Oakton Community College; Michael Mendelson, University of California at San Diego; William Parent, Santa Clara University; Anthony Preus, State University of New York at Binghamton; Dennis Rothermel, California State University at Chico; James D. Ryan, Bronx Community College; James Spencer, Cuyahoga Community College; K. Sundaram, Lake Michigan College; Ken Stikkers, Seattle University; Robert Sweet, University of Dayton; Howard Tuttle, University of New Mexico; Jerome B. Wichelms, Jefferson Community College.

My thanks to the many people at the Wadsworth Publishing Company who played a role in the book's production. In particular, I appreciate the encouragement and support I received from Peter Adams, my editor.

The acknowledgments would be incomplete if I did not express my thanks to those individuals who have been particularly supportive throughout my career. My first exposure to philosophy was under the instruction of Arthur Holmes, my undergraduate chair, who ignited my love for the history of philosophy. The late Irwin C. Lieb guided me throughout my career as a graduate student, first as my professor, then as my department chair, and finally as graduate dean. Years of team teaching with David Schlafer, my former colleague, provided exciting lecture performances that have influenced what and how I teach. I have benefitted from good philosophical discussions with present and past colleagues, particularly Michael Harrington, Michael Lynch, Louis Pojman, and Robert Westmoreland. I also need to thank the many bright students who taught me how to teach.

This book is dedicated to my parents, James and Cecelia Lawhead, who first introduced me to the two dimensions of philosophy, love and wisdom; to my wife, Pam, who knows that love sometimes means being close and sometimes it means giving space; and to my sons, Joel and Andy, who taught me how much I do not know.

William Lawhead

Introduction to
The Ancient Voyage

This volume covers the history of Western philosophy from the ancient Greeks to the Hellenistic and Roman period. While many of the positions developed by these ancient thinkers have long since been abandoned, the questions they set in motion remain with us today. Pioneers are always to be admired, whether they are the first person to discover a new planet, the first to get an airplane off the ground, or the first to inaugurate a new style of painting or literature. These early philosophers asked questions that had never been asked before and worked out methods for answering these questions. You can be a reasonably good chemist without knowing the history of chemistry. However, you will not proceed very well in addressing the important philosophical questions without an understanding of the attempts of earlier thinkers to answer these questions. Art students will sometimes sit for hours in a museum painting a duplicate of a great work of art. They do so in order to learn the technique and point of view of a famous painter so that this knowledge will inform the student's own original work.

While the philosophers discussed in this volume are all dead, many of their ideas are not, for they have a life of their own. From the first chapter of this volume to the last, the ideas of these thinkers have permeated the soil from which our thinking has grown. For example, Plato and Aristotle still inform the thinking of many today, in fields ranging from mathematics to ethics. Similarly, the terms *cynical, epicurean, stoical,* and *skeptical* are still used today to describe different types of people or stances toward life. These terms are derived from different philosophies discussed in the last chapter of this volume.

In short, studying these ancient thinkers will help you to (1) get a clearer picture of your own beliefs, (2) understand their origins, and (3) see what strengths and weaknesses others have discovered in them. Hence, studying the history of philosophy is like reading a consumer's magazine to find out about other people's experiences with a product you are thinking of buying.

While there are many practical benefits of studying great philosophers, it is important to add that the study of ideas can be rewarding in itself. When a reporter asked mountain climber George Mallory why he risked his life and went to such great expense to climb Mount Everest, his terse reply was, "Because it's there." The best reason for working through a significant thinker's philosophy is not that it will train your mind (although it will do that), but because "it's there." Like mountains, philosophical ideas contain challenges, beauty, mysteries, majesty, and drama that we can appreciate for their own sake, beyond any practical utility they may have.

P | A | R | T

I

THE ANCIENT PERIOD

1

The Greek Cultural Context: From Poetry to Philosophy

IT WAS MAY 28, 585 B.C., AND THE SUN BEAT down unmercifully as the six-year battle between the Medes and the Lydians waged on fiercely on the west coast of Asia Minor. Suddenly, a shroud of darkness began to cover the battlefield. Puzzled, the warriors on both sides lowered their weapons and looked up to the sky, where they discovered a black void where the sun had once stood. Was this a sign from the gods? Would worse calamities follow? Not wanting to know the answers to these questions, the soldiers of both armies threw down their arms and fled. Prudence, not military might, won the battle that day. However, in this same region a middle-aged merchant and engineer, who would later be known as a sage, was also looking upward. In contrast to the warriors, his face was not contorted with fear but sported a knowing smile as he nodded approval at the cosmic event. Who was this wise man, and why was he the only one to welcome the darkness of the sun?

The sage in question was named Thales. Many ancient sources consider Thales the first philosopher in Western history. One of the most notable achievements attributed to Thales is his predic-

tion of this solar event. Scientists calculate that an eclipse did occur on May 28, 585 B.C., and we can assume this was the one that gave Thales his fame. He surely did not predict the date exactly, but possibly he knew enough astronomy to pick the correct month. Given all this, does Thales belong in a book on the history of astronomy? What possible connection could there be between his prediction and the birth of Western philosophy? To understand the significance of his prediction, we must back up to see what preceded it.

The Role of the Poets

The story of philosophy begins with poetry. The poets held a central position in Greek culture. They were not only tellers of interesting tales in flowery language (it is questionable whether any good poetry is only that). Instead, the poets developed, preserved, and conveyed the historical, scientific, and religious truths of the time. They were concerned with history, because their tales gave an account of the past and how various traditions, races, and cultures came to be. Furthermore, they

3

Science Library/Photo Researchers, Inc.

When the philosopher Thales predicted a solar eclipse in 585 B.C., he demonstrated that the world exhibits a consistent, natural order that our minds can understand.

and false stories. They are more than this, however. They represent the attempt to explain the unfamiliar and mysterious in terms of what is familiar and observable. They are symbolic expressions of how the deepest concerns of human life fit into a large-scale picture of the cosmos. The primary model of explanation available to pre-scientific people was that of human motives and actions. Hence, their Greek gods were very human. They acted according to their purposes and aims. However, they were also anthropomorphic in the sense that they were driven by passion, lust, petty jealousies, were easily offended, vengeful, deceitful, played favorites, in short, their enormous power was equaled only by their raging immaturity. The Greek gods had a division of labor: there was a separate god for each area of life—war, love, trade, hunting, and agriculture. Both the favorable and the unfortunate events in life were attributed to the anger or the goodwill of this or that god. In short, even though they seem like extravagant fantasies to us, the myths of the poets tried to provide a comprehensive view of the world and the individual's place in it.

attempted to answer cosmological questions by speaking about the origins, structure, and workings of the universe. Hence, they explained the causes that lay behind thunderstorms, abundant crops, drought, health, and sickness. They also served an important religious function. The poets told the stories of the gods, and their accounts were taken to be authoritative. The Greeks thought that the poets were inspired by the Muses. These were the goddesses of literature and the arts. "Inspired" means "breathed into." Hence, to the Greeks, the poets were inspired or filled with a divine spirit no less than the biblical writers in the Christian tradition. Finally, all this served an ethical function. By explaining how great heroes triumphed or fell, how the universe worked, and how human destiny was controlled by the gods and fate, the poets helped make clear what course people should take in life and what actions were appropriate or improper, advantageous or ruinous.

The poets explained the world through myths. Many people think of myths as simply fanciful

THE NATURAL ORDER ACCORDING TO HOMER

To set the stage for philosophy, it is worth looking at the most important Greek poet, Homer.* His authority within Greek culture is underscored by the fact that later philosophers found it important either to defend or to criticize his views. One of the earliest Greek philosophers, Xenophanes (about 570–478 B.C.), explains that he criticizes Homer because "All at first have learnt according to Homer."[1] Homer's poems suggest several broad conceptions about the nature of the universe. First, what order we find in nature (the pattern of the seasons, for example) is the product of the

---

*The Homeric poems *The Iliad* and *The Odyssey* were originally songs that were passed on orally from generation to generation. We believe they were put in written form sometime in the eighth century B.C. Because of tradition, we attribute them to a blind bard known as Homer. But scholars suspect that they are actually the product of more than one poet.

steady purposes and aims of the gods. However, nature is sometimes unpredictable, because the gods are fickle and impulsive. A devastating earthquake or a sudden storm, for example, is caused by the god Poseidon, but they do not fit into any long-term, rational purpose of his that would make his initiation of these events intelligible.

Second, the Homeric gods are a far cry from the omnipotent deity of the Judeo-Christian tradition. Not only can they be thwarted by other gods, including their own family members, but they are subject to such forces as fate or necessity. Although the fates are sometimes presented as several personal beings, their actions are usually so unintelligible and unpredictable that the human mind cannot penetrate their mysteries. Thus, from our standpoint, the collection of forces called *fate* is more a principle of randomness than it is a law of nature.

THE MORAL IDEAL ACCORDING TO HOMER

The Homeric notion of virtue is quite a bit different from that found in later moral traditions. Homer's virtues were the virtues of the warrior-hero and can be summarized under the heading of *excellence*. Excellence was defined in terms of success, honor, power, wealth, moderation, and security. Homer's heroes may be called on to look after the welfare of others and to take risks to meet the demands of loyalty. However, these moral duties are always for the sake of preserving one's honor and status, not because of the outcome for others.

Homer's conception of the gods was consistent with this picture. The gods' interests revolved around their own honor and status. They sat up on Mount Olympus, looking down on the spectacle of human affairs like spectators at the chariot races. Although the gods were able to suffer frustration, no one doubted that their lives were basically happy. Thus, when a mortal aspired to be godlike, this had more to do with enhancing his or her own status than it did with concern for others. When it came to their interaction with mortals, the gods did not reward virtue and punish evil as much as they expressed favoritism and reacted

negatively when annoyed. Flattery, bribery, cajoling, and coaxing worked as well to win the gods' favor as did moral goodness. Service to the gods was motivated not by their goodness but by their power. Consequently, all interactions between mortals and the gods was, for both sides, solely a matter of calculating self-interest.

Homer's account of Zeus, however, provides some exceptions to this general picture. Zeus was the supreme god among Homer's collection of deities. Although he was stronger than all the rest and they looked to him for advice and approval, he still was limited both by external forces and his own personality flaws. Nevertheless, we sometimes get glimpses of his concern to see justice prevail within human affairs. He becomes angry at the moral wrongs that mortals inflict on one another.[2] Homer's near contemporary, the eighth-century (B.C.) poet Hesiod, develops this line of thought even further. According to Hesiod, Zeus directs the other gods to measure humans' actions against a universal law of justice. As Hesiod states in his *Works and Days*,

> The deathless gods are never far away;
> They mark the crooked judges who grind down
> Their fellow-men and do not fear the gods.[3]

In these sorts of passages, the will of the gods takes on the character of a uniform, moral order operating in the world. This picture provided fertile soil for developing the notion of an impersonal natural order, independent of the gods' will.

CONFLICTS WITHIN HOMER'S PICTURE

To simplify and summarize, Homer and the other poets established four notions of world order: (1) Some events in the world are caused by purposeful, though frequently capricious, human or divine agents. (2) There is an element of randomness in the world such that some events are as purposeless as the throw of a pair of dice. (3) The fates represent an unyielding, amoral order in the world to which both mortals and the gods, including Zeus, are subject. (4) In some passages, the gods respond to a moral order and judge mortals by a standard of objective justice. Unfortunately, Homer does not make clear what happens when two or more of these forces conflict.

Despite the crudeness of Homer's picture of the universe, it provided a starting point for Greek scientific and philosophical thought.[4] It did this in two ways. First, the conflicts between his principles cry out for a more coherent view of the world. An inconsistent answer is no answer at all. Second, his last two principles (fate and justice) suggest a new sense of order that would lead beyond the Homeric myths. The notion of fate as an inescapable causal order is, in spite of its superstitious colorings, the predecessor of the notion of impersonal, natural laws. Also the idea that Zeus sometimes lays aside petty, personal interests and is concerned with justice, points toward the development of objective, ethical principles. Nevertheless, what we find in Homer are at best the seeds of theoretical thought. Only when these seeds break through the soil of mythological thought and rise above the darkness in which they took root will the fruits of philosophy begin to appear.

The Birth of Western Philosophy

Traditionally, the birth of Western philosophy has been located in the sixth century B.C. The problem is, to say *when* Western philosophy began requires an understanding of *what* philosophy is. However, to ask, "What is philosophy?" is to raise a philosophically controversial question. Hence, when and where one locates the birth of philosophy within a culture will depend on how narrowly or broadly one defines "philosophy." There are strains of philosophy in the poetry of Homer and Hesiod, and there are remnants of traditional, mythical thought throughout Greek philosophy. However, everyone agrees that Western philosophy did not leap into being from out of nowhere. Transitions in the history of thought are rarely that abrupt and do not arise from a vacuum. Historically, philosophy emerged within Western civilization the same way it emerges within our personal lives. Becoming philosophical is a gradual process in which cultures and individuals learn to look at the world in

a new way by becoming self-conscious and critical. Although we cannot pinpoint the birth of Western philosophy the way we can a solar eclipse, we can point to significant landmarks on the continuum from mythological tales to fully aware, self-critical philosophical thought.

To return to the solar eclipse, Thales' prediction was a significant event in the story of philosophy because it represented a new concept of order. If Thales was able to predict this natural phenomenon, it meant that he realized (unlike many of his contemporaries) that events in the world were neither the result of the irrational and unpredictable will of the gods, blind chance, nor the work of a largely inscrutable fate. Instead, Thales realized that such events were the product of a consistent, impersonal, natural order that can be studied and made the basis of generalizations and predictions. This raised the question of what this order must be like that allows the world to be open to rational inspection and understanding.

As with any philosopher, Thales owed an intellectual debt to many sources. In his time, the Greeks benefited both economically and intellectually from their trade with other cultures. Because of the thriving commercial life of their coastal cities, they were in touch with the leading centers of civilization: Egypt and Phoenicia; Lydia, Persia, and Babylon. Thales, no doubt, acquired much of his knowledge about mathematics from the Egyptians and his knowledge of astronomy from the Babylonians. It is quite possible that his philosophical speculations about the universe were nourished by the traditions of the different cultures around him. Furthermore, the suggestions in Homer's and Hesiod's myths that Zeus applies a consistent rule of justice to the world may have inspired Thales to search for an impersonal order in nature.

Although Thales applied and continued some of the ideas of his predecessors, he brought to these materials the spark of a new way of thinking. This new style of thought was that of original, theoretical inquiry. Rather than appealing to tradition or the stories of the gods to support his conclusions, he sent his opinions out into the world to stand or fall on their own merits. Thales' contemporaries and successors produced a whirl of questions, arguments, theories, and critical dialogue, making clear that a new way of answering questions and resolving disputes was emerging in Western history. From the womb of this spirit of inquiry and argument, both science and philosophy were brought to birth.

Outline of Classical Philosophy

From its early beginnings with Thales to its end in the Middle Ages, classical philosophy went through a number of distinct phases. This development is briefly summarized in the following outline:

1. *Cosmological Period* (585 B.C. to the middle of the fifth century B.C.)—Chapter 2
    *   Concerned with external nature
    *   Wanted to know what is fundamentally real

2. *Anthropological Period*—Chapter 3
    *   Concerned with human-centered issues
    *   Asked questions about knowledge and conduct
        a. Sophists (fifth century B.C.)—skeptical and practical
        b. Socrates (470–399 B.C.)—concerned to find objective knowledge and values

3. *Systematic Period*—Chapters 4 and 5
    *   Concerned to develop a comprehensive, philosophical system
    *   The first to raise all the basic questions of philosophy
        a. Plato (427–347 B.C.)
        b. Aristotle (384–322 B.C.)

4. *Post-Aristotelian or Hellenistic-Roman Philosophy* (320 B.C.–A.D. 529)—Chapter 6
    *   Concerned with individualistic, practical issues
    *   Metaphysical concerns subordinated to ethical concerns
        Cynicism, Epicureanism, Stoicism, Skepticism, Neoplatonism

Questions for Understanding

1. Why were the poets so important in ancient Greek culture?
2. What was Homer's view of the order of the world?
3. What was Homer's view of the moral order?
4. How did Thales' approach to understanding the world differ from that of Homer?
5. What were the four main stages in ancient Greek philosophy? What were the primary concerns of each stage?

Questions for Reflection

1. Homer provides accounts of the nature of the world, morality, and the meaning of human life. Given the account of philosophy in the introductory chapter of this book, in what sense were Homer's views philosophical and in what sense were they not?
2. Are most people in our contemporary society more like the ancient poets or are they more like Thales? In other words, do people tend to base their beliefs more on tradition and popular opinions or on critical thinking? Why is this? What are the strengths and weaknesses of each approach?
3. In this chapter we have examined philosophical thinking in its infancy. In an analogous sense, what sorts of philosophical questions came to your mind when you were a child? When in your life did you, like Thales, first begin to critically examine some of the traditional beliefs you had taken for granted up until then?

Notes

1. Quoted in John Burnet, *Early Greek Philosophy*, 4th ed. (New York: Meridian Books, 1930), 118.
2. See Homer, *Iliad* 16.384–393.
3. Hesiod, *Works and Days* in *Hesiod and Theognis*, trans. Dorthea Wender (New York: Penguin Classics, 1973), 66.
4. For the points made in this section, I am indebted to Terence Irwin's discussion in Chapter 2 of his *Classical Thought*, A History of Western Philosophy:1 (Oxford, England: Oxford University Press, 1989).

CHAPTER

2

Greek Philosophy Before Socrates

THE MILESIAN PHILOSOPHERS

Thales

We have already encountered Thales in Chapter 1. He was the Greek philosopher who predicted the solar eclipse. He is also considered by many ancient authorities to be the first Western philosopher. The dates of his life are only approximate, but most scholars place him somewhere between the years 624 and 545 B.C. His native city of Miletus was a thriving Greek seaport in Ionia, on the western coast of Asia Minor. Because of their geographical location, Thales and his two successors are called the Milesian philosophers (and sometimes the Ionians). Miletus was a city noted for its commerce, wealth, and cosmopolitan ideas. Because the trading industry put them in contact with other countries, many Milesians were receptive to new ideas and the city was the perfect breeding ground for fresh perspectives.

Thales had a very practical mind. Besides predicting the eclipse, stories abound that he solved a number of engineering problems for the military and invented navigational instruments and techniques. However, it was not his technological achievements that earned him his place in history. He is important for understanding the Western intellectual heritage because he set in motion an ongoing debate about the ultimate nature of things. Many theories of these early thinkers may seem as much an example of early science as they are of philosophy. This is not surprising, for the disciplines were not clearly distinguished, as they are today. What we call *science* was considered to be "natural philosophy" for most of human history. Even today, a student receiving the highest degree in chemistry will get a Ph.D., which is a "doctor of philosophy" degree. This period represents both the birth of science and of philosophy because these early thinkers embarked on the quest for universal principles and rationally defensible theories rather than simply making observations and collecting data.

THALES' QUESTION

Thales' concern was to find the unity that underlies all the multiplicity of things in our experience. This is sometimes called the problem of "the one and the many." We encounter many things in the world: fish, sand, trees, stars, grapes, storms, rocks, and plants. But what unifies it all? Why do we consider this a *universe*, not a *multiverse*? What basic principle accounts for all this? What fundamental "stuff" underlies everything we find in the world? This is the primary issue that occupies all the Pre-Socratic philosophers.

THALES' ANSWER

The answer Thales gave, Aristotle tells us, is that water is the source of all things.* At first this answer may seem naive and improbable. However, before we criticize any of these early philosophers, we must remember that we stand on top of some twenty-five hundred years of philosophical speculation and scientific discoveries. Hence, these early attempts to answer these questions are remarkable in their originality and cleverness. Aristotle speculates that Thales reasoned from the fact that water is essential to life and the seeds of all things are moist to the conclusion that water is the fundamental element. Additional reasons may have occurred to Thales to support his conclusion that everything is transformed water. For example, liquid water can be transformed into a gas (steam), and it also can be changed into a solid (ice). Furthermore, water comes from the air in the form of rain and returns back to the air as mist. When water evaporates from a dish, it leaves a sediment (apparently turning into earth), while digging down into the earth will lead us to water. Finally, living in Miletus and being surrounded by water may have made it seem probable to Thales that everything comes from water. Although we don't know what Thales' real arguments were, the fact that his immediate successors offered rational support for their theories makes it likely that Thales did too.

THE PROBLEM OF CHANGE

Some further issues are involved in Thales' speculation. If water is the one permanent and basic substance, what causes the changes in water's appearance that transforms it into all the other things in our experience? This is the question of "permanence and change" or "being and becoming." A possible answer can be found in Thales' claim that all things are "full of gods." Contrary

*Aristotle could be considered the first systematic historian of philosophy. He was born close to 250 years after Thales and is discussed in Chapter 5.

to appearances, it is likely that he was not reverting to a naive theological explanation here. He noticed, for example, that magnetic stones have the power to move iron. He considered this power to be an animate, causal agent in a seemingly inert stone. Thus, he seemed to believe that the principle of animation and change resides in things themselves. However, the only vocabulary he had for expressing this was to say that things are alive and divinely animated in some fashion.

THALES' SIGNIFICANCE

We can summarize Thales' impact and contribution in terms of several key points. First, Thales' position was an early example of metaphysical monism. **Monism** is the name for any position that claims there is only one principle of explanation. His is a metaphysical monism because he is claiming that reality can be explained by one principle (water). Thales' immediate successors adopted this assumption without questioning it. They continued to look for the one principle that explains everything, and only differed with Thales on the details of what this is. Second, Thales assumed that this one principle is a material substance. This is called **material monism**. Again, this assumption went unquestioned for quite a while. Third, Thales made a contribution in the questions he asked. The turning points in the development of human thought are to be found in original questions as much as in insightful answers. Thales asked some practical questions, such as "What will the olive harvest be like?" However, when he asked, "What is the ultimate substance underlying all the appearances?", this question had no immediate, practical payoff. It represented a search for theoretical understanding for its own sake. Such a quest opens doors that the more practical questions never will.

Finally, Thales is a key figure in the history of thought because of the nature of his answers. The important point here is not his claim that water is the ultimate substance. After all, his contemporaries discarded this answer. What is important is that he did not appeal to tradition or authority for his answer nor did he simply spew forth opinions. He put forth a theory that others could examine and debate, and he provided rational grounds for his speculations. Thales made the first serve in the history of philosophical exchanges. It was up to his successors to return the shot. Arthur Koestler once said that the history of thought is full of barren truths and fruitful errors. Thales' theory is obviously an example of a fruitful error. His contemporaries did not accept his answer, but it set in motion the philosophical dialogue that continues on even in our own time.

Anaximander

Anaximander's dates are approximately 610 to 545 B.C. He was a younger contemporary of Thales and, perhaps, the latter's student. He was well known in Miletus and published a book on the evolution of the world. At the same time, significantly, prose was emerging as a form of literature to rival that of poetry. This shows that the way people made sense out of the world was shifting.

ANAXIMANDER'S QUESTION

Anaximander took up the task of his teacher by addressing the question "What is the single, basic stuff that is fundamental to all other things?" Notice that he also absorbed Thales' assumption that the key to the universe would be a *single* type of entity. Anaximander was not satisfied with his teacher's solution, however. Water is just another particular thing that we find in the world along with earth, air, and fire. How can one kind of thing explain all the other things? It is a contradiction to suppose that something that is clearly not water (for example, fire) really is water. Whatever is fundamental and universal cannot have the particular properties water has. Water itself needs to be explained. Thus, with Thales' pupil the process of philosophical criticism begins.

ANAXIMANDER'S ANSWER

According to Anaximander, the ultimate reality must be an eternal, imperishable source from which all things are made and to which all things return. This ultimate ground of all being is the *Apeiron*, which means the Boundless, the Infinite, or the Indefinite. It is without any internal boundaries or divisions and is a space-filling, dynamic mass. It is infinite in time, otherwise there would have to be something more fundamental that produced it. Furthermore, it is indefinite in quantity. The Boundless can be thought of as a reservoir from which all things and their qualities are produced. But what are the properties that describe it? Is it cold? No, Anaximander would say, for then it could not produce the property of heat. Is it wet? No, for then it could not produce the property of dryness. Since it contains or produces all specific properties, it itself cannot be identified with any one of them. Hence, it is undefinable, since we can only define things that have specific properties.

THE PROBLEM OF CHANGE

Anaximander has a much more developed theory of change than did his teacher. He says the world is made up of warring opposites (cold versus heat, night versus day). Since they are opposites, one cannot give birth to the other, but they must all come from something else more fundamental. Therefore, change is the process of various qualities separating out from and returning to the primordial substance. Originally, everything was part of the whirling mass of the Boundless, and in the act of creation the different qualities were flung out from it much as particles are separated out from a solution in a centrifuge. This whirling motion explains how the planets originally received their motion. Through this process all the warring opposites such as hot and cold, wet and dry were produced. Combinations of these qualities produced the objects in our experience. For example, from the combination of cold and wet came the earth and clouds. From the hot and dry came a ring of fire that enclosed the whole. This burst into smaller rings of fire, creating the heavenly bodies. From the warm and the wet came life. Interestingly, Anaximander included a primitive evolutionary theory in his account of the world, claiming that all life forms, including humans, originally came from the sea.

Anaximander gave a very modern answer to the age-old problem: What does the earth rest on? His answer was that it rests on nothing. Since the earth is the center of a spherical universe, it has no reason to go one way or another. Since any direction is equally attractive, it stays where it is. Anaximander recognized that from the standpoint of the universe as a whole, there can be no absolute directions of up or down.

The universe is an everlasting motion made up of the cycle of creation and destruction. This is the first philosophical account in the Western tradition of the cyclical view of history (a common theory among the Greeks). Although he is attempting to give a natural explanation of things, he retains the notion of a moral force in the universe as did his poetic predecessors. He uses the principle of justice to explain the world cycle. Since everything "borrowed" its existence from the Boundless, it must return the loan. Hence, everything ultimately returns to its original source.

ANAXIMANDER'S SIGNIFICANCE

Anaximander's first contribution was the fact that his theory moves in the direction of a more abstract mode of thought. This may seem like a deficiency, but actually it is not. We cannot imagine the Boundless, nor see it, nor feel it. Similarly, however, neither can we imagine nor directly sense most of the forces and particles that our contemporary physicists talk about. By going beyond Thales' crude principle of water, Anaximander frees reason to think about that which transcends our everyday experience. Second, he began the process of philosophical criticism. He learned from Thales but found his solutions inadequate. Therefore, he contributed to philosophical progress by building on his predecessor while improving the latter's theory. Third, Anaximander addressed more seriously the problem of change and tried to give a more detailed and adequate explanation of it. Fourth, with his principle of justice he struggled to articulate an early version of a natural, scientific law. True, he still characterized it as a moral law (a relapse back to a poetic, anthropomorphic view of things). Nevertheless, it was an impersonal principle that operated independently of the caprice of the gods, making it more scientific in character.

Anaximenes

Anaximenes' dates are hard to pin down, but he was active around 545 B.C., making him a younger contemporary of Anaximander and the third member of the Milesians or Ionians. He is said to have written a book, but it has not survived. Nevertheless, his contemporaries say that it had a simple, unpretentious style, and it seems to have been more scientific in tone and less poetic than the work of his predecessors.

ANAXIMENES' QUESTION

As with his fellow Milesians, Anaximenes is concerned primarily with the question "What is the basic substance that is the foundation of all reality?" He agrees with Anaximander that the basic reality must be eternal, unlimited, and singular. However (continuing the process of philosophical criticism), he finds his colleague's answer to be inadequate. To say that the basic reality is the Boundless is not to say much at all. If there is a basic substance, we must be able to say something about it if we know that it is there at all. Thus, using the criterion of clarity, Anaximenes has the task of finding a less vague and more convincing answer to the fundamental question.

ANAXIMENES' ANSWER

The answer he gives is simple: the basic reality is *air*. He may have come to this theory on the basis of several observations. First, air is much more pervasive than water, so it is a better candidate for the fundamental substance. Second, air is central to all nature. It is necessary for the existence of fire and can be found in water and in the earth. Third, he may have noticed that water falls when not supported, but air is self-supporting. Therefore, water cannot support the earth as Thales claimed. However, since air can support itself, it can conceivably support the heavenly bodies as well, just as a light breeze can float a leaf. Finally, air sustains life. It is the primary difference between the living and the dead. Anaximenes believed the soul was identical to air. When we breathe our last breath and then expire, air (which is the soul) leaves the body.

THE PROBLEM OF CHANGE

Anaximenes accounted for the process of change by two principles that produce changes in the density of the basic substance. One is *rarefaction* (or expansion), and the other is *condensation* (or compression). For example, extremely rarified air becomes warm and eventually becomes fire. As air becomes increasingly condensed, it becomes colder and successively changes into wind, water, earth, and finally stone. Not content to simply throw out opinions, Anaximenes provided the first recorded scientific experiment to provide evidence for his claims. He observed that when you open your mouth wide and blow on your hand, your breath will feel warm. But when you close your mouth as if you were going to whistle and blow on your hand, your condensed breath feels cold. Hence, by appealing to the quantitative changes produced by rarefaction and condensation, he believes we can account for all qualitative changes in the world.

ANAXIMENES' SIGNIFICANCE

Anaximenes' contributions are twofold. First, he showed that we must temper abstract thought with conceptual clarification. If the ultimate reality is indefinite, as Anaximander claimed, then we cannot know much about it and this concept explains very little. Second, Anaximenes treated the problem of change more explicitly and adequately than his predecessors. Instead of simply saying that all things contain the principle of change, as Thales seemed to conclude, or that some cosmic moral principle accounts for the world process, as Anaximander claimed, Anaximenes tries to give an explanation that has some degree of scientific basis.

Summary of the Milesians' Methods

None of these first three philosophers directly address the problem of how we obtain knowledge about the world. Nevertheless, they do illustrate the beginning emergence of epistemological and methodological concerns. Thales' and Anaximenes' positions could be viewed as examples of a primitive empiricism. **Empiricism** is the position that claims that sense experience is the best way to arrive at knowledge. Since they took observable substances (water and air) to be ultimate, they obviously were concerned that their theories stick close to what we can see and touch. In contrast, Anaximander's position might be seen as a crude and early version of rationalism. **Rationalism** claims that reason is the best method for obtaining knowledge. Since Anaximander's Boundless cannot be sensed but is postulated sheerly on the basis of a rational argument, his philosophical method differs from that of his two colleagues. Although the terms *empiricism* and *rationalism* are too precise to describe these early theories correctly, these philosophies contain seeds of an issue that will become very important in all philosophy from Plato to our century.

Summary of the Milesians' Metaphysics

Although they differed on the details, the Milesians were similar in many respects. First, the Milesians introduced the problem of appearance versus reality. They all agreed on how the world *appears* to be, but what they wanted to know was "What is reality ultimately like?" Water, the Boundless, and air were their respective attempts to answer this question. Second, despite their differences all three Milesians assumed they could explain everything in the universe, without exception, on the basis of a *single* principle. Third, they each assumed this monistic principle was a physical substance of some sort. Although later philosophers questioned these assumptions, the Milesians made the first attempt to reduce the multiplicity of nature to a simpler unity. Finally, they all had something to say about how change occurs. For Thales, change was sheer spontaneous transformation, because things were "full of gods." Anaximander explained change as the separation of qualities out of the reservoir of the Boundless. Anaximenes accounted for most changes with the processes of rarefaction and condensation. Despite their innovative brilliance, these answers were but halting attempts to deal with problems that would require a much more developed treatment by later philosophers.

PYTHAGORAS AND HIS SCHOOL
|||

Pythagoras: Mathematician and Mystic

The Pythagorean movement was begun by a philosophical, mathematical, religious mystic by the name of Pythagoras. Most people are familiar with him as the alleged discoverer of the Pythagorean theorem. However, we know very little about him apart from various tales and legends that developed around him. The best we can tell, he lived somewhere between 570 and 495 B.C. Born on the island of Samos, near the Ionian coast, he eventually migrated to Croton in southern Italy, where he founded a religious community that was open to both men and women. Many of his followers believed that Pythagoras was divine. For this reason, it is hard to separate his thoughts from those of his followers, since they tended to attribute all their ideas to their founder. Although spurious works were written in his name, it is generally thought that he did not produce any books. Instead, he passed on his teachings orally, along with a vow of secrecy. The Pythagorean religious community combined the Greek scientific spirit with religious mysticism. Hence, it functioned both as a school of mathematics and a religious order. The movement was a hardy one, lasting about two hundred years. The sect died out in the late fourth century B.C., but remnants of Pythagorean thought continued on into the Christian era.

PHILOSOPHY AND SALVATION

For the Pythagoreans, the goal of religion was purification, and the goal of purification was the salvation of one's soul. They believed that the soul was immortal and that after death it migrates into another body, possibly an animal's body. The only way to achieve release from this "wheel of birth" and the prison of the body was to purify the soul. They did this through various purification rites, resulting in an ascetic life filled with many taboos and dietary restrictions. Most important, Pythagoras taught that the soul achieved purity through an intellectual process of obtaining philosophical wisdom. Pythagoras is thought to be the first to call himself a "philosopher," which literally means "a lover of wisdom." The "right way of life" required harmony with the universe, and this implied the need to understand it. For the Pythagoreans there was no division between religion and science or between worship and the intellect. Their intellectual life was on one continuum with their religious worship.

REALITY IS MATHEMATICAL

The Pythagoreans taught that there was an order and unity to the cosmos and that it was mathematical in nature. Hence, numbers lie at the base of reality. In fact, they believed numbers have a reality of their own. This notion may seem strange to the average person. But consider the fact that numbers have objective properties that must be discovered. They are not something that we invent or make up. According to the Pythagoreans, mathematical points produce lines, conjunctions of lines create plane figures, and multiple plane figures form solids. Hence, from mathematical points we can understand our entire universe. We can reason about lines and planes without thinking of physical bodies, but we cannot understand physical objects without understanding the lines and planes embedded within them.

The Pythagoreans thought that music provided clues to the mathematical nature of the universe. In Greek music the three major tone intervals are the octave, the fourth, and the fifth. The Pythagoreans discovered that the differences between musical tones are functions of exact numerical ratios. When a string is doubled in length, the sound it makes is an octave lower. Two strings whose lengths are in a ratio of 4 to 3 make sounds four notes apart. Lengths in the ratio of 3 to 2 produce sounds a fifth apart. The physical material of the strings does not matter as long as the mathematical properties follow the correct pattern. If numbers are the basis of music, perhaps they are the basis of everything else, the Pythagoreans reasoned. Further considerations reinforced this speculation, for according to their crude measurements, the distances between the planets were in the same proportion as the notes in a musical scale. They called this "the harmony of the spheres." Furthermore, they taught that the body is healthy when all its parts are acting in harmony, as in a well-tuned musical instrument. Hence, music, astronomy, medicine, and all existence seemed to be controlled by mathematical ratios.

The Pythagoreans saw the universe as governed by a continual conflict between order and disorder. They summarized this in the "table of opposites":

Order	*Disorder*
Limit	Unlimited
Odd	Even
One	Many
Right	Left
Male	Female
Rest	Motion
Straight	Crooked
Light	Darkness
Good	Evil
Square	Oblong

Since the two columns represent two sorts of forces in the universe, this is a type of **metaphysical dualism**. Since one side is identified with good and the other with evil, this is also a moral dualism. The placement of male and female in this scheme of oppositions speaks volumes about the typical Greek male's attitude toward women. Although the two lists represent an eternal conflict between two fundamental forces, it seemed to the Pythagoreans that harmony had the edge over chaos. The battle between rational order and chaos also takes place within our own souls. The soul takes on the form of whatever it contemplates. Therefore, by studying the mathematical harmony of the universe, our souls will become like that order and we will achieve an inner harmony. Furthermore, since mathematics weans us away from the senses and the physical world (which was thought to be the soul's prison), pursuing the life of the mind can be a spiritually purifying and liberating activity.

The Pythagoreans' Significance

The Pythagoreans were innovative in several ways. First, they realized that metaphysical theory has a bearing on one's life. Whereas previous philosophers such as Thales focused on theoretical issues for their own sake, the Pythagoreans believed philosophy was not merely a matter of intellectual curiosity but a way of life. Hence, this is the first time we see individual, ethical concerns appearing in philosophy. Second, Pythagoras emphasized form over matter. Instead of trying to understand the universe in terms of a basic, material element, he sought to understand it in terms of its mathematical order. Hence, he gave mathematics a more exalted task than simply calculating the size of a grape orchard. Although he may have learned many of his mathematical ideas from the Mesopotamians and Egyptians, Pythagoras helped advance the study of mathematics. Viewing nature as a vast mathematical order was an amazing achievement. Pythagoras is said to be the first to apply the term *cosmos* (which means "order," "fitness," "beauty") to the universe. Without the revival of this Pythagorean perspective, modern science never would have gotten off the ground. In the seventeenth century, the astronomer Galileo followed the Pythagoreans when he said that the book of the universe "is written in the mathematical language" and if one doesn't understand its symbols "one wanders in vain through a dark labyrinth."[1]

XENOPHANES

The Destroyer of Myths

Xenophanes was born in Colophon, a little over forty miles north of Miletus. Although his exact dates are only approximate, we do know he lived a long life and probably lived from 570 to 478 B.C. He fled to Italy when the Persians conquered Ionia in 546 B.C. There and in Sicily, he spent most of his life wandering about, supporting himself by reciting his own poetry and speaking at banquets. Although he was a contemporary of Pythagoras, the two philosophers differed greatly in spirit. Xenophanes was said to be irreverent and cynical and was famous for his sharp, satirical wit. He enjoyed criticizing and mocking his contemporaries and predecessors. Among his targets were the theological myths of Homer and Hesiod, the glorification of athletes in his time, and the decadent vanity of people in his culture. Although he was famous because of his rational theology, he was also a serious student of physical nature. He dabbled in astronomy and meteorology and deduced conclusions about the changes in the earth and the origins of life from the fossil record. Although, as always, a good deal of information about him comes from ancient secondary sources, we are fortunate to have some fragments of his own writings.

Theory of Knowledge

Although Xenophanes has only a few brief remarks to make about the nature of knowledge, he is significant for being the first philosopher thus far who directly addresses the issue. In a significant passage, Xenophanes asserts, "If God had not made yellow honey, men would think figs were much sweeter" (G38; 1.401).[2] In other words, sense perception is relative. What we consider sweet (or heavy, or tall) may depend on what else in experience contrasts with it. This bespeaks an epistemological sophistication on Xenophanes' part that was rare at the time. In another passage he claims,

Certain truth has no man seen, nor will there ever be a man who knows [from immediate experience] about the gods and about everything of which I speak; for even if he should fully succeed in saying what is true, even so he himself does not know it, but in all things there is opinion. (G34; 1.395)

Here he is making an important contrast between knowledge and opinion. Some later Greeks thought he was expressing **skepticism** (the view that knowledge is unattainable). However, Xenophanes clearly does not mean to say that all opinions are equal in value or even worthless. Instead, he is providing a helpful corrective to the extreme dogmatism of his philosophical predecessors. Although humans can never have perfect knowledge or total certainty, through careful investigation we can achieve a close approximation of the truth. Hence, Xenophanes advised (presumably about his own teachings), "Let these things be believed as resembling the truth" (G35; 1.396).

Philosophy of Religion

Xenophanes' major contribution was in his philosophical theology. Previous philosophers had simply ignored the gods of popular religion, but Xenophanes subjects them to philosophical criticism. His criticisms are threefold. First, he says that his contemporaries used mythological explanations to explain events when natural explanations would suffice. For example, many Greeks thought the rainbow was really the radiant goddess Iris (the messenger to the other gods). However, as Xenophanes explains in his typical iconoclastic manner, "She whom men call Iris also is a cloud, purple and red and yellow to behold" (G32; 1.392).

Second, he deplored the immorality of the traditional gods: "Homer and Hesiod have ascribed to the gods all deeds that among men are a reproach and disgrace: Thieving, adultery, and mutual deception" (G11; 1.371). Third, he ridiculed the poets for creating the gods in their own image:

Men suppose that gods are brought to birth, and have clothes and voice and shape like their own. (G14; 1.371)

But if oxen and horses or lions had hands, or could draw and fashion works as men do, horses would draw the gods shaped like horses, and lions like lions, making the bodies of the gods resemble their own forms. (G15; 1.371)

Although most of his points are negative, Xenophanes does offer some positive theological claims of his own:

God is one . . . in no way like mortals either in body or in mind. . . . He sees as a whole, perceives as a whole, hears as a whole. . . . Always he remains in the same place, not moving at all . . . but without toil he makes all things shiver by the impulse of his mind. (G23 25; 1.374)

In contrast to the anthropomorphic polytheism of the Greek poets, Xenophanes presents a vision of one eternal and unmovable god. At times, it is true, he speaks of the gods in the plural. But this is generally thought to be simply a flippant concession to the popular figure of speech. Having

said this, however, it would be a mistake to identify his position with Judeo-Christian monotheism. For Xenophanes, the deity is not beyond the cosmos but is identical with it. Reality is a god–cosmos unity.

Xenophanes' Significance

Xenophanes' position evokes two crucial questions: (1) What sense does it make to say the universe is divine? In other words, is Xenophanes doing any more than tagging the universe with the three-letter label of "God"? (2) How can an unmoving god be identical with a moving and changing world? Although these are serious questions, to be aware of these problems would require a level of philosophical precision not possible at this time, even for such an innovative thinker as Xenophanes. More positively, he contributed to the philosophical conversation in two ways. He raised crucial, epistemological questions, and he attempted to construct a rational theology that did not simply take for granted the traditional answers.

HERACLITUS

The Lover of Paradoxes

Heraclitus was an Ionian Greek who was born into a noble family in Ephesus. He was well familiar with the philosophers we have already discussed, because his hometown was 25 miles up the coast from Miletus, close to Pythagoras's native island of Samos and Xenophanes' Colophon. He lived his entire life in and about Ephesus and was said to be in his prime around 500 B.C. His exact dates are unclear, but the period from 540 to 480 B.C. is as good a guess as any.

Heraclitus did not seem to be a very pleasant person, for he had a proud, arrogant, and contemptuous mind, which he employed to produce

critical and dogmatic sayings. Although his attitude was very aristocratic, he stubbornly refused the honors bestowed on him by society, including an inherited position of religious and political distinction. His harsh disposition and utter disdain for humanity (both the common folk and his philosophical contemporaries) guaranteed that he would attract no disciples in his lifetime. He thought most people were no better than cattle. Nevertheless, even if he lived a lonely and withdrawn life, his writings and sayings seemed to have provoked a good deal of discussion among later generations.

Although the amount of material we have from him exceeds that of many early Greeks (over a hundred fragments), he has the reputation of being one of the most difficult philosophers to interpret. What is worse, there is every reason to believe he wanted it that way. He delighted in throwing out paradoxes and aphorisms (terse, pithy statements) rather than developing a patient, continuous line of argument. For this reason, the ancients called him "the Dark One," "the Riddler," "the Obscure." Although his style does not conform to the philosophical ideal of clarity, Heraclitus represents an interesting stage in the history of thought in that he put forth some dramatically innovative alternatives.

Reason Is the Path to Knowledge

According to Heraclitus, wisdom is the goal of philosophy. However, we cannot obtain wisdom by acquiring factual information, but by seeing the hidden meaning behind the appearances. According to Heraclitus, the world comes to us in the form of a riddle. "Reality loves to conceal itself" (G123; 1.418). The secret to reality is found by understanding the **Logos**. This very important Greek word is so rich in meaning that it is difficult to translate. Briefly, the Greek word *logos* means "statement" or "discourse," but it also refers to "reason" or "the rational content of what is spoken."* However, logos is not limited to what goes on in our minds—it also suggests the rational order or structure of the world itself. Fragment 2 gets to the heart of Heraclitus's point: "One must follow what is common; but although the Logos is common, most men live as if they had a private understanding of their own" (G2; 1.425). Thus, this universal, rational order is available to all, but most people prefer to follow their individual, idiosyncratic opinions. In our contemporary culture, we often hear that everyone has their own, personal opinion and one opinion is just as good as another. But Heraclitus would not accept this. We could imagine him saying,

If we are all rational and calculate 6 + 5, we should all get the same answer. Only a company of fools would come up with different, personal answers. On any issue there is but one truth, not many.

The key to wisdom, then, is searching out the principle of reason that lies hidden within the universe and within our own souls.

Reality as Change and Conflict

THE PRIMACY OF CHANGE

What is it that we must understand about reality that will give us wisdom about life? The Milesians sought for the one, material substance, the fundamental "stuff" that was permanent throughout all the changing appearances. For them, permanence was fundamental and change was a secondary phenomenon. According to Heraclitus, however, they had it all backward. He asserted that change is ultimate and most of our experiences of stability and permanence are merely how things *appear* to be. Heraclitus critiqued our tendency to divide the world into separate and distinct *things*. We talk of coins, fish, olives, rocks, and many particular things, but these are not what is ultimate. To focus in on a very ordinary example, we commonly talk about "the weather" with our acquaintances. This noun gives us the impression that we are referring to some distinct object. However, we know that "the weather" is really a collection of many different, interacting processes: high and low pressure fronts, humidity, temperature, precipitation, wind direction and velocity, and so on. Heraclitus suggested that all the "objects" we talk about are really a collection of processes.

Heraclitus used the metaphor of a river to make his point. Although scholars are divided on what his exact words were, he said something to the effect that "you cannot step into the same river twice." In one sense, the river may seem to be the same over time. We can identify it by name, such as "the Mississippi River." However, in another sense, while the name remains the same, the waters are constantly changing and we are not dealing with the same physical entity.

---

*The notion of "rational discourse" comes out in many English words that were derived from the word *logos,* such as "logic," "geology," "psychology," and "biology."

One writer in the first century A.D. quoted Heraclitus as saying, "We step and do not step into the same rivers, we are and are not" (G49a; 1.490). This suggests that *we* are like that river, constantly changing and never staying the same. For example, when I look at my high school picture taken in the 1960s, I recognize that person as being *me*. Yet in another sense, I am not the same person. Besides the fact that my hair is grayer and thinner, many of my values and beliefs are different. Even though there is some resemblance physically and psychologically, a good deal of change also has occurred. In another passage, Heraclitus makes the same point by saying, "The sun is new every day" (G6; 1.484). The problem of continuity within change later became such a problem that Aristotle made it one of the major issues in philosophy.

THE UNITY OF OPPOSITES

Going along with his emphasis on change, Heraclitus puts forth the thesis of "the unity of opposites." He gives us abundant evidence of this from common experience. For example, different aspects of the same thing can have opposite characteristics. The pen moves in a straight line across the page when we are considering the sentence, but it moves in a crooked line when we are considering the forming of individual letters. Some opposites are merely different stages in one, continuous process. In this sense, night and day are one (G57; 1.442), and hot and cold are relative qualities that coexist on the same continuum (G126; 1.445). Heraclitus taught not only that there is a unity of opposites, but also that the conflict between opposites is good. For example, he suggests that the bow and lyre show there is harmony in conflict (G51; 1.439). The bow leaning against the wall appears stable and passive. However, the illusion of stability results from the balanced opposition of forces. Only if they maintain their tension or conflict is the bow usable. If the force of the bent bow overpowers the weakened string, it snaps, and the power is unleashed, but in a chaotic, uncontrolled way. Similarly, a lyre can produce music only if there is tension in the strings.

FIRE

Heraclitus, ever the riddler and poet, adds to the river and war metaphors yet another puzzling image to capture the nature of reality. Whereas the Milesians debated whether the world is fundamentally water or air, Heraclitus says it is an everlasting *fire*. "This world-order, the same for all, none of the gods nor of men has made, but it was always and is and shall be: an ever-living fire, which is being kindled in measures and extinguished in measures" (G30; 1.454). It is not clear whether he meant this literally as an alternative to the answers of previous philosophers or whether he meant it in a more figurative sense. Either way, the image of a fire does capture a large portion of Heraclitus's vision of the world. A fire is a process rather than a substantial object. It is constantly changing yet remains the same. Finally, fire transforms everything it touches. Substances are fed into the fire and are changed into something else. Yet although things change, there is a balance to nature and the total amount of reality remains the same.

LOGOS AGAIN

Like Xenophanes, Heraclitus has nothing but disdain for popular religion. He ridicules those who pray to statues, saying that this confused piety "does not understand what gods and heroes really are" (G5; 1.472). Yet despite his harsh, critical mind, Heraclitus had a profound and passionate religious vision of his own. Throughout the changing world, one thing does not change. However, it is not a "thing"; it is the principle or law of change itself. Thus, although the river is in constant flux, the law that governs its flowing is constant. Like the Pythagoreans, he seeks the ultimate unity not in the physical things that are ordered, but in the rationality of that order. These are the beginnings of the concept of a physical law. He identifies this ultimate unity with the Logos or the rational order of the world. However, it is an active rationality, for Heraclitus says that "everything comes to pass in accordance with this Logos" (G1; 1.419). Furthermore, he advises people that if they will listen not to him but to the Logos, they will discover all things are one (G50; 1.425). He clearly identifies the Logos with the ever-living fire, for both have the attributes of a singular divinity. The fire "will come and judge and convict all things" (G66; 1.455). Although he speaks of "the gods" in typically Greek fashion, he believes there is one supreme deity over them all. Like Xenophanes' deity, Heraclitus's god is immanent and identified with the order of nature. "God is day and night, winter and summer, war and peace, satiety and hunger . . . but he changes just as fire, when it is mingled with perfumes, is named according to the scent of each" (G67; 1.444).

Moral and Social Philosophy

As we have seen, Heraclitus believes the conflict of opposites is necessary and good. In his mind, those who prefer stability and peace are "tender-minded" individuals (whom he despises), while those who relish change and strife are "hard-headed" realists. Pythagoras thought that harmony is a blending of opposites and a diminishing of differences. But Heraclitus believes harmony and justice can only come about when opposites sharply conflict. "One must know that war is common, and justice strife, and that all things come about by way of strife and necessity" (G80; 1.447). Heraclitus's outlook is alive in our own day among those who believe that a balance of equal destruc-

tive power among the supernations will ensure world stability and peace. Furthermore, our advocate system of law illustrates his point that "justice is strife." Through the conflict of two opposing lawyers, we believe truth and justice will emerge.

Heraclitus introduces the notion that the civil law is a reflection of the divine law, which foreshadows the Stoics' and the medievals' position: ". . . all human laws are nourished by one, the divine, . . ." (G114; 1.425). However, he balances off this thought with another one: "To God all things are fair and good and just, but men have supposed some unjust and some just" (G102; 1.413). This seems to suggest there is no real distinction between good and evil in this world. In other words, Heraclitus seems to be saying, "Whatever *is*, is good" (a problematic conclusion at best).

Heraclitus's Significance

Despite the obscurity of some of his broad, sweeping generalizations, Heraclitus made several contributions. First, like Pythagoras, he sought for the unity of reality not in a material substance but in a formal pattern. Second, he developed further the notion that a universal rationality pervades the universe that our finite minds can understand. This approach encouraged scientists and philosophers to understand this order. Third, he was the most comprehensive philosopher thus far, because he addressed the issues of epistemology, metaphysics, ethics, politics, and theology.

PARMENIDES AND THE ELEATICS

Parmenides: The Rigorous Rationalist

Parmenides was born and lived in Elea, a city on the western coast of Italy. He founded a movement known as the Eleatic school of philosophy, which was named after his hometown. His birthdate is

estimated to be about 515 B.C. and he probably lived until sometime after 450 B.C. Legend has it that he was influenced by a Pythagorean as a young man. His dates indicate that he was a younger contemporary of Heraclitus, whose work he seems to have known and criticized. In a dialogue named after Parmenides, Plato says that the philosopher—

"very distinguished looking" at 65—and his disciple Zeno visited Athens for a festival. There, according to Plato's report, he met the young Socrates. Although some have doubted this account, most scholars rely on it for Parmenides' dates.

At first glance, Parmenides' ideas will seem implausible and even absurd. Even though most philosophers did not accept his conclusions, he is considered one of the most influential of the Pre-Socratics. Parmenides uses logic more powerfully than any thinker thus far. In spite of his unacceptable conclusions, his style of reasoning accounts for his influence in the development of philosophy.

Reality Is Unchanging

Parmenides' starting point is the essence of simplicity. His position can be distilled into the claim "Whatever exists, *exists*, and there is nothing apart from that which exists." That is difficult to argue with! However, Parmenides squeezes some very startling conclusions from that obvious truth. We can summarize his first argument in this way:

(1) Anything we can think or speak about either exists or doesn't exist.

(2) Anything that doesn't exist is nothing.

(3) We cannot think or speak about nothing.

(4) So, we cannot think or speak about what doesn't exist.

(5) Therefore, anything we can think or speak about exists.

The first premise presents two mutually exclusive alternatives. The second premise is true by definition. So far, we may see no problem in granting Parmenides these points. However, the third and fourth premises are the controversial ones, and yet they are the key to all of Parmenides' metaphysics. Why can't we think about nothing—premise (3)? Parmenides' reasoning seems to be that all thought requires an object. If I really were thinking about sheer nothingness, my thought would have no content and would not be a thought. What about

premise (4)? It certainly seems possible to think about things that don't exist. For example, I can think about a hamburger stand on Mars. Parmenides would point out, however, that I am not thinking about nothing. I am thinking about Mars and a hamburger stand existing there, even if what I am picturing is inaccurate. It only appears to be the case that we can talk about what does not exist, for to talk about "what is not" is to talk about nothing. But if we are talking about nothing, we are merely tossing words around and speaking nonsense.

In premise (1) Parmenides only pretended it was really possible to think and speak about what does not exist. He did so only to lead us to see the absurdity of attempting it. Parmenides' position is a very rigorous rationalism. He claims that anything that can be the object of rational thought is identical to what exists and anything that cannot be thought cannot exist. For example, if I construct a mathematical proof to show that all the angles of any triangle add up to 180 degrees, I will always find that reality is consistent with this conclusion. And when I realize that the notion of "a round square" is unthinkable, I will be certain that nothing like that could ever exist.

For Parmenides, the fundamental reality of Being can be spoken of as the "what is" or "the One." He sometimes simply refers to this as "It," meaning everything and anything. However, note that he never refers to it as "God." From this initial argument, Parmenides draws out a number of logical consequences:

1. *Being is uncreated.* Parmenides uses what will come to be known as the "principle of causality." If Being began at some point or was created, it would either have to come from (a) something or (b) pop into being from nothing. But if Being is all there is, then condition (a) could not be true, for there could be no other cause from which Being came into existence. Furthermore, Being could not have come from *nothing*, because that does not exist and could not cause anything. So condition (b) cannot be true either. Parmenides also uses what later philosophers called the "principle of

sufficient reason." There must be a reason why Being appeared when it did and not, say, three minutes ago. But if nothingness precedes Being, there could be no reason for Being to come into existence at one time as opposed to another. Hence, Being cannot have an origin.

2. *Being is unchangeable and imperishable.* If it could change, what could it change into? It could not change into Being, because it is that already. Hence, if it ever changed or was destroyed, it would have to become nothing. But is this conceivable? No, for Parmenides has previously shown that non-Being cannot exist or be thought. It appears that Parmenides' Being is timeless, since time requires moments coming to be and passing away into nothingness. But if there can be no creation or destruction, there cannot be time as we know it. All of reality is like the eternal objects of mathematics. We cannot ask about circularity and the number 2, "How old are they?" or "What will they be like in the future?"

3. *Being is one and is indivisible.* If Being is a plurality or is divided, what could mark the divisions within it? If the thing marking the division is Being, this is the same as what is being divided. If something is continuous, it can have no divisions. To use an analogy, trying to divide a pool of water into two parts with another quantity of water would be useless. We would still end up with one quantity of water. Yet if the division is not made up of *what is*, then it must be nothing—in which case it is not a division at all.

4. *Being is motionless.* Motion would require empty space. But since empty space would necessarily contain nothing (which cannot be something that exists), there can be no motion.

5. *Being is a finite body.* Parmenides assumes the material monism of the Milesians and conceives of his Being as a physical body. He also assumes it is finite, because the Greeks were very nervous about the concept of an infinite quantity. They thought that anything infinite would be indefinite and incomplete. Since Being is homogenous and evenly distributed throughout the universe,

Parmenides compares it to a perfectly round sphere.

Reason Versus the Senses

How could Parmenides possibly believe all this? Our common sense tells us we live in a world of changing, plural objects. Does he really want to deny what our senses so clearly tell us about the world? Parmenides' answer is that we have a basic choice to make. We have, on the one hand, the world as it appears to our senses. On the other hand, we have a description of reality that his logical arguments present. Which source of knowledge should we trust? With regard to the first alternative, he cautions, "Let not habit born of much experience force thee along this way, to ply a heedless eye and sounding ear and tongue" (G7, 2.21). Instead, we are to "judge by reason" (*logos*) the controversial conclusions he puts forth. When we see a magician pull a rabbit out of a previously empty hat, our senses tell us that Being came from non-Being. However, our reason vetoes the senses and tells us this is only an appearance. Parmenides asks us to do this with all our sense experience. He is, without a doubt, the most uncompromising rationalist in the history of philosophy. His position raised to prominence the question "What roles do sense experience and reason play in coming to know reality?" Other philosophers do not necessarily agree with his conclusions, but serious thinkers had to come to terms with his arguments.

Zeno of Elea: Coming to Parmenides' Defense

Parmenides was the object of a great deal of ridicule because of his outrageous conclusions. However, he had a very able defender in a disciple who was twenty-five years younger. Zeno of Elea (approximately 490–430 B.C.) wrote a book in which he produced a barrage of arguments (perhaps close to fifty of them) to refute his master's critics. His arguments are so extremely clever and penetrating that countless twentieth-century mathematicians and logicians have spent a great deal of time and ink trying to get to the bottom of them. The main strategy Zeno uses is to adopt the position of Parmenides' critics. From there he shows that one or more conclusions logically follow. However, the conclusions turn out to contradict one another or to be patently absurd. This type of argument has been called *reductio ad absurdum* or "reducing to an absurdity." The collection of these arguments have been labeled "Zeno's Paradoxes." A few examples will illustrate his technique.

1. *Arguments Against the Senses.* If we drop a small millet seed on the ground, it will make no noise. However, if we drop a bushel of millet seeds, they will make a thud. Either (1) millet seeds do not make a sound when dropped, or (2) millet seeds do make a sound when they are dropped. Which of the two experiences are we to believe? If condition (1) is true, then our senses deceived us when we heard a sound. If condition (2) is true, then our senses deceived us when we did not hear a sound. Either way, the senses are unreliable.

2. *Arguments Against Plurality.* Zeno is said to have offered forty arguments to show that the notion of plurality is full of paradoxes. To take the simplest argument, let's suppose numerous objects exist. They each must have some particular size. But any one of these objects can be infinitely divided into multiple parts and this leads, Zeno argues, to an absurdity. For example, take a 6-foot board. We can saw it in half, and then we can take each one of these pieces and saw them in half again, and do this repeatedly. In principle (although not in practice), we could divide each piece an infinite number of times. However, if the original board contained an infinite number of parts, each having some magnitude, then the original board must have been infinitely large. Since this conclusion is absurd, it must mean that the starting assumption—that there are multiple, divisible objects—is absurd also.

3. *Paradoxes of Motion.* Zeno produced four arguments to show that motion is impossible. The easiest to describe is called "the racecourse." Let us suppose a runner tries to run from the starting point A to a distant goal Z. Before he can get from

A to Z, he must first traverse half the distance. But before he can get halfway, he must first cross half that distance, and so on. At any given point in the race, his immediate goal is a certain distance that can be divided in half and this length can itself be divided into an infinite number of points. Since he always has an infinite number of points to cross, which will take an infinite amount of time, the poor runner will not be able to get anywhere at all. Therefore, contrary to our uncritical beliefs, it is impossible to make any rational sense out of motion.

Before we dismiss Zeno with a disgusted wave of the hand, it is worth pointing out that all great advances in human thought have gone against entrenched common sense. It is not immediately obvious to the senses that the earth is in motion, nor are some of the theories of present-day physicists any more palatable to common sense than Parmenides' conclusions. Nevertheless, while most philosophers have been sure that there is something wrong with Zeno's arguments, it has been hard to find agreement on where the problem lies. Contemporary analyses of the arguments have depended on the revolutionary work on infinite sets done by the mathematician Georg Cantor (1845–1918).

Evaluation and Significance of the Eleatics

A major problem in the Eleatics' arguments is that they confused grammar, logic, and metaphysics. This caused them to make fallacious leaps from language to reality. For example, they thought it was contradictory to say, "There *is* nothing." The problem was that the Greeks at this stage of philosophy could not conceive that a word might have more than one meaning. However, "to be" can have at least three meanings:

1. To exist—"There *is* a God."
2. Identity—"The butler *is* the murderer."
3. The attribution of a quality—"John *is* tall, and Mary *is* tall."

However, the early Greeks often confused these three uses of "is." For example, the fact that John and Mary are both tall does not imply that the two people are identical. Similarly, although it is true that "a unicorn is a one-horned beast," this does not mean that such a beast exists, just as the claim "there is nothing in the refrigerator" does not mean that *nothing* is some *thing* that exists. Plato attempted to clear up some of these points in his dialogue called the *Sophist*.

In spite of their problems, we must not overlook the Eleatics' positive contributions: (1) They were the first to reflect on the logical implications of words and concepts. (2) They had the courage to follow their assumptions to their logical conclusions, even though they seemed counterintuitive. Science cannot advance unless people are willing to forsake the obvious, the immediate, and the commonsensical. (3) They were very influential, even if in a negative way. The rigor of Parmenides' arguments forced Plato and Aristotle to wrestle with them to lay these problems to rest. The Eleatic philosophy is another example of a fertile error, for their philosophy was so cleverly argued yet so outrageous that it provoked hard thinking.

THE PLURALISTS

The Pluralists' Task

Parmenides showed what happens when we start with monism and consistently work out all its implications. It seemed clear to the philosophers who analyzed Parmenides' arguments that he and his followers must have started off in the wrong direction if they ended with the conclusion that the world of sense experience is one, massive illusion and that change does not really occur. The remedy, offered by a group of philosophers we call the *pluralists*, was to reject the starting point of radical monism.

Empedocles (495–435 B.C.)

Empedocles, a native of Sicily, was known as a philosopher, religious mystic, poet, and magician. Although he agreed with Parmenides that there can be no *absolute* creation or destruction of reality, Empedocles claimed there is *relative* change. In postulating both change and permanence, he achieved a compromise between Heraclitus and Parmenides. However, contrary to the Eleatics, he postulated that there is not one thing that is permanent but four things: earth, air, fire, and water. These are the eternal "root" substances or elements, and all change is explained as the combination and separation of these permanent elements. He even worked out some of the details of how this might come about. For example, bone consists of two parts earth, two parts water, and four parts fire.*

However, this explanation of the composition of things is not enough to explain the world of our experience. Empedocles realizes we need a separate set of principles to explain change and motion. On the one hand, we find the world consists of certain unified objects such as chairs, trees, stones, and so forth. We need something to explain how the individual elements combine and stick together: a *principle of unification*. On the other hand, the world is not one, giant unity, as Parmenides thought. It is composed of individual objects. Furthermore, even these smaller unities disintegrate and break down into their separate components. Therefore, we also need a *principle of individuation*. Empedocles was insightful in realizing that both principles were essential.

According to Empedocles, *love* is the principle of unity and *strife* is the principle of individuation. The interaction of these two opposing forces results in a continual amount of flux in the world.

---

*We might suppose that if Empedocles had been familiar with our method of symbolizing chemical compounds, he would designate bone as $E_2W_2F_4$!

The present world is in an intermediate stage between total unity and separation. Concerning the direction in which it is headed, Empedocles was a pessimist. He says, "Things are becoming worse." Even though he speaks of these forces as deities, he also thinks of them as materialistic forces, for he says, "Love and strife run through all things like quicksilver." Many Greeks at this time still had difficulty imagining any other kind of reality except large material objects and very fine material objects. Notice that the forces that control the physical universe are moral forces (love and hate). Even though the Greek philosophers of this period had moved away from the fantastic stories of the gods controlling all events, their explanations were still tinged with a heavy dose of anthropomorphism. We may smile at some of their primitive notions until we realize how hard it is to escape the use of metaphors in describing the world. In contemporary physics, the notions of love and strife find their way into our talk of subatomic particles "attracting" and "repelling" one another.

Empedocles had three other theories worth mentioning. First, he denied that there could be empty space. He understood motion as one clump of matter moving between other clumps of matter, much like a fish moving through water. Although the Pythagoreans had postulated empty space, the notion that a void (nonbeing) could exist was difficult to accept at this time. Second, in terms of the written records we have, he developed the first theory of sense perception. According to his account, when particles of matter fly off an object and strike our sense organs, perception occurs. Thus, when you see a red tomato, this is the result of red particles from the tomato actually contacting your eyeballs. Finally, he proposed a theory of evolution based on a crude version of what we now call the "law of natural selection." He imagined that once there were random products of nature that consisted of creatures with heads of cattle and branches for arms and other fantastic combinations. For obvious reasons, these could not function very successfully, and so they died off and their species became extinct. The species that now exist are those whose random arrangements of bodily parts that were most advantageous for survival.

Anaxagoras (500–428 B.C.)

Anaxagoras was an Ionian who moved to Athens and became a part of the intellectual circle surrounding Pericles, a major political figure of this time. Anaxagoras had a hardheaded, naturalistic approach to the world that is best illustrated by two stories. First, we are told that he was exiled from Athens on charges of impiety for promoting the heresy that the sun was a white-hot stone and not a deity. Then there is the story of a one-horned ram that was given to Pericles. A soothsayer proclaimed that this unusual creature was a sign from the gods and predicted that if either Pericles or Thucydides possessed it, they would be victorious in battle. Anaxagoras was unimpressed and swiftly dissected its skull, finding that the lack of two horns was caused by a brain tumor. It was a natural phenomenon, not a miraculous sign, he explained.

Anaxagoras carried pluralism one step further. Instead of four elements, he said that every kind of thing has its own element. Thus, there is an indefinite number of elements or "seeds" (*spermata*). There are seeds for grass, bone, hair, gold, mud, and so on. How is it that when we eat food it becomes part of our bodies and is converted into flesh, bone, hair, and blood? The answer is that the particles of these things were already in the food to begin with. Thus, everything is in everything. When we see grass, the grass elements predominate in it and so that is all we see. However, if the cow eats grass and produces milk and the horse eats grass and it produces muscle, then bits of milk and muscle must be mixed in with the grass elements.

Anaxagoras introduced Mind (or *Nous*) as the source of motion and the principle of order. *Nous* does not create the world but is a free, spontaneous, active, perfect, and all-knowing force. Although this is the beginning of a vague dualism of mind and matter, in the final analysis *Nous* comes out to be merely a kind of rarefied matter.

EVALUATION OF ANAXAGORAS

There are several problems in Anaxagoras's philosophy: (1) He leaves us without any sort of unified explanation of reality. An extreme pluralism that claims there is an element for every kind of thing loses all explanatory value. Explanations are supposed to make the world simpler and more unified, not hand it back to us as diverse as when we first began. (2) Both Socrates and Aristotle point out that Anaxagoras brings in *Nous* or Mind only when mechanical explanations fail. Thus, it is an emergency principle that is called in only to fill in the blanks in our knowledge. Despite these problems, his principle of Mind led philosophers to ask what else besides matter is necessary to explain the world.

DEMOCRITUS AND THE ATOMISTS

|||

The founder of the Atomist movement is thought to be a philosopher by the name of Leucippus, but we know very little about him. Therefore, Democritus (460–360 B.C.) is our source for most of the Atomists' ideas.* He was a younger contemporary of Anaxagoras who wrote on physics, epistemology, metaphysics, ethics, and history, besides being ranked highly as a mathematician.

Being

According to the Atomists, two principles explain reality: atoms and the void. Notice that by making the void or empty space a component of being, the Atomists disagree with Parmenides, for they are claiming that what-is-not *does* exist! Atoms have several features. First, they are indivisible, eternal, and unchanging (making them almost small editions of Parmenidean Being). However, they are infinite in number (the unlimited expanse of space allows this). Second, there are quantitative differences between them (they come in various sizes and shapes). Third, they are qualitatively alike or neutral (they have no color, taste, temperature, or odor).

Becoming

Change was understood as a result of the differing relationships between the atoms. Democritus's ar-

gument concerning change is as follows: (1) There is no up or down in any absolute sense, and, therefore, motion is directionless. (2) It follows that atoms do not have weight in any absolute sense.† (3) Since there is no natural, final resting place for the atoms, the motion of atoms is eternal (like dust particles dancing in the sunlight). Aristotle was not satisfied with this answer and complained, "They lazily shelved the question of the origin of motion."

The World of Appearances

The world we see about us can be explained on the basis of the previous principles: (1) the motion of the atoms and their geometrical properties produce (2) various interactions and combinations that produce (3) all the qualities found in sense experience. For example, solid matter results when atoms that have rough surfaces or hooks become interlocked. Liquids are made up of spherical atoms with smooth surfaces that continually roll over one another. Sweet-tasting substances are made up of smooth atoms, while bitter herbs, of course, are made up of atoms with sharp points that irritate our mouth atoms. For Democritus, there is no ordering principle in the world. What patterns there seem to be are simply products of the material properties of atoms and the chance collisions that result from their motions.

---

*Democritus is not truly a Pre-Socratic, because he was a younger contemporary of Socrates.

†We now know he is right. As space travel illustrates, weight is a relative property.

Theory of Knowledge

Democritus's epistemology follows from his materialism. He has an emanation theory of perception in which atoms from objects fly off and collide with our sense organs. The motion from this impact is then transmitted to our material soul atoms, and we experience an image of the original object. However, if this is true, then the senses do not give us direct knowledge of the world. They only produce certain appearances within us. Lemons taste bitter, while honey tastes sweet. Apples appear to be red, and water appears to be blue. However, these experiences are really produced by the objective spatial qualities of the atoms and the subjective effects of their impact on our sense organs. This is why the same food can taste different to different people. The colors, smells, and tastes we experience are not the real properties of the objects out there. For this reason, Democritus asserts there are two kinds of knowledge:

Trueborn	Bastard
Objective	Subjective
Things as they are	Things as they appear
Atoms and	Qualities: colors,
the void	sounds, smells,
	tastes, textures

What Democritus calls "bastard knowledge" is really sense experience. Thus, to know the true nature of things, reason must penetrate beneath the sensory appearances to discern the quantitative nature of the atoms. The implications of this distinction reverberated all the way into the modern age. In the seventeenth century, Galileo and Descartes made the same distinctions in terms of primary and secondary qualities. For both Democritus and these seventeenth-century mechanists, the world as viewed by the poet, the artist, or our unrefined senses is subjective. Only the world as given to us by scientific and mathematical reason is real. However, this epistemology caused some problems for Democritus. Sense experience gives us only appearances, but reason has no materials to work except those provided by the senses. Thus, according to one account, Democritus has the senses taunting reason: "Wretched mind, do you take your evidence from us and then throw us down? That throw is your overthrow" (G145; 2.460). In despair Democritus concludes, "In reality we know nothing, for truth is in the depths" (G117; 2.460).

Ethics

Democritus started with an attempt to develop a hardheaded scientific view of the world. However, he was also well aware that this had implications for all of life. His writings on morality seek to work this out consistently. As he says in one passage,

> Equanimity comes to men through proportionate pleasure and moderation in life. Excesses and defects are apt to change and cause great disturbances in the soul. Those souls which are moved over great distances have neither stability nor equanimity.[3]

The key term here is "moved." He is attempting to provide ethical advice on the basis of physics. His theory is based on three assumptions:

1. All experience is produced by the movement of atoms.
2. The good life is one in which this experience is pleasing.
3. Tranquility of the soul (gentle motions) is more pleasing than all the pleasures of the body (large-scale motions).

This view is known as "prudent hedonism." **Hedonism** is the theory that pleasure is the only value in life. What other sort of ethics could a materialist have but one that reduced ethical values to material, physiological motions? However, it is a *prudent* hedonism because he realizes that not all pleasures are worthy of being pursued. As far as our ultimate destiny is concerned, the Atomists theorized that the soul is only a bundle of very fine atoms. Since this compound (and hence the person) disperses at death, there is no personal immortality. Therefore, living our life here and now with as much joy and as little trouble as possible is the only goal we need worry about.

Significance of the Atomists

Plato ignored the Atomists and Aristotle rejected them because they found that an atomistic, mechanistic materialism was inadequate to explain the world. However, the Atomists' metaphysics and moral philosophy were revived in the Hellenistic period, mainly through the teachings of the Epicureans. Atomism as a foundation for science was reborn in the sixteenth and seventeenth centuries and virtually remained unchanged until the nineteenth century. Hence, we will defer any evaluation of their thought until we look at these later outworkings of their theory.

Summary of the Pre-Socratics

The philosophers that preceded Socrates set philosophy in motion by offering arguments for their theories and by criticizing one another. Although their arguments are not always cogent, they *did* present reasons for their positions as well as for the refutations of their contemporaries. This was a great advance over previous explanations of the universe, which simply relied on the noncritical transmission of the mythical and poetic traditions of the culture. However, along with their insights came a number of problems. The wide range of conflicting opinions that developed during this period would lead the next group of philosophers to be very skeptical about whether we could ever arrive at any truths that were more than simply personal opinions. These developments also made philosophers realize that more work needed to be done on the foundations of knowledge.

Questions for Understanding

1. What was Thales' basic question? What was his answer? What reasons might he have had to support his position?

2. How does Thales explain change?

3. What is metaphysical monism? Why could Thales' position be called "material monism"?

4. What does Anaximander mean by the Apeiron?

5. How does Anaximander explain change?

6. What is the basic substance according to Anaximenes?

7. According to Anaximenes, what two principles explain change?

8. What points of agreement were there among the Milesians?

9. In what sense did the Pythagoreans combine philosophy and religion?

10. What did the Pythagoreans mean when they said reality is mathematical? Why did they believe this?

11. Why are the Pythagoreans called metaphysical dualists?

12. What was the Pythagorean view of the soul?

13. In what ways were the Pythagoreans innovative?

14. What was Xenophanes' view of knowledge?

15. In what ways did Xenophanes' views differ from the typical Greek view of the gods?

16. According to Heraclitus, what is the Logos? Why is it important?

17. Why did Heraclitus say "you cannot step into the same river twice"? How does this represent his basic view of reality?

18. What does Heraclitus mean by the "unity of opposites"?

19. What does the image of fire symbolize in Heraclitus's philosophy?

20. What are the main themes in Heraclitus's moral and social philosophy?

21. Why does Parmenides believe reality is unchanging?

22. What are some examples of Zeno's paradoxes? How does he use them to defend Parmenides' philosophy?

23. According to Empedocles, what substances are fundamental?

24. What two principles does Empedocles use to explain change?

25. What is Anaxagoras's view of the basic elements?

26. What does Anaxagoras mean by Nous?

27. According to Democritus and the atomists, what two principles explain reality?

28. How does Democritus use the geometrical properties of atoms to explain the properties of the objects of everyday experience?

29. How does Democritus use his theory of atoms to explain knowledge? What features of reality are objective and what features are subjective?

30. What sort of account does Democritus give of ethics?

31. What is hedonism?

Questions for Reflection

1. If you were living during the time of the Pre-Socratics, which of their philosophies would you think was most plausible? Which would seem the least plausible. Why?

2. The Pre-Socratics' greatest contribution was not their answers, but their questions. What were some of the questions they raised that were particularly innovative, important, and that we still ask today?

Notes

1. Quoted in Edwin A. Burtt, *The Metaphysical Foundations of Modern Physical Science*, rev. ed. (Garden City, NY: Doubleday Anchor Books, 1932), 75.

2. Quotations of the Pre-Socratic philosophers are from W. K. C. Guthrie, *A History of Greek Philosophy*, vols. 1 and 2 (Cambridge, England: Cambridge University Press, 1962). This is abbreviated in the text with the letter "G." The first number of the reference is the fragment of the particular philosopher's work being quoted. The second set of numbers represents the volume and page in Guthrie where the quote can be found.

3. Quoted in John Mansley Robinson, *An Introduction to Early Greek Philosophy* (Boston: Houghton Mifflin, 1968), 220.

3

The Sophists and Socrates

THE SOPHISTS

Skepticism and the Keys to Success

In the fifth century, while philosophers from Parmenides to Democritus were debating traditional questions about physical nature, a major juncture or turning point in the history of philosophy was emerging. To understand this change in direction, we need to look at what was happening to the culture during this century. By this time, the city-state of Athens had risen to become the commercial, intellectual, and artistic center of Greek culture. This period was rich with advances in medicine, architecture, art, poetry, and drama. Furthermore, Athenian democracy came to birth as a new form of political governance. For these reasons, this century is known as the Golden Age of Greece. Ironically, the flood of social and political changes brought with them a moral and cultural malaise. As the century wore on, the old ideal of respect for the Athenian laws, religion, and customs began to disintegrate. Writing in the latter third of the century, after the outbreak of the Peloponnesian War, the historian Thucydides described a society that had lost its moorings:

> The common meaning of words was turned about at men's pleasure; the most reckless bravado was deemed the most desirable friend; a man of prudence

> and moderation was styled a coward; a man who listened to reason was a good-for-nothing simpleton.[1]

Likewise, in his play *Medea*, Euripides mourned the changes that had taken place in his culture:

> Life, life is changed and the laws of it o'ertrod. . . .
> Man hath forgotten God. . . .[2]

At least four causes produced these changes: (1) Respect for the culture's authorities (the poetic traditions concerning the gods) declined. This resulted in the loss of a metaphysical foundation for values. (2) Increased contact with different cultures, customs, and laws led to the conclusion that most beliefs and standards once thought to be universal and absolute were actually relative to the local culture. (3) The rise of democratic lawmaking made it difficult to assume the divine origins of one's society. Furthermore, the democratic spirit led to a new sense of individualism and opened up new opportunities for personal power and success. (4) The plurality of opinions among the philosophers and scientists concerning the nature of reality led to the skeptical conclusion that no one can ever know the truth. All this caused a loss of interest in metaphysical questions. Taking its place was an increased interest in the more practical concerns of individuals and their culture.

Into this philosophical turmoil stepped a group of educators called the Sophists. With the decline of the old aristocracy, political leadership was no longer a result of one's birth. One could now rise to power by winning the favor of the crowd and by prevailing in the judicial system. Accordingly, the Sophists offered guidance in practical matters to the rising class of politicians. Many of them traveled from town to town, offering their instruction for a fee. When the Sophist Protagoras was asked what a student would learn from him, he is said to have replied, "The proper care of his personal affairs, so that he may best manage his own household, and also of the state's affairs, so as to become a real power in the city, both as a speaker and man of action."[3]

The word "Sophist" is derived from the Greek word *sophia*, which means "wisdom."* Originally it had a neutral meaning and meant something like "professor." After Socrates' quarrels with the Sophists, however, they came into disrepute, and many people used the word as a term of abuse. For example, Plato referred to them as "shopkeepers with spiritual wares."[4] Aristotle complained that the training provided by Sophists such as Protagoras was a "fraud" because it taught the skill of "making the worse argument seem the better."[5] In their defense, we should note that most of our information on them comes from prejudiced sources.

In its worst forms, the Sophists' philosophy could be summed up in two words: *skepticism* and *success*. **Skepticism** is the claim that true knowledge is unattainable. When the thinkers of the fifth century looked back over their own, brief philosophical history, the jumble of conflicting opinions gave credibility to skepticism. Thales was refuted by Anaximander, who was refuted by Anaximenes. Heraclitus said everything is changing, and Parmenides said everything is permanent. It seemed as though no one really knew. So all truth is relative, claimed the Sophists. Likewise, all values and standards are relative. What is "truth," "justice," or

"moral goodness"? According to many of the Sophists, they are just sounds we make.

The second main theme of the Sophists was that achieving success is the goal in life. If knowledge is impossible, then it is useless to seek for what you can't find. Instead, one should just try to get along. The Sophists taught that you should not ask of an idea, "Is it true?" Instead, you should ask, "Will advocating this idea help me?" Don't ask of an action, "Is it right?" Instead, you should ask, "Will performing this action be advantageous to me?" To the success-driven young people of Athens, the search for truth gave way to the marketing of one's opinions. The search for moral correctness gave way to promoting one's interests. Accordingly, the Sophists taught the skills of rhetoric, debate, public speaking, and persuasion.

An important issue to the Sophists was the distinction between *physis* and *nomos*. *Physis* is commonly translated as "nature" and refers to the features of the world that are independent of human traditions and decisions. Appropriately, our word "physics" is derived from it. *Nomos*, in contrast, refers to that which is based on human customs or conventions. The fact that Americans hold their fork in their right hand when eating and Europeans keep it in their left hand is a matter of *nomos*. However, the fact that eating is necessary to sustain life is a matter of *physis*. An important application of this distinction is found in the question "Are the laws of morality simply a matter of *nomos* (human convention), or can we find their basis in *physis* (the natural order of things)?" All the Sophists agreed that traditional morality was based only in convention or *nomos*. The conservatives among them said success was to be gained in accepting the morality of one's society. However, those with a more cynical bent said we should give lip service to conventional morality but should not allow it to limit our behavior.

PROTAGORAS

The first and most famous of the Sophists was Protagoras. His dates are in dispute, but most believe he was born in the early part of the fifth century B.C. (probably not later than 490) and may have

*Our English words *sophomore* and *sophisticated* share this same root.

died around the year 420 B.C. He became famous for his assertion "Man is the measure of all things, of those that are that they are, of those that are not that they are not." Two interpretations have been given of this slogan: (1) each individual person provides his or her own standard for interpreting things, or (2) society as a whole is the measure of all things. Under either interpretation, he expresses a radical humanism and relativism that says there is no standard other than those that individuals or societies invent. Actually, Protagoras seems to have embraced both alternatives. As we will see, he affirmed an individualistic subjectivism with respect to perception and a social subjectivism with respect to ethics.

Protagoras accepted without question the thesis that our only contact with the world is through perception. From this he drew the conclusion that everything is relative to the individual. To me the wind may feel warm, but to you it may seem cold. There is no correct answer here, for however it *seems* to you, that is the way it *is* (to you), and no one can say you are wrong. In his brief slogan, Protagoras swept away with a flourish all the debates of the previous philosophers. The cosmologists (such as Parmenides) were trying to find out how reality truly is, apart from how it appears to be. Protagoras argued that we can make no such distinction.* All we have are appearances and individual opinions. Hence, all beliefs are equally true.

Such a radical individualism would seem to lead to moral and social anarchy. However, Protagoras surprises us with a rather conservative position on ethics. Even though moral judgments are purely relative and a product of convention, society's traditions and laws are as good as any. Therefore, we should uphold and follow the traditions of our particular society because a peaceful and orderly society is good. As he is reported to have taught, "Whatever practices seem right and laudable to any particular state are so, for that state, so long as it holds by them."[6] No doubt, he would have approved of the advice "When in Rome do as the Romans do." Therefore, he comes down on the side of *nomos* (convention), since it is all we have to guide our lives. Protagoras believed that even though it is useless to worry about whether an idea is true or not, he thought it obvious that some ideas are better or more expedient than others. Therefore, our humanly invented standards can be given a pragmatic justification by virtue of the fact that they seem to work for our good.[†]

His skepticism led him to dismiss the possibility of theoretical discussions of theology:

> Concerning the gods I am unable to discover whether they exist or not, or what they are like in form; for there are many hindrances to knowledge, the obscurity of the subject and the brevity of human life.[7]

Nevertheless, he thought traditional religion should not be abandoned. Although he was not sure the gods existed, he did seem assured they should be worshiped. Religious belief was an integral part of the civilized society and political community of his time. Therefore, belief in the gods is necessary for social stability. Once again, his interests were practical and not theoretical.

GORGIAS

The Sophist Gorgias is thought to have lived over a hundred years, from around 483 to somewhere around 375 B.C. He was led to his skepticism by Zeno's arguments and even seems to have adopted the latter's style and method. Having given up on the pursuit of truth, he also gave up philosophy and became a teacher of rhetoric. His book was titled *On the Non-Existent or On Nature*, which seems to be a parody of the title *On Nature or the Existent*, which is thought to be the name Parmenides gave to his own book. Here, Gorgias appears to be following the advice he gave his students, which was "to destroy an opponent's seriousness by laughter."[8]

---

*In referring to "things that are and things that are not" in the "Man is the measure" formula, Protagoras may have been referring to Parmenides' discussion of Being and non-Being. Thus, in contrast to the Eleatics' teachings, Protagoras is saying that what exists and what doesn't exist is simply a matter of individual or social opinion.

†F. C. S. Schiller, one of the founders of the twentieth-century movement of pragmatism, called himself a disciple of Protagoras.

Whereas Protagoras argued that "everything is true," Gorgias delighted in proving that "nothing is true." Accordingly, he argued for three outrageous theses:

1. Nothing exists.
2. If anything exists, it is unknowable.
3. If it is knowable, it cannot be communicated.

We have a report of the arguments he provided for these conclusions, but they are too lengthy to reproduce here. It is not clear whether he meant these arguments to be regarded seriously, or whether he was showing off his rhetorical skills and offering a parody of Parmenides and the entire cosmological tradition. Nevertheless, it does seem that the point of each one of his theses is to promote a cynical skepticism. With the first conclusion, he is showing that rational argument is limited. Parmenides argued that Being exists, but Gorgias attempts to show that it is just as easy to argue that nothing exists. Hence, reason can prove anything and metaphysics is impossible. The second thesis implies that reason and experience are inadequate to tell us about the world. Thus, knowledge is impossible. The third thesis claims that human language is inadequate and each of us is trapped within our own subjective world of impressions. Nevertheless, according to Gorgias, a skilled rhetorician can reason to any conclusion. Persuasion, not truth, is the goal of discourse.

ANTIPHON

A distinction is often made between the earlier Sophists and the later ones. The earlier ones, such as Protagoras, tended to be more conservative. They endorsed *nomos* since, in the absence of any real knowledge, it is better for us to simply stick with the conventions of our society. The later Sophists, however, saw the laws of society (*nomos*) as being in tension with the laws of nature (*physis*) and said we are better off following nature. A good example of this viewpoint is found in Antiphon, a contemporary of Socrates. He argues that we naturally seek what is advantageous to us. We are all subject to the law of self-preservation. However, this law was not passed by any human legislators but is a law of nature itself. If we violate this law, the penalty is death, and, unlike human courts, nature's penalties follow swiftly and automatically:

> *Most of the things which are just by law are hostile to nature. . . . But life and death are the concern of nature, and living creatures live by what is advantageous to them and die from what is not advantageous; and the advantages which accrue from law are chains upon nature, whereas those which accrue from nature are free.*[9]

The problem is that many of the conventional laws work against the law of nature. For example, society tells me I cannot attack a malicious enemy except in self-defense. However, nature dictates that it is in the interest of my self-preservation to strike first. Consequently, Antiphon offers the following moral policy:

> *A man will be just, then, in a way most advantageous to himself if, in the presence of witnesses, he holds the laws of the city in high esteem, and in the absence of witnesses, when he is alone, those of nature.*[10]

Further cynical sentiments were expressed by Thrasymachus (represented in Plato's *Republic*) and Callicles (in Plato's *Gorgias*). Thrasymachus emphasized the sociological fact that those people who have the most power are in a position to dictate what we will call just or not. Hence, since morality is just a matter of social convention, then "justice" will be whatever serves the interests of the powerful. Callicles stressed that not only *will* the interests of the stronger persons prevail, but that they *should* prevail. In other words, the laws of nature dictate that "might makes right."

EVALUATION AND SIGNIFICANCE OF THE SOPHISTS

Socrates and Plato provided the negative critique of the Sophists. In brief, they said that: (1) The Sophists overemphasized the accidental, subjective, and personal elements in knowledge and conduct. (2) They failed to realize that objective standards are inescapable, for they are required for any judgment—including critical ones. (3) The Sophists claimed to teach success in life, but never examined this concept. Hence, they were uncritical in their criticisms.

Even if we agree with these criticisms of the Sophists, the perspective of history shows that they did make some positive philosophical contributions: (1) They raised critical questions in epistemology, ethics, and politics that had been ignored or taken for granted by their predecessors. (2) The Sophists focused on questions concerning human affairs (knowledge, values, and actions) and thereby expanded the range of philosophy beyond merely cosmological concerns. (3) They provided a "philosophical weeding service" by undercutting beliefs that were naively based on dogma and tradition. (4) The corrosive skepticism of the Sophists and their ethical relativism forced later philosophers to think more carefully about the foundations of knowledge and values. Thus, the Sophists, along with their opponent Socrates, represented a transitional stage to the more systematic philosophies of Plato and Aristotle. (5) The Sophists' study of language and argument contributed to the development of logic, rhetoric, and grammar. (6) They were a progressive force against entrenched tradition. Because they traveled about, they could look beyond the boundaries of the much too provincial city-states. Furthermore, their critique of blind faith in tradition led to more practical political solutions in the form of Panhellenism or a greater sense of unity between the Greek states. (7) Finally, the problems evoked by the Sophists' skepticism were a motivating force behind Socrates' philosophical quest. Hence, his reaction to them produced one of the most influential philosophies in human history. We now turn to this philosophical giant that occupied the body of an eccentric little man.

SOCRATES (470–399 B.C.)

Socrates on Trial

The year is 399 B.C. In the Athenian courtroom, the crowd murmurs as the former sculptor turned marketplace philosopher makes his way to the center of the room to face his accusers. To the unfeeling spectators, the defendant seems to be physically unimpressive as the light shines off his bald head and a disheveled and worn garment hangs awkwardly on his seventy-year-old, short and stocky frame. It would be a humorous scene except for the solemnity of the occasion. The "criminal" is Socrates, and he is arguing for his life before an Athenian jury made up of five hundred citizens, chosen at random. The charges are "Socrates is guilty of corrupting the youth, and of believing not in the gods whom the state believes in, but in other new divinities."[11] Although he is initially a comical figure, one's assessment of him changes when he begins to speak. He addresses the charges while weaving in the details of his life. The twinkle in his eye almost makes us forget that capital charges hang over him. As his voice increases in its intensity and urgency, we have a sense that it is not this aged philosopher that sits in judgment, but that the court and the citizens of Athens are on trial. How they make their decision will reveal both their own character and that of their society. The defendant speaks:

Athenians, I hold you in the highest regard and affection, but I will be persuaded by the god rather than you. As long as I have breath and strength I will not give up philosophy and exhorting you and declaring the truth to every one of you whom I meet, saying, as I am accustomed, "My good friend . . . are you not ashamed of caring so much for the making of money and for fame and prestige, when you neither think nor care about wisdom and truth and the improvement of your soul?" If he disputes my words and says that he does care about these things, I shall not at once release him and go away: I shall question him and cross-examine him and test him. If I think that he has not attained excellence, though he says that he has, I shall reproach him for undervaluing the most valuable things, and overvaluing those that are less valuable. This I shall do to everyone whom I meet, young or old, citizen or stranger. . . . For I spend my whole life in going about and persuading you all to give your first and greatest care to the improvement of your souls, and not till you have done that to think of your bodies or your wealth.[12]

And now, Athenians, I am not arguing in my own defense at all, as you might expect me to do, but rather in yours in order [that] you may not make a mistake about the gift of the god to you by condemning me. For if you put me to death, you will not easily find another who . . . clings to the state as a sort of gadfly to a horse that is large and well-bred but rather sluggish because of its size, so that it needs to be aroused. It seems to me that the god has attached me like that to the state, for I am constantly alighting upon you at every point to arouse, persuade, and reproach each of you all day long. You will not easily find anyone else, my friends, to fill my place; and if you are persuaded by me, you will spare my life.[13]

Apparently the majority did not appreciate Socrates' role as a gadfly in their midst, stinging them out of their complacency, for the vote of the jury was 280 votes for conviction and 220 votes for acquittal. Socrates spent the next thirty days in prison, discoursing with his friends and awaiting his execution. When the day arrived, he was surrounded by his weeping friends as he drank the poison hemlock and went to a quiet and peaceful death.

Having looked at the circumstances that brought about his death, what do we know about his life? Socrates was born in 470 B.C. in Athens. Unlike Plato, his student, he came from humble economic circumstances. His father was a sculptor and his mother a midwife. Socrates was eccentric in manner and appearance, yet he had a captivating effect on people. Even his friends testify that his clothes were always rumpled and that his walk was like the strut of a pelican. Nevertheless, he was

physically robust. Although he rarely drank, he could consume enormous quantities of wine without getting drunk. He was in his seventies when he died, and he left behind a wife and three children; the oldest was a young man, and the youngest was still in arms.

Once a friend of his asked the oracle of Delphi if there was anyone wiser than Socrates. The priestess replied there was not. Socrates was speechless, for he was aware of his own, considerable ignorance. Deeply puzzled, he set about to clear up this riddle. His goal was to find someone wiser than he was, and thus prove that the oracle was mistaken. First he sought out a politician who had a reputation for being wise. As he says in his own words,

When I conversed with him I came to see that, though a great many persons, and most of all he himself, thought that he was wise, yet he was not wise. Then I tried to prove to him that he was not wise, though he fancied that he was. By so doing I made him indignant, and many of the bystanders. So when I went away, I thought to myself, "I am wiser than this man: neither of us knows anything that is really worth knowing, but he thinks that he has knowledge when he has not, while I, having no knowledge, do not think that I have. I seem, at any rate to be a little wiser than he is on this point: I do not think that I know what I do not know."[14]

Like a man obsessed, he sought out other politicians, and then poets, and finally skilled craftsmen, all of whom were well respected in Athens, in search of someone wiser than him. But the results were always the same as in the first case. Finally, he realized that he was better off with his honest ignorance than were the pompous leaders with their shallow and smug "wisdom."

This experience was the turning point in his life as a philosopher. Henceforth, he felt compelled by a divine calling to seek knowledge by questioning his contemporaries. Accordingly, he walked the streets of Athens questioning them on everything from politics to poetry. For Socrates, philosophy was not just a detached discussion of ideas but was a passionate search for wisdom that affected every area of life.

THE SOURCES OF SOCRATES' THOUGHT

Since Socrates believed that philosophy was best done in conversation and not by writing books, he never set down his ideas in print.* Accordingly, everything we know about Socrates comes to us by way of the writings of Plato and other contemporaries. It is particularly problematic to decide when Plato is giving us a faithful transcription of Socrates' ideas and when he is simply using the figure of Socrates as a mouthpiece for his own philosophy. While scholars differ on this issue, the most common opinion is that Plato's earliest dialogues are intended to represent the historical Socrates.† Likewise, it is commonly concluded that the voice of Socrates in the remaining dialogues represents Plato's philosophical maturity and contains his original philosophical reflections.‡ These distinctions are based on the different styles that appear in each period of Plato's writings.

Socrates' Task: Exposing Ignorance

We are told that Socrates studied under the Sophist Prodicus, but because of poverty could only take the cheap course and not the more complete one.[15] Nevertheless, the more he became familiar with the teachings of the Sophists, the more he was troubled by their "schools for success." He thought that they were both intellectually mistaken and morally harmful. These smooth-talking rhetoricians had never honestly sought after genuine knowledge, yet they presumed to instruct people in worldly success. Socrates worried that the people of Athens, under the influence of the Sophists, were mistaking false images and shadows for reality. It was as though the Sophists were selling people maps of the fictional land of Atlantis and claiming that these would help their customers to find their way around Greece. Learning from the Sophists how to speak smoothly and persuasively was dangerous to society and to oneself if one merely spouts eloquent errors.

Socrates was convinced that one could act only on the basis of the truth or, at least, our most carefully examined opinions. We must know *what* knowledge is available, *how* we can obtain it, and *why* it is true. To Socrates, the people in his society were ignorant of the one thing it is most important to know: how to conduct their lives or "tend" their own souls. Only one thing is worse than having cancer, and that is having cancer but not knowing it. If we know we have the disease, we can seek treatment. For Socrates, ignorance is a disease of the soul. It prevents the soul from functioning properly. The problem was that the people of Athens were inflicted with a multiple ignorance. They were ignorant and did not know it. So, Socrates was like a pathologist, he was trying to make people aware of their condition. Some were able to accept the diagnosis and seek for intellectual and spiritual health, while others were too vain to face the painful truths about themselves.

Socrates' Method

SOCRATIC QUESTIONING

Socrates' method for leading people to knowledge was so effective that it has become one of the classic techniques of education commonly known as the "Socratic method" or "Socratic questioning." Plato later referred to this method as **dialectic**. It is a conversational method that proceeds by means

---

*The importance of dialogue to Socrates is illustrated by his complaint that eloquent orators and books are alike in that they provide massive amounts of information, "but if one asks any of them an additional question, . . . they cannot either answer or ask a question on their own account." Plato, *Protagoras* 329a, trans. W. K. C. Guthrie, in *Collected Dialogues of Plato*, ed. Edith Hamilton and Huntington Cairns (New York: Bollingen Foundation, 1961).

†These are *Apology, Crito, Euthyphro, Laches, Charmides, Ion, Hippias Minor, Lysis, Euthydemus*, and, to some extent, the *Protagoras* and *Gorgias*.

‡These include the middle dialogues (*Meno, Hippias Major, Cratylus, Phaedo, Symposium, Republic*) and the late dialogues (*Parmenides, Phaedrus, Theaetetus, Sophist, Statesman, Timaeus, Philebus, Laws*).

of a series of questions and answers in which the inadequacy of the pupil's successive answers are exposed, progressively leading both the pupil and the teacher to answers that have greater clarity and refinement. The most powerful feature of the method is that instead of simply being given information, the pupils discover for themselves their own ignorance and are skillfully led to discover the truth on their own.

For Socrates, the method was employed to arrive at an understanding of the most important concepts in human life. He was scandalized by the fact that the leading figures in his society loved to hold forth in political speeches or orations in the law courts, using terms such as *wisdom*, *justice*, *goodness*, or *virtue*. Yet, when questioned by Socrates, they could not explain what these terms meant. How do we debate or resolve these issues unless we know what we are talking about or what it is we are seeking? Typically, Socrates' method of questioning moved through the following six stages.

1. Socrates meets someone on the street or at a party and begins a conversation with him. Soon Socrates steers the conversation into an area that has some philosophical significance. The genius of Socrates was his ability to find the philosophical issues lurking in even the most mundane of topics.

2. Socrates then isolates a key term on which the discussion hinges and that needs clarification before the conversation can proceed. Thus, the question is posed "What is *X*?" where *X* refers to some property or category. For example, in the *Charmides* the issue is temperance, in the *Laches* it is courage, in the *Lysis* it is friendship, in the *Euthyphro* it is piety, in the *Meno* it is virtue, in the *Symposium* it is love, and in the *Republic* it is justice.

3. Socrates then complains that he is ignorant and confused about the issue and begs the help of his companion in clearing up the matter. Typically, this feeds the arrogance and the smugness of his companion, causing the person to confidently put forth a definition of *X*.

4. Socrates then thanks him profusely for his assistance but says that he needs just one or two more points to be clarified. This leads to an examination of the definition and the discovery that it is inadequate.

5. Typically, the subject then produces another definition that improves on the earlier one. This leads back to step 4, and on close examination the definition is once again found to fail.

6. Steps 4 and 5 are repeated several times until the "victim" realizes that he doesn't really know what he is talking about. Typically, the dialogues end either when Socrates' companion finds some excuse for ending the conversation so that he can get out of Socrates' spotlight or the two agree that they need to seriously continue their search for a solution.

SOCRATES' METHOD OF ARGUMENT

Although a few of his arguments are a little thin, Socrates' methods for disposing of inadequate definitions and theories are fascinating examples of philosophical analysis. Basically, there are three ways that he attacks a definition. First, he sometimes finds a structural flaw in the definition. Sometimes the problem is that it is circular, as in "Justice is what a just person does." Another structural flaw is that a part is identified with the whole, as when justice is used to explain virtue when it is really only an aspect of virtue. Finally, a definition fails structurally when a mere list of examples is offered instead of the defining property that is common to them all. For example, Euthyphro seeks to define piety (or obligation) to Socrates by pointing out that his own actions of taking his own father to court are pious. To this Socrates replies,

> *I did not ask you to tell me one or two of all the many pious actions that there are; I want to know what is characteristic of piety which makes all pious actions pious. . . . Well, then, explain to me what is this characteristic, that I may have it to turn to, and to use as a standard whereby to judge your actions and those of other men, and be able to say that whatever action resembles it is pious, and whatever does not, is not pious.*[16]

Second, Socrates attacks his companion's position by employing the form of argument we now call *reductio ad absurdum* (or "reducing to an absurdity"). To use this technique, you begin by assuming that your opponent's position is true and then you show that it logically implies either an absurd conclusion or one that contradicts itself or other conclusions held by the opponent. If we can deduce a clearly false statement from a proposition, this is definitive proof that the original assumption was false. Plato provides a good example of this Socratic technique in his masterpiece, the *Republic*.[17] The Sophist Thrasymachus puts forth the cynical thesis that

(1) Justice means doing what is in the interest of those in power. (Thrasymachus's definition)

Socrates then elicits the following corollary to the definition from Thrasymachus:

(2) To be just is to obey the laws of those in power. (inference from thesis 1)

Next, Socrates has him agree to the common-sense observation that

(3) Those in power can make mistakes. (observation)

From this, the following two inferences may be drawn:

(4) Those in power may mistakenly make laws that are *not* in their own interest. (inference from 3)

(5) To obey such laws is not to act in the interest of those in power. (inference from 4)

Finally, Socrates elicits a contradiction:

(6) Therefore, to be just is to do what is in the interest of those in power. (paraphrase of 1)

and

To be just is to do what is *not* in the interest of those in power. (inference from 2 and 5)

Third, Socrates frequently uses the method of counterexample to show that a definition is either too narrow or too broad. In other words, if his opponent is defining some term X, Socrates shows that the definition of X excludes cases that clearly should be called X or he will show that the definition includes cases that are not examples of X. In his discussion with Socrates, Meno puts forth the definition that the virtuous (or excellent) person is the one that has the capacity to govern.[18] However, Socrates points out that while it makes sense to talk of a virtuous child, a child does not have the capacity to govern others. Thus, the definition is too narrow. Furthermore, he points out that the original definition should have said, "The virtuous person is the one who has the capacity to govern *justly*." Otherwise, the definition would allow us to include tyrants among the company of just people. Hence, the first definition was also too broad.

A typical response of those that were the target of this Socratic analysis was given by Nicias (an Athenian general and admirer of Socrates):

Anyone who is close to Socrates and enters into conversation with him is liable to be drawn into an argument, and whatever subject he may start, he will be continually carried round and round by him, until at last he finds that he has to give an account both of his present and past life, and when he is once entangled, Socrates will not let him go until he has completely and thoroughly sifted him.[19]

Some of Socrates' contemporaries compared him to a stingray that leaves its victims numb from its sting, and others said he was like the legendary Daedalus, who could make statues move, just as Socrates makes one's firmly held convictions move and slip away.[20]

Young people flocked around Socrates to see him prick the pretentious, inflated opinions of their smug, pompous leaders. Of course, this did not earn him the favor of the establishment. However, if he often appears to play the part of the classroom smart aleck, it is not hard to believe that he had a genuine love for those he examined. Despite his skill at intellectual gamesmanship, truth—not the humiliation of his opponents—

was his goal. Nevertheless, the process of finding the truth is often unpleasant. If ignorance is like a disease, then pain is sometimes a necessary accompaniment to the healing process. At times, Socrates seems like a chess master who can see the conclusion of the game several moves ahead of his opponent. However, even if Socrates knows where the argument is leading, it would do no good to simply announce the answer to his partner, for Socrates realizes that this will not be effective in the person's life until he discovers it for himself. Much of the time, however, Socrates does not seem to know where the conversation will lead, for some of the intellectual dead ends they discover were the result of suggestions made by Socrates himself. He often insists that he is exploring territory that is as unfamiliar to him as it is to his dialogue partner.[21]

If Socrates' companions rarely get the final answer to their questions, he does not leave them unchanged, for he has forced them to examine their own lives, beliefs, and intellectual poverty. One of his opponents, Callicles, expressed the effect of Socrates on him in this way:

> Tell me, Socrates, are we to consider you serious now or jesting? For if you are serious and what you say is true, then surely the life of us mortals must be turned upside down and apparently we are everywhere doing the opposite of what we should.[22]

Although Socrates rarely arrives at firm answers, he does perform a weeding service. Confused ideas must be uprooted to prepare the soil for healthy intellectual fruits to grow. Even the answers Socrates rejects contain some truth in them, for they draw us closer to the goal. Rather than being like a skin that is peeled off and disposed of to get at the fruit, the initial answers of Socrates and his companions are more like rough approximations that need to be refined.

Socrates' Theory of Knowledge

Aristotle credits Socrates with making two contributions to philosophy: inductive arguments and universal definitions.[23] Inductive arguments, as Socrates employed them, reason from information about *some* examples of a class to general conclusions about *all* members of that class. In trying to understand justice, for example, Socrates examines several cases in which we would call a particular individual's actions just and when we would not. On Socrates' view, when we apply a universal term like *justice* to a number of different, particular examples, one of two things is occurring. One possibility is that the term has a different meaning each time it is applied. For example the word *bank* does not mean the same thing when applied to a financial institution as it does when applied to the edge of a river. But if there was never any common meaning between two applications of a term, then language would break down completely. The second possibility, then, is that the word *justice* refers to some quality or property that is found in all genuine cases of justice. If two actions performed by different people at different times are both just, it is because they share something in common. Socrates believes that the word *justice* refers to a common quality each time it is used and that it can be captured in a universal definition.

In searching for universal definitions, Socrates assumes that particular things can be grouped into certain natural and, hence, nonarbitrary categories. He further assumes that our universal concepts and definitions both allow us to identify the kind of thing something is, as well as to evaluate how well it fulfills its purpose. For example, if I say that "Holmes is a teacher" I am not only identifying the group to which he belongs but also a set of ideals or criteria for evaluating him. Plato later treats these common qualities uniting things as substantial realities, capable of existing independently of the particular things that exemplify them. However, Socrates does not offer us a full-fledged metaphysical theory as much as an attempt to unearth the assumptions and necessary conditions underlying our speech and actions.

To understand Socrates' view of the nature of knowledge and how it is to be obtained, it is important to note that he calls himself "the midwife of ideas."[24] A midwife does not bear a baby herself but merely helps another in the labor of bringing a baby to birth. Thus, Socrates claims that he does not have answers or wisdom to give but can help others find the truth within themselves. A conclusion that can be drawn from this metaphor is that Socrates believed the truth was not something to be found outside of us, through the senses. On the contrary, we already possess the truth, it is deep within us and written on our souls. All we need is assistance in discovering the truth within and bringing it to the light of day. This later became known as the doctrine of **innate ideas** and became one of the dominant theses within the rationalist theory of knowledge. The midwife analogy falls short on one point. Each biological baby is a unique individual. However, Socrates believed that when we pursue his method of dialectical questioning, we would all find within us one set of identical truths and moral virtues. In other words, the innate knowledge he is helping others discover is presumed to be the same for everyone.

Socrates' Metaphysics

As was mentioned earlier, we will not find much in Socrates that falls under the heading of metaphysics. He was too concerned with the more concrete problems of human life to engage in theoretical speculations about the nature of reality. Plato would take up the task of developing the metaphysical underpinnings of Socrates' philosophy. Nevertheless, Socrates did touch on metaphysical topics, particularly in his discussion of the soul.

THE HUMAN SOUL

For Socrates, the most important task in life is to care for one's soul. In many previous Greek accounts, the *psyche* (which we translate as "soul") was the breath of life, while the body was identified with the real person. The soul accompanied the body like a shadow, was useless apart from the body, and had no connection with the thoughts or emotions of the person. After death the soul was thought to exist as a kind of ghost that could be summoned back to prophesy or to take vengeance on the living. However, the soul was not really identified with the original person in many early Greek accounts.

Socrates reversed this picture of the relationship of the soul and the body. For him, the soul was the true self and the body was now merely thought to be its accompaniment.* The body is an instrument that the person uses in negotiating with the physical world. To care for the body and to pursue riches and fame while failing to attend to the soul is like spending all our time and resources polishing our shoe while our foot is infected and rotting from neglect. An excellent soul is well-ordered, has wisdom, and maintains control over the emotions and bodily desires. One must be careful not to read too much theological content into Socrates' notion of the soul. As Gregory Vlastos says,

> The soul is as worth caring for if it were to last just twenty-four more hours, as if it were to outlast eternity. If you have just one more day to live, and can expect nothing but a blank after that, Socrates feels that you would still have all the reason you need for improving your soul; you have yourself to live with that one day, so why live with a worse self, if you could live with a better one instead?[25]

Is the soul immortal for Socrates? In some of his remarks, Socrates seems undecided about this issue. Most of the time, however, he is confident that people survive physical death. For example, a humorous but telling remark occurs in the dialogue *Phaedo.* The very practical Crito asks Socrates, "How shall we bury you?" To which Socrates answers, "As you please, only you must catch me first, and not let me escape you." Thereon he explains that the dead body they will be left with is something quite different from the real Socrates whose immaterial self will swiftly escape both the prison walls and the confines of the body to dwell in "the happiness of the blessed." Even if many of the arguments in this dialogue are Plato's, the playful, quick wit and philosophical punch of the preceding remark are characteristically Socratic. This issue brings into sharp relief the problem of the relationship between the person (including the soul or the

---

*Socrates' account of the soul had many predecessors, such as the Pythagorean philosophy, for example. Nevertheless, Socrates' version is historically important for the powerful way it stated that the body is not the real person.

mind) and the physical body. Plato addresses the problem, and it remains one of the central problems in philosophy.

Ethics and the Good Life

VIRTUE AND EXCELLENCE

The concern of ethics is to determine how we ought to live our lives. In the *Crito* Socrates asserts that the most important goal for humans is not just living but "living well."[26] For Socrates, "living well" is an ethical notion, for it involves some notion of human excellence. Accordingly, in this same passage he asserts that "living well and honorably and justly mean the same thing." To understand how to live justly, therefore, we must understand what constitutes our perfect end or what standard of excellence we should be trying to fulfill. The Greeks used the word *arete* to capture this. It is usually translated into English as "virtue." In our time, to say that someone is "virtuous" suggests that they are very pious or, perhaps, sexually pure. However, for the Greeks the word had a much broader meaning. If something had "virtue," this meant it was good at a particular task or had a certain sort of excellence or fulfilled its function well. Thus, the virtue of a knife is its ability to cut things. The virtue of a racehorse is to run very fast. The virtue of a shoemaker is the skill of making high-quality shoes. While the shipbuilder, the wrestler, the physician, the musician each have a particular kind of virtue related to their specific task, Socrates is concerned with the question "What does it mean to be a virtuous human being?" In other words, being fully human is a task or a skill in itself. Just as we evaluate the knife in terms of the end or function of knives, so we can evaluate people in terms of the appropriate end or function of a human being. By speaking about a good person in the same way he speaks about a good knife, Socrates makes clear that morality arises out of nonmoral, naturalistic considerations. Morality is not something disclosed to us in a religious revelation, nor alien to our deepest interests or our fundamental nature. Instead, he argues that being moral boils down to

being successful at the art of living. However, it will become clear that his notion of "success" is quite different from that of the typical Sophist.

Understanding this viewpoint shows us how Socrates would answer the question "Why be moral?" Socrates' view (which was the typical Greek view) is that since being virtuous means fulfilling our nature, it is the only thing that can guarantee our happiness. We will find little disagreement from any Greek moral theorist that happiness is the one end that all people pursue and that it is the one end that needs no justification. Hence, for the Greek, morality would never require a sacrifice of our own interests in the name of duty, because the very purpose of all morality is self-fulfillment. However, for Socrates, this does not mean that life should be lived selfishly. In fact, he claims that it is better to suffer a wrong than to inflict it.[27] Since he went to his death rather than violate his moral principles, it is obvious that he does not equate the good life with simply experiencing pleasure and also that he has a very complex notion of what constitutes one's real interest. The problem is that we can be mistaken about what is truly the good life. In being unjust or pursuing our bodily appetites, we may think we are serving our best interests. However, according to Socrates, in the process of living this way our soul is becoming corrupted and nothing is more miserable than a diseased soul.[28]

KNOWING AND DOING

At this point the link between morality and knowledge becomes clear. Socrates' position is sometimes called "ethical intellectualism," because of the role he thinks the intellect plays in our moral life. According to Socrates, knowledge and virtue are one. Without knowledge, all other virtues (temperance, justice, courage) are useless and may lead to harm.[29] A well-intentioned judge who is ignorant of the law and of the circumstances of the case will not mete out justice. Someone who is courageous because they are ignorant of the danger at hand, will act foolishly. There is not only a necessary unity between the virtues and knowledge, but there is also a unity among all the virtues themselves. Someone who is brave but un-just might end up being a dangerous tyrant. Each virtue requires the others. Plato will adopt all these conclusions and will consistently defend them throughout all his writings.

If every person naturally pursues his or her own good, and being virtuous is what is our good, then it follows that the wise person who *knows* what is right, will *do* what is right. In other words, *to know the good is to do the good.* The person who has learned the art of medicine is a physician. The person who knows what justice is, will be just.[30] The corollary is the startling claim that *no one chooses to do evil knowingly.* "For myself I am fairly certain that no wise man believes anyone sins will-ingly or willingly perpetrates any evil or base act. They know very well that all evil or base action is involuntary."[31] This view strikes many people as being counterintuitive, for our own moral experi-ence of yielding to temptation seems to count against its truth. For this reason, Socrates' posi-tion was criticized by many of his contemporaries. Euripides, for example, a Greek playwright and contemporary of Socrates, had one of his charac-ters proclaim, "By teaching and experience we learn the right but neglect it in practice, some from sloth, others from preferring pleasure of some kind or other to duty."[32]

Although many find Socrates' view implausi-ble, maybe some things can be said in support of it. In the early part of the twentieth century in the United States, there was a notorious bank robber by the name of Willie Sutton. Supposedly a re-porter asked him, "Why do you rob banks, Willie?" The criminal replied impatiently, "Because that's where the money is." This illustrates Socrates' point perfectly. The thief believes that money is the supreme good in life. If that is true, then it logi-cally follows that one ought to do whatever is nec-essary to obtain the supreme good. If banks are where the money is, then robbing banks is good. Hence, the problem with the thief is that he is pur-suing false values. He is mistaken about what is truly good. Socrates would argue that it would be inconceivable that anyone could say, "This is not a good goal and it will be harmful to me and make me unhappy, but I choose it nevertheless."

The key to making sense out of Socrates' claim that knowing the good is sufficient for doing the good is to realize that, for him, knowl-edge is more than simply having information or assenting to certain facts. On the contrary, true knowledge is identical to wisdom. One cannot be a wise person and a moral infant. For Socrates' formula to make sense, we must assume that the person is in the grip of a real personal conviction and that reason controls his or her soul. Moral knowledge is like the art of medicine: it involves practice, skill, and experienced judgment, and not just the acquisition of facts. I may know that pizza is bad for me because I have high choles-terol and high blood pressure. But if I choose to eat it, it is because my intellect is clouded and confused by my physical appetites, and for the moment I think that the immediate pleasure is what is good for me. Nevertheless, Aristotle was not convinced by Socrates' arguments. The for-mer believed that it is possible for moral weak-ness and an insufficiently developed character to let us do wrong even when we know it is wrong. He complains that Socrates' view "plainly contra-dicts the observed facts."[33]

Political Philosophy

We will not find a well-developed political theory in Socrates. This task would be taken up later by Plato. Nevertheless, Socrates does express a num-ber of convictions about our proper relationship to the state. Foremost among these was his dis-trust of popular democracy. Since he ties compe-tence in any task to having the appropriate sort of knowledge, it follows that ruling the state requires a special sort of knowledge that only a few will have. We would not entrust our medical care to the vote of the inexperienced crowd. Similarly, Socrates taught, we should not choose public offi-cials by casting lots or by a popular vote as was common in that time. Only those who have philo-sophical wisdom are competent to rule. Obvi-ously, this doctrine did not endear him to the popular leaders of Athens.

Generally, Socrates took a very conservative stance toward the laws of society, saying that they merit our total obedience. In the scene described by Plato in the *Crito*, Socrates' friend Crito visits him in prison and tries to persuade him to avoid his unjust punishment by escaping. However, Socrates refuses to do this and, thereby, reveals to us some of his political theory. He argues that we only have two options if we disagree with the laws of our country. We can either try to persuade our legislators to change the laws, or we can register our dissent by lawfully leaving the country and revoking our citizenship.[34] Even though he had been unjustly condemned by his enemies who were administering the law, Socrates believed that if he subverted their decision he would be trampling on the laws themselves and thus wrongfully encouraging disrespect for the state.[35] The principle that guides him is that it is always wrong to return injustice for injustice. Or, as we might say, "Two wrongs do not make a right." When we commit injustice, we are corrupting our own souls and are only ending up worse than before. As he says, "It is a much harder thing to escape from wickedness than from death."[36]

In his trial, Socrates made one exception to his principle of unconditional obedience to the law. Arguing before the jury, he made it clear that he would refuse to obey any order to give up philosophizing, even if obedience would mean that he would be acquitted and disobedience would mean death.[37] However, he saw this situation as different from illegally escaping from prison. His principle in the trial was that his personal god had commanded him to do philosophy and obedience to this god took precedence over the state. Also, continuing to do philosophy would benefit the state, by showing where it was wrong. Finally, continuing to philosophize would still show respect for the law because, even though it would challenge the edict of the court, its public nature would demonstrate a willingness to accept the legal consequences. By contrast, escaping from prison would be an attempt to evade the law by doing an end run around it.

We can find in Socrates two notions of political philosophy in germinal form that became important later in history. The first is an implicit notion of the **social contract theory** of political

obligation. This theory claims that our relationship to the government is a contractual one. We have a tacit agreement that the state will provide certain services for us and, in return, we will fulfill our agreed-on obligations to the state. Accordingly, Socrates argued that we ought to always keep our just agreements. By living seventy years in Athens, he had benefited from the nurture and protection of the state. At any time, he could have left and moved to Sparta or Crete, but he chose to stay. Therefore, even though he disagreed with the judgments of the state in his case, he still felt an obligation to abide by its laws.[38]

The second sort of political theory that appears in Socrates is built around the notion of natural law. The term **natural law** in moral and political theory refers to the claim that there is a universal moral law that can be known through reason and experience. It is not created by governments. On the contrary, governments are deemed just by natural law theorists only to the extent that their civil laws conform to the natural law. Socrates believed that the laws of his society conformed to this universal standard of justice. However, even though his trial was legal in terms of its procedures, he claimed that his verdict was unjust. He could say this because he believed that there were laws above the laws of society. For this reason he imagined these universal laws saying to him that he was "a victim of the injustice, not of the laws, but of men."[39]

Socrates' Legacy

In terms of the doctrinal legacy of Socrates' thought, he influenced the ethical theories of a number of schools. Included among these are the Megarians, the Cyrenaics, and the Cynics (this latter group is discussed in a later chapter). Plato, of course, was the disciple who developed Socrates' insights into a full-blown philosophical system. Having mentioned these movements, however, it is important to note that Socrates is one of those rare individuals in the history of thought whose contribution lay less in his doctrines than in his personality. To be sure, there are plenty of intellectual fruits in Socratic philosophy for scholars to pick apart under their analytic microscopes. Nevertheless, the Socratic dialogues always seem to end abruptly before any definitive conclusions are nailed down. Instead, what he primarily gave us was the paradigm of the philosophical life—the passion to know, the conviction that everything else paled in importance compared to the search for wisdom, and the commitment to follow one's questions wherever they may lead. The history of philosophy took a decisive turn with Socrates. The early Greek thinkers primarily sought to know external nature. Although Socrates acknowledged that there was some value in this, he taught that there was a much more important goal in life. This was nothing less than achieving self-knowledge. To be sure, the Sophists also turned away from questions about the cosmos to focus on the human situation. However, Socrates was able to do this while avoiding the dead ends of their uncritical relativism, subjectivism, skepticism, and cynicism.

In the temple of Apollo at Delphi, where Socrates first understood his mission, was the inscription "Know thyself." This became the motto by which Socrates lived his life. However, Socrates never claimed to have this knowledge but merely the dialectical method of questioning that would lead each person toward this goal. For him, all philosophy began with the confession of ignorance. Only then would we be cleansed of the comfortable and familiar ideas that lead to intellectual and spiritual apathy. In the closing moments of his trial, he left us with the words that have become the driving conviction behind the philosophical journey: "An unexamined life is not worth living."[40]

Questions for Understanding

1. What four causes produced cultural changes in fifth-century Greece?

2. Who were the Sophists? What were the main themes of their philosophy?

3. What distinction is represented by the terms *physis* and *nomos*? How did the Sophists apply this distinction to morality?

4. What did Protagoras mean by saying "man is the measure of all things"?

5. What was Protagoras's view of ethics and religion?

6. What were Gorgias's three theses? What was his point in making these assertions?

7. What position did Antiphon, Thrasymachus, and Callicles take on justice and the laws of society?

8. What did Socrates finally conclude about the oracle of Delphi's claim that he was the wisest person in Athens?

9. According to Socrates, what is the "disease" that can inflict the soul?

10. What is the Socratic method?

11. Why was Socrates so concerned with definitions?

12. What is a *reductio ad absurdum* argument? How does Socrates use it against Thrasymacus?

13. What are innate ideas? How does this notion relate to Socrates' description of himself as a "midwife of ideas"?

14. What is Socrates' view of the soul?

15. Why did Socrates claim that no one chooses to do evil knowingly?

16. Why did Socrates argue that it would be wrong for him to escape from prison even though he considered his sentence to be unjust?

Questions for Reflection

1. What is wisdom? Why did Socrates consider it to be the most important goal in life? Was he correct about this? In what ways are you pursuing wisdom or not pursuing it in your life? What persons in history do you think were wise? Why?

2. Who would Socrates identify as the Sophists in our day?

3. Do you agree or disagree with Socrates' statement that "to know the good is to do the good"? Why?

4. Was Socrates correct in claiming that being moral or living up to the highest standards of human excellence is necessary for happiness and fulfillment?

5. Do you agree or disagree with Socrates' claim that morality is objective and not a matter of subjective opinion as the Sophists thought? Why?

6. Is it ever morally justified to break the law? If so, under what conditions? Assuming that Socrates' sentence was unjust, do you agree with his reasons for not escaping from prison?

Notes

1. Thucydides, *History of the Peloponnesian War*, bk. 3, line 82, quoted in Frank Thilly and Ledger Wood, *A History of Philosophy*, 3rd ed. (New York: Holt, Rinehart and Winston, 1957), 55.

2. Euripides, *Medea*, trans. Gilbert Murray, in *Ten Greek Plays*, ed. Lane Cooper (New York: Oxford University Press, 1940), 326.

3. Quoted by Plato in *Protagoras* 318e, trans. W. K. C. Guthrie, in *Collected Dialogues of Plato*, ed. Edith Hamilton and Huntington Cairns (New York: Bollingen Foundation, 1961).

4. Plato, *Protagoras* 313c.

5. Aristotle, *Rhetoric* 2:24, section 9, trans. W. Rhys Roberts, in *The Basic Works of Aristotle*, ed. Richard McKeon (New York: Random House, 1941), 1431.

6. Quoted by Plato in *Theaetetus* 167c, trans. F. M. Cornford, in *Collected Dialogues of Plato*.

7. Quoted in W. K. C. Guthrie, *A History of Greek Philosophy* (Cambridge, England: Cambridge University Press, 1969), 3:234.

8. Ibid., 3.194.

9. Antiphon, quoted in John Mansley Robinson, An Introduction to Early Greek Philosophy (Boston: Houghton Mifflin, 1968), 251.

10. Ibid., 250–251.

11. Plato, *Apology*, trans. F. J. Church, trans. rev. Robert D. Cumming, in *Euthyphro, Apology, Crito* (Indianapolis: Bobbs-Merrill, Library of Liberal Arts, 1956), 29.

12. Ibid., 35–36.

13. Ibid., 37.

14. Ibid., 26.

15. Plato, *Cratylus* 384b.

16. Plato, *Euthyphro* in *Euthyphro, Apology, Crito*, 7.

17. Plato, *Republic* 338c–339d.

18. Plato, *Meno* 71e–73d.

19. Plato, *Laches* 187e–188a, trans. Benjamin Jowett, in *Collected Dialogues of Plato*.

20. Plato, *Meno* 80a and *Euthyphro* 11b-d.

21. Plato, *Meno* 80c, *Charmides* 165b, 166c-d, and *Protagoras* 348c.

22. Plato, *Gorgias* 481c, trans. W. D. Woodhead, in *Collected Dialogues of Plato*.

23. Aristotle, *Metaphysics* 13:4.

24. Plato, *Theaetetus* 149–151.

25. Gregory Vlastos, "Introduction: The Paradox of Socrates," in *The Philosophy of Socrates*, ed. Gregory Vlastos (Garden City, NY: Anchor Books, Doubleday, 1971), 5–6.

26. Plato, *Crito* 48b.

27. Plato, *Gorgias* 469b.

28. Plato, *Gorgias* 479b.

29. Plato, *Meno* 88a-89a.

30. Plato, *Gorgias* 460b.

31. Plato, *Protagoras* 345e; cf. *Meno* 78a.

32. Euripides, *Hippolytus*, trans. E. P. Coleridge, line 380, in *The Complete Greek Drama*, ed. Whitney J. Oates and Eugene O'Neill, Jr. (New York: Random House, 1938), 1:773–774.

33. Aristotle, *Nicomachean Ethics* 7.1, trans. W. D. Ross, in *The Basic Works of Aristotle*.

34. Plato, *Crito* 52a, 51d.

35. Ibid., 50b–c.

36. Plato, *Apology* 39a.

37. Ibid., 29c–d.

38. Plato, *Crito* 49e–52e.

39. Plato, *Crito* 54b, in *Euthyphro, Apology, Crito*, 65.

40. Plato, *Apology* 38a.

4

Plato: The Search for Ultimate Truth and Reality

Plato's Life: From Student to University President

When Socrates was put to death, his student Plato was not quite thirty. The politically motivated death of his mentor may have been the turning point in Plato's life. As a result of his friendship with Socrates, he had taken up the elderly philosopher's challenge to pursue wisdom in his own life by facing hard questions. At Socrates' trial, Plato and three friends offered to pay a substantial fine to the court as an alternative to the death penalty. But to Plato's dismay, this attempt to change the court's mind failed and his brilliant teacher's life came to a tragic end. Plato's feelings, no doubt, were the same as those he attributes to Phaedo when Socrates breathed his last breath: "Such was the end . . . of our friend, who was, I think, of all the men of our time, the best, the wisest, and the most just." Because of these events, many questions haunted Plato: "What kind of society was it that could not tolerate a Socrates in its midst? What kind of society ought we to have if philosophical wisdom is to prevail in human affairs?" Consequently, he spent the rest of his life trying to answer these questions.

Plato had not always planned a career as a philosopher. Born in 428 or 427 B.C. into an aristocratic Athenian family, he was educated and groomed to become a great political leader. After Socrates' death, however, he decided to devote all his energies to philosophy. Initially, he traveled for a while. Some think he may have made it as far as Egypt. Whether this is true or not, we do know he went to Italy in 388 and to the city of Syracuse in Sicily. On returning to Athens, he founded a school, the first university in the Western world. Plato's school was called the Academy, having been located outside the city walls in a grove sacred to the hero Academus. Nine hundred years later, the institutional heir of Plato's school was still operating, and its fame lives on today, signified by the fact that "the Academy" and "academics" are still terms used to refer to higher education.

Plato spent the remainder of his life teaching and directing the Academy as well as writing philosophical works. Among the most famous of his works was the *Republic*. In this book he argued that society would never be just unless people with philosophical vision became rulers or rulers acquired philosophical wisdom. In 368 and again in 361, he tried to realize this goal by returning to Syracuse in response to the request to educate Dionysius the Younger, the young ruler who had inherited the throne. Sadly, Plato's mission failed, for the ruler was too committed to tyranny and little interested in philosophy. On his second visit, the two did not get along at all, and Plato barely escaped with his life. Plato returned to the Academy, where he continued to teach until he died suddenly but peacefully around 348 or 347 B.C.

Plato's Task: Making Philosophy Comprehensive

Following in the steps of his teacher Socrates, Plato had an intense interest in ethical questions. However, Socrates' fate also taught him that good people will not survive unless society itself is transformed. Therefore, political philosophy was also a major concern in Plato's works. But Plato puts these issues into a much broader context than Socrates ever did. If goodness and justice are sheerly a matter of convention, as the Sophists claimed, then it is useless spending much time thinking about them. However, Plato believed that the answers to our ethical and political questions could be found in an adequate understanding of the nature of reality itself. Therefore, he devoted a substantial portion of his philosophical energies on metaphysical questions. However, we must establish the foundations of knowledge before we can make any progress with the other philosophical issues. Previous philosophers have had brief skirmishes with the problems of epistemology, but Plato was the first to make an all-out assault on these problems.

Theory of Knowledge: Reason Versus Opinion

To understand Plato's theory of knowledge, we first have to understand three positions that he rejects. He was concerned first with the relativism of the Sophists. Contrary to their emphasis on personal or cultural opinion, Plato believed that our lives and societies must be founded on knowledge and that this knowledge must be universal (true for all people at all times). Second, he tried to disabuse us of our confidence in sense experience. The sort of knowledge we need must be eternal and unchangeable, and we cannot find that in experience. Finally, he argued that knowledge is more than true belief, for it must be grounded in rational insight.

REJECTION OF RELATIVISM

In the dialogue *Theaetetus*, he critically examines the claim of Protagoras the Sophist that "man is the measure of all things." This is a very concrete way of expressing the position of relativism. There is some initial plausibility to this position. For example, the same wind may seem chilly to one person and pleasant to a more warm-blooded person (Th 151e–152c).[1] If you say it is chilly *to you*, you cannot be mistaken about this judgment, and it would be very boorish of me to insist that you are wrong. Each person's opinion about how the wind appears to him or her is equally correct. Protagoras, of course, does not limit his claim to matters of comfort but applies the same sort of argument to all judgments, including judgments about morality. Plato, however, finds the relativist's position flawed. First of all, the position refutes itself. In the *Theaetetus* (171a,b), Plato gives this exchange between Socrates and the mathematician Theodorus:

> *Socrates*: Protagoras, for his part, admitting as he does that everybody's opinion is true, must acknowledge the truth of his opponents' belief about his own belief, where they think he is wrong.
>
> *Theodorus*: Certainly.
>
> *Socrates*: That is to say, he would acknowledge his own belief to be false, if he admits that the belief of those who think him wrong is true?
>
> *Theodorus*: Necessarily.

In other words, relativists do not really believe all opinions are equally true. Relativists believe they are *correct* and their opponents are *wrong* in their opinions about knowledge. Protagoras proposed to teach people what they needed to know and even expected them to pay him generous sums of money for this knowledge. But once the relativists have claimed that their opinions are better than others, they have abandoned their relativism.

Socrates goes on in the dialogue to point out that everyone recognizes a difference between wisdom and ignorance and between true belief and false belief. Suppose your physician believes your foot is broken, and you believe it is not. Does that mean it is true for your physician that your foot is broken, but equally true for you that it is not? Who would have the best opinion on whether a wine will turn out sweet or dry—the keeper of the vineyard or a flute player? Who could best tell if a musical score will be melodious or not—a musician or a gymnastics coach? (Th 178c–e). Plato's point is that not all opinions are of equal value.

REJECTION OF SENSE EXPERIENCE

The second position Plato rejects is one that would later be called *empiricism.* Empiricists claim that we derive all our knowledge from sense experience. However, Plato provides several reasons why we can never derive true knowledge from the data of the five senses. First, sense perception only gives us the world of constant change that Heraclitus described. In this realm we can never say with confidence what is true because it is always in flux. Hence, what is true at one time will become false at a later time. The minute I say, "The coffee in this cup is hot," it has already begun to cool, and shortly my description will no longer be correct. Furthermore, all claims about the sensory world are relative to the perceiver. The coffee I consider hot may seem tepid to you. Similarly, our perceptions are relative to the circumstances. For example, lukewarm coffee seems hot in comparison to iced tea but cool in comparison to boiling water. The dress that looked black inside the store now looks dark blue in the sunlight. If we were limited to sense experience, then the relativism of Protagoras would be inescapable. I could say only what seems to be the case or how things appear to me

and not what is definitely true. Hence, for Plato, the so-called knowledge gained from perception is too fleeting and ephemeral to take seriously.

Plato's second problem with sense experience follows from his conviction that the object of knowledge must be something universal that we can capture in an unchanging description or definition. However, if language only referred to the constantly changing particulars in the physical world, then the meaning of our terms would be in flux and language would not function. Hence, we achieve understanding through universal concepts. To clarify what Plato is saying here, let's perform some thought experiments. First, what would you call the object in Figure 4-1? Most likely, you would say it is a circle. However, Plato says that is incorrect. More accurately, it is an *attempt* to represent a circle. Why isn't it a true circle? Well, if you looked at it through a powerful magnifying glass, you would see that the line is somewhat jagged. The particles of ink are not all equidistant from the center. Furthermore, the line has a width that could be measured in minute fractions of an inch. Also, the line has depth, for it is made up of a layer of ink imposed on the paper. Finally, the ink can fade or the paper can burn, changing or destroying the printed figure. However, the points forming a true circle are perfectly equidistant from the center, have neither width nor depth, and cannot change or be destroyed. The figure is a fairly close approximation of a circle, but it is not a genuine circle. The point is that we cannot see true circularity; we can only know it conceptually, with the mind. This is why mathematicians do not need laboratories to make their discoveries. They use reason and not the senses to study their objects. If you saw a mathematician

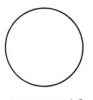

FIGURE 4-1

cutting out cardboard circles and *then* measuring them, you would know this person did not really understand what mathematics is all about.

Let's try another thought experiment. Compare the different nations of the world in terms of the amount of justice they exhibit. Or compare the quantity and quality of justice in the United States during the era of slavery with the degree of justice in our present laws and institutions. How are you able to perform this comparison? Can you see justice with your eyes? What color is it? How tall is it? How much does it weigh? Clearly, these questions can apply to physical things, but it is meaningless to describe justice in terms of observable properties. We can see the actions of people and say that those actions exhibit justice or injustice. But we cannot literally see justice itself. Microscopes and telescopes help us to see features of the physical world that the naked eye cannot see. However, there are no "justice scopes" or "justice meters" that will make justice visible.

Furthermore, no nation is perfectly just. We have never seen an example of perfect justice in human history, only frail, human attempts to approximate it. Therefore, our concept of perfect justice could not have come from our experience. Nations differ in the degree of justice they manifest. Individual nations can change in the direction of becoming more just or more unjust. Nations, like all other particular things, are constantly changing. According to Plato, however, the standard of justice itself does not change. Only if that standard is singular and constant can we evaluate the moral changes in a nation. For such reasons, Plato agrees with Heraclitus that the eyes and ears are poor witnesses if they are not informed by the understanding that only reason can bring.

Plato is convinced that if justice is not something fixed that transcends the physical world, then the Sophists are right in saying that moral qualities such as justice are merely sounds or puffs of air. We can put Plato's position into the following argument form:

(1) Either justice is something real and objective, or it is a mere word.

(2) If the second alternative is true, then our moral judgments have no value. There is no real difference between Hitler and a saint except certain sounds we conventionally apply to them.

(3) But statement 2 is absurd. There *is* a difference between Hitler and a saint.

(4) So justice is something real and objective.

(5) That which is real must be either physical or nonphysical.

(6) Clearly, justice cannot be physical.

(7) Therefore, justice must be something real, objective, and nonphysical.

KNOWLEDGE IS NOT TRUE BELIEF

Finally, Plato insists on a very firm distinction between knowledge and belief. Beliefs can be either true or false, but knowledge must always be true. Could we then say that knowledge is the same as true belief? Plato does not think so. For example, let's suppose I believe that at this present moment the U.S. President is telephoning the governor of California. However, I have no grounds for this belief. It is just an arbitrary guess. Nevertheless, it *could* be a true belief by virtue of a fortunate coincidence. Clearly, we would not want to dignify such a lucky guess with the title of "knowledge." We could also imagine that a child has memorized the Pythagorean theorem and knows how to apply it. But if he (or she) does not understand the rational grounds for the truth of this theorem, then it is merely a secondhand true opinion, according to Plato. Even if the child had memorized the proof for this theorem, if he did not fully understand the logic of the proof, he still would not have knowledge. To be knowledge, it must be grounded in some sort of rational insight. For this reason Plato says,

> For true opinions, as long as they remain, are a fine thing and all they do is good, but they are not willing to remain long, and they escape from a man's mind, so that they are not worth much until one ties them down by (giving) an account of the reason why. . . . That is why knowledge is prized higher than correct opinion, and knowledge differs from correct opinion in being tied down.[2]

UNIVERSAL FORMS ARE THE BASIS OF KNOWLEDGE

Following Socrates' method, Plato is honing in on the correct understanding of knowledge by eliminating inadequate conceptions. From what has been said so far, Plato clearly believes that genuine knowledge is

1. Objective
2. Unavailable to the senses
3. Universal
4. Unchanging
5 Grounded in a rational understanding

Having made a strong distinction between the here-and-now realm of sense experience and the unchanging realm of rational knowledge, Plato goes on to show that they are intertwined in a special way. He says that the world of sense experience is not one of total flux or pure individuality. We find that particulars fall into a number of stable, universal categories. If this were not so, we could not identify anything nor talk about it at all. For example, Tom, Dick, Susan, and Jane are all distinct individuals, yet we can use the universal term "human being" to refer to each of them. In spite of their differences, something about them is the same. Corresponding to each common name (such as "human," "dog," "justice") is a **Universal** that consists of the essential, common properties of anything within that category.* Circular objects (coins, rings, wreathes, planetary orbits) all have the Universal of Circularity in common. Particular objects that are beautiful (roses, seashells, persons, sunsets, paintings) all share the Universal of Beauty. Particulars come into being, change, and pass away but Universals reside in an eternal, unchanging world. The rose grows from a bud, becomes a beautiful flower, and then turns brown and ugly and fades away. Yet the Universal of Beauty remains eternally the same.

Plato uses a number of terms to refer to these constants within experience. He calls them "Universals" because they are what is common to all the particulars in a certain category. Sometimes, he refers to "Justice Itself" (or "Beauty Itself" or "Goodness Itself"). Plato uses these terms to suggest that he is talking about the purest embodiment of the quality in question. For example, Justice Itself differs from the deficient, limited versions of justice we experience in human affairs.

Plato frequently uses the term "Ideas" (as in the "Idea of Justice," the "Idea of Goodness") to talk about the objects of knowledge. Hence, this whole discussion concerns what is sometimes called Plato's "theory of Ideas." This wording captures the sense that Plato is referring to nonphysical entities. The Idea of Humanity, for example, transcends the flesh-and-blood individuals that make up the human race. Unfortunately, however, the English term "idea" also refers to the subjective contents of one's mind. In this sense of the term, your ideas no longer exist if you become unconscious. Platonic Ideas, however, are realities that exist independently of the minds that know them. In Plato's account, if there were no circular objects, and no one ever thought of circularity, the objective, geometrical properties of circularity would still exist, waiting to be discovered. Fortunately, Plato uses another term for the Ideas, which can be translated as "Forms." Since this does not have the misleading associations of the former term, we will refer to Plato's account as the "theory of Forms" from now on. Be aware that the "Form" of something does not necessarily refer to its shape. If we are talking about the Form of Triangularity, then shape is a necessary aspect of it. Obviously, however, the Form of Justice has nothing to do with shape.

KNOWLEDGE COMES THROUGH RECOLLECTION

In the dialogue named after him, a young man by the name of Meno confronts Socrates with a paradox used by some of the Sophists to show that the search for knowledge is impossible. Meno states the dilemma in this way:

> *How will you look for something when you don't in the least know what it is? How on earth are you going*

---

*Henceforth, I will capitalize terms such as "Universal," "Form," and "Justice" that Plato uses in a special, technical sense.

to set up something you don't know as the object of your search? To put it another way, even if you come right up against it, how will you know that what you have found is the thing you didn't know?[3]

In other words, if we are seeking the meaning of justice, we either know it or we don't. If we already know what it is, we don't need to seek it, but if we don't know what justice is, how will we recognize it when we find it? The answer that Plato gives is that both horns of the dilemma are true; we both know the universal Forms and we don't know them. First, we know them because they are imprinted on the soul. In other words, we have **innate knowledge** of what is ultimately true, real, and of intrinsic value. Plato believed that before the soul entered the body, we were directly acquainted with the Forms, but on entering the physical world we forgot this knowledge. This explains the second half of the dilemma—why we feel as though we don't have this knowledge. Nevertheless, this knowledge of the Forms is still there, waiting to be recovered through the process of *recollection*. When Plato talks about the pre-existence of the soul, he does so in myths and stories, recognizing that we cannot have detailed scientific knowledge of these states of affairs. The important point, however, is that gaining an understanding of what life is all about is more similar to remembering something than to discovering new data. We have all had the experience of coming to understand clearly something for the first time only to realize that we had sort of known it all along but had not grasped it at the level of full, conscious awareness. It is this sort of experience that Plato thinks illustrates the nature of knowledge. Certain truths are available to the rational mind and can be known independent of sense experience.

How do we trigger this recollection of the Forms? Plato's answer is that we do so by engaging in the sort of dialectical questioning that Socrates initiated. In the *Meno* Socrates converses with an uneducated slave boy who comes to recognize a geometrical truth when Socrates, the intellectual midwife, assists him by means of a series of questions. In the *Phaedo* Socrates argues that we can have a notion of such things as Absolute Justice, Beauty, Goodness, and Equality, even though we have never seen any of these with our eyes. Sense experience and Socrates' method of dialectical questioning cannot give us knowledge of the Forms, for this is already in our possession. Instead, they remind us of what we dimly knew but could not consciously apprehend.

PLATO'S DIVIDED LINE

Ironically, even though Plato was disdainful of the world of the senses, some of the most revealing passages he provides for understanding his theory of knowledge use concrete images. One of his most famous symbols is his account of the divided line. Plato asks us to imagine the following:

Take a line divided into two unequal parts, one to represent the visible order, the other the intelligible; and divide each part again in the same proportion, symbolizing degrees of comparative clearness or obscurity. (R 6.509d–e)

In his description of the divided line, Plato correlates the degrees or levels of knowledge with the different levels of reality. Although our interest in this section is in Plato's theory of knowledge, it is impossible to separate this from what he also believes about reality. Accordingly, Plato seeks to demonstrate that epistemology and metaphysics parallel each other. As we go up the ladder of awareness, our cognitive state more nearly approximates genuine knowledge. Similarly, the objects corresponding to the higher levels of awareness are more fully real. A diagram of the divided line is shown in Figure 4-2.

As is clear from the figure, the journey of the human mind along the vertical line from 1 to 2 passes through several modes of awareness that correspond to various levels of reality. The continuum from total ignorance (A) to pure knowledge (D) is divided into two main cognitive states, those of opinion and of knowledge. These correspond to the two main levels of reality, which are the visible (or physical) world (A' and B') and the intelligible world (C' and D'). However, each of these divisions is further divided. The lowest level of opinion could be called imagination or conjecture (A). This epistemological state corresponds

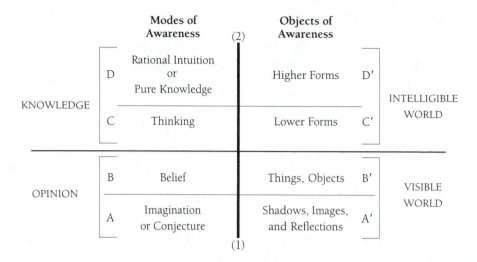

FIGURE 4-2 Diagram of Plato's divided line

to borderline "realities" such as shadows, images, reflections, optical illusions, dreams, and fantasies. Mistaking a desert mirage for water would be an obvious example of a person at this level of cognition and reality. Similarly, someone becoming emotionally involved in the lives of the soap opera characters on television, taking them to be real people, would be another example. However, we can be deceived not only by physical images but also by images created with clever words. Hence, those people who believe the slick rhetoric of a Sophist politician and his false images of what justice is about are trapped at the lower level of the line. They are confusing a distorted shadow of Justice with the real thing.

The second level (B) is that of commonsense belief. In terms of reality, it corresponds to the realm of natural objects as well as cultural objects. A person who recognizes individual horses or particular nations that practice justice but does not see these as imperfect representations of the Ideal Horse or of Perfect Justice is at this level. Such a person can have true opinions, but he (or she) does not have knowledge. This is because he does not understand the reason why things are this way and sees only particulars but not the Forms. There is a ratio here. The reflection of the horse in the water (segment A') is to the physical horse (seg-

ment B') as the entire world of visible things (A' and B') is to the intelligible world (C' and D').

When we have attained the third level (C), we have begun to find our way into the realm of knowledge. It is a transitional stage to the higher realm of awareness and represents the sort of reasoning employed in mathematics and the special sciences. This realm of cognition has two characteristics. First, the mind uses objects in the visible world as a means to arrive at an understanding of the intelligible world. For example, Plato says that the student of geometry uses diagrams and drawings of triangles to prove various theorems. But the visible lines he draws are really not the objects of his knowledge. It is the pure Form of Triangularity he is studying. Second, knowledge at this level is fragmented and based on assumptions that are taken to be self-evident. To be perfected, such knowledge will ultimately have to be derived from a nonhypothetical first principle.

In the final stage (D), the mind soars beyond all assumptions and sensory crutches to a rational intuition of the pure Forms. These Forms are the ultimate principles that we use to derive all subsidiary and specialized knowledge. The final destination of this process of dialectic is the apprehension of "the first principle of the whole." It needs no further explanation or justification and everything else depends on it. Plato calls this ultimate source of knowledge and reality "the Good" (R 7.508e, 518c). The only way we can describe it is by means of an analogy. Think of the Good as the sun, Plato says. The sun makes possible the existence of all living things and enables us to see them. Similarly, the Good is the source of the being and reality of all things and, like the light of the sun, enables our minds to see the truth. The knowledge discovered here cannot be put into words, because the Good is the transcendent source of all partial truths that words can convey. We can only encounter it "after a long period of attendance on instruction in the subject itself and of close companionship, when, suddenly, like a blaze kindled by a leaping spark, it is generated in the soul and at once becomes self-sustaining" (L 7.341c–d). Later Christian Platonists will identify Plato's Good with God. It is important to understand, however, that Plato's Good is an impersonal, rational principle that is the foundation of reality, but it is not a benevolent, anthropomorphic deity.

Metaphysics: Shadows and Reality

THE REALITY OF THE FORMS

Plato's attempt to work out Socrates' insights drove him to pursue their metaphysical foundations. Plato shared Socrates' concern to capture universal concepts in carefully constructed and rationally derived definitions. However, Socrates never had much interest in metaphysics. So he never paid much attention to the question of what sort of reality these Universals or Forms have. Plato, however, argued that if the Forms are the true objects of knowledge, then knowledge must be of something real. Therefore, the Forms must be objective, independently existing realities. What does the mathematician study when she reasons about the geometrical properties of circles? She doesn't examine the circular hoops, rings, or wheels she finds in experience. Instead, with her mind she contemplates the eternal Form of Circularity itself. Circular objects can be changed or destroyed, but what the mathematician studies cannot be changed.

If the Forms are real, then where do they exist? The question is meaningless because "where" and "when" questions apply only to spatiotemporal objects. You cannot ask, for example, where the multiplication tables exist. True, we have them in our minds and write them on our blackboards. But if our minds forgot them and the copies were destroyed, the truths in the multiplication tables would still endure. We did not invent them, but we *discovered* them. Hence, they do not depend on our minds for their existence. Every science and every craft accomplishes its task with reference to the Forms. The biologist studies frogs but is not interested in simply this or that particular frog for its own sake. Instead, the biologist seeks to know what is universally true about all frogs. He seeks to understand the Form characteristic of frogs. Similarly, the carpenter has a familiarity with the Form of Chairness and the Form of Tableness and seeks to instantiate these in his wood.

THE PROBLEM OF CHANGE

Plato was also driven to metaphysics by the unsolved problems that previous philosophers left behind. Looming large among these problems was the problem of change. Like a pebble in one's shoe, it was a constant irritant in Greek philosophy that refused to go away. There is a paradox about change. When you visit relatives whom you've not seen since you were very young, they may say, "My, how you have changed!" But what are they saying? Obviously, they are saying you are different from the way you were. However, you are not different from your younger self in the way you are different from your sister. In some sense you are the same person. You are the same, and you are not the same. Both Heraclitus and Parmenides sought to dissolve the paradox of change with extreme solutions. Heraclitus said that everything in the world of experience is changing and permanence is merely an illusion. Parmenides and his fellow Eleatics eliminated the problem by claiming that permanence is fundamental and change is merely an appearance.

Although their positions were diametrically opposite, both assumed monism, the claim that reality is essentially one sort of thing. If the Heraclitean position is correct, then knowledge is impossible because there is nothing stable about the world that we could know. Yet Parmenides' solution is not satisfactory either, because change is obviously a fact of life. Plato believes that they are both wrong and they are both right. They are wrong in their monism, because they too quickly assume that all reality is one sort of thing. However, they are each right in describing one-half of the total picture. Plato was a genius at synthesizing the insights of his predecessors. He adopted their insights but modified them to eliminate their weaknesses.

In seeking a compromise between Heraclitus and Parmenides, Plato embraces **metaphysical dualism**, the claim that there are two completely different kinds of reality. His solution is to propose that there is a world in constant flux, at the same time there is a world that is eternal and unchanging. The world of flux is the physical world that we encounter in sense experience. Because it is constantly changing, we cannot have rational knowledge of it. The world that is eternal and unchanging is a nonphysical reality. It is not located in space or time. Plato sometimes refers to this as the "intelligible world" because only this reality is intelligible to reason.

THE RELATIONSHIP OF PARTICULARS TO THE FORMS

At this point, Plato faces the problem of all dualisms. Once you have separated reality into two different realms, how do you understand the relationship between them? For Plato, the universe is not a democracy, for these two kinds of reality are not equal. The physical world is less real than the world of Forms and depends on the higher world. The reality that transcends experience produces whatever order and reality we find in the world of experience.

It sounds strange to us to hear talk about "degrees of reality." After all, doesn't common sense tell us a thing either *is* or *is not* real? Even Parmenides, that great opponent of common sense, would agree. But according to Plato, the objects

of sensation occupy a gray area between the real and the unreal. Maybe it would help to examine some ways in which Plato's notion of degrees of reality finds its way into common experience and ordinary conversation. If we find ourselves stuck with a counterfeit $20 bill, we obviously have *something* in our wallet. Insofar as it is a piece of paper, it has as much reality as any paper does. However, as an example of legal currency it is not a *real* dollar bill. The counterfeit bill is only an imitation of the genuine article. If we have a photograph of someone we love, it is a kind of reality because it sits on our dresser and evokes warm memories within us. But, unfortunately again, it is not the *real* person, only a representation of them. What fascinates us about the picture is that it shares in some of the reality of the person we love. It was directly derived from the person and bears his or her image. Similarly, reflections in a mirror or shadows have some reality, but they are only vague images of something more substantial than they are. To use Plato's term, the photograph and the reflected images *participate* in the realities they represent. The better the picture, the more fully it participates in the real object and represents the features of the original.

Thus far, we have been comparing two physical objects, one of which is a copy of or derived from something else. These examples illustrate Plato's point that something is a lower level of reality if it depends on something else for its existence and bears the image of that higher reality. However, because these examples are confined to the physical world, they do not fully capture Plato's point. To better illustrate his position, let's look at some examples that compare a physical reality with a nonphysical, perfect, reality. I once overheard a frustrated student who had been given the runaround by an unfeeling, inefficient, college bureaucracy in her attempts to register for courses. Her comment was "This is *unreal!*" Plato would say she was comparing the spatiotemporal events in her experience with the way things ought to be. The vision of a humane, caring college, known only with her mind, was the standard against which she compared the present, deficient institution she was experiencing. As a result of this comparison, her school was so far from what a real college should be that she described it as "unreal." We tend to think of ideals as imaginary objects that exist only in our daydreams. But according to Plato, the ideal of a college genuinely serving its students constitutes what a *real* college is. The institutions you and I know are more or less real college communities to the degree that they approximate this higher reality.

Let us look at a second example. We frequently use the term "inhuman" to describe tyrants such as Adolf Hitler. Now, a very dull biologist might respond, "Oh, no, you're wrong—Hitler was human. He had two lungs, a four-chambered heart, the correct sort of chromosomes." But this person would have missed the point. To say Hitler was inhuman has nothing to do with what we would discover in an autopsy. For Plato, to be fully human depends not so much on physical characteristics as it does on one's nonphysical features such as the condition of one's soul, the degree of a person's rationality, and one's values.

We could contrast Hitler with a notable humanitarian such as Dr. Bill Walsh. Walsh was an American cardiologist who quit a lucrative medical practice in the 1960s to start a medical relief organization called Project HOPE. With donated money, supplies, and volunteer labor, he converted a former naval ship into the SS *HOPE*, a hospital ship that sailed all over the world, bringing medical treatment and training to needy people. In terms of Plato's philosophy we could say Walsh was more fully a real human being because of his exemplary moral qualities. Compared to him, Hitler was subhuman. Although he was a great humanitarian, Walsh could have only a partial hold on what it means to be human. According to Plato, no earthly, physical being (human or otherwise) ever attains the perfect reality of its Form, for to be physical is always to be limited, deficient, and changing. Accordingly, we could say Hitler was but a shadow of what a human is, whereas someone such as Bill Walsh is like a very clear photograph. He's not the full reality itself, but a very good likeness of it.

We can now summarize the relationship between particulars and their Forms. First, the Forms are the *cause* of the existence of particular things, analogous to the way a statue causes its shadow. Second, physical objects *resemble* their Forms, analogous to the way a photograph is the likeness of the person. Third, particular objects *participate* in their Forms. Compare the three shapes in Figure 4-3. Obviously, the one on the right participates in the Form of Circularity more fully than the other two. We might describe the middle one as "sort of a circle" because there is some likeness. However, the one on the left falls quite a bit short of the ideal circle. In fact, it falls so short of any recognizable Form that it would be hard to describe. Similarly, if we were to rank humans according to their participation in the Form of Humanity, Adolf Hitler would be on the left, the average person somewhere in the middle, and a saintly person would represent the fullest participation in the Form. Fourth, as the previous examples illustrate, Forms represent the *standards of evaluation* we use to judge particulars as excellent or deficient. Engineers evaluate ball bearings in comparison to the Perfect Sphere, and horse breeders judge their stock in comparison to the Ideal Horse. Finally, the Forms make particulars *intelligible*. Try to describe a close friend. No matter how unique they may be, you must resort to a list of universal qualities to say anything about them (for example, "tall," "brilliant," "female," "athletic"). Without the Forms we could not think, speak, or make sense out of anything.

THE ALLEGORY OF THE CAVE

Plato spells out his theory of knowledge and reality in the Allegory of the Cave, one of the most striking stories in the history of Western literature (R 7.514a–521b) (See Figure 4-4 on page 56). In the story, there is a group of prisoners that have lived all their life in the bottom of a cave where they have been chained so that they can only see the back wall of the cave. Behind them, some unnamed men parade statues of animals and other objects in front of a fire. However, the prisoners cannot see the fire or the artificial objects. They can only see the shadows projected on the wall, and consequently they believe these to be the sum

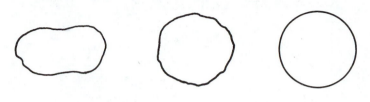

FIGURE 4-3

total of reality. Now imagine that one of these prisoners was liberated. At first the sight of the wooden objects would be confusing and the fire would hurt his eyes. He would be inclined to think that the familiar shadows were the true reality and that what he is seeing now are frightening illusions.

Now if he were dragged up to the opening of the cave and out into the sunlight, he would be even more amazed. The light of the sun would be even more disorienting than that of the fire. Eventually, however, he would become accustomed to this new level of reality. He would see real animals, trees, flowers, and stars for the first time and would realize that these colored, three-dimensional objects are more real than the shadows or even the wooden replicas in the cave. He would now see how pathetic is the life of those in the cave, for their vision of reality is limited to the shadows. Plato imagines they have a practice of awarding prizes and honors to those who are most skillful at recognizing and anticipating particular shadows. However, these honors are worthless to one who has encountered the fuller realities. Plato asks, "Would he not . . . far sooner 'be on earth as a hired servant in the house of landless man' or endure anything rather than go back to his old beliefs and live in the old way?" If this man would return to the cave, he would be the subject of ridicule, for his eyes would no longer be accustomed to the darkness and it would be difficult for him to discern the shadows as well as the prisoners. Furthermore, his former friends would think he had gone mad when he talked of the green grass, the glassy lakes, and the bright sunlight. Finally, Plato says, "If they could lay hands on the man who was trying to set them free and lead them up, they would kill him."

Plato makes several applications of this allegory. First, with respect to metaphysics, the story represents Plato's theory of the levels of reality. The shadows are imperfect representations of the wooden puppets, but these in turn are themselves just copies of real animals, trees, flowers, and so on. Hence, the cave world represents the physical world, a world made up of different levels of copies and images. The land above represents the realm of the Forms, the realities that are only imperfectly represented down below. Finally, the sun represents the Good, that supreme Form that gives life and intelligibility to everything else. In terms of epistemology, the story shows that simply accumulating more and more knowledge of the shadows will not produce understanding. What is required is a new perspective, a higher vision of the genuine realities. Hence, Plato says,

> Education is not what it is said to be by some, who profess to put knowledge into a soul which does not possess it, as if they could put sight into blind eyes. On the contrary, our own account signifies that the soul of every man does possess the power of learning the truth and the organ to see it with; and that, just as one might have to turn the whole body round in order that the eye should see light instead of darkness, so the entire soul must be turned away from this changing world, until its eye can bear to contemplate reality and that supreme splendour which we have called the Good. (R 7.518c)

Just as the person who has climbed up out of the cave is the only one that can really understand the shadows for what they are, so the person with wisdom is one who has mentally gone beyond the physical world and understood the Forms that make all things intelligible. The man in the story

FIGURE 4-4 This diagram of Plato's Allegory of the Cave represents a chained prisoner whose only reality is (A) the shadows, which are projected by (B) replicas of objects, and (in the upper left corner) the steep and rugged passage out of the cave to the upper world. If the prisoner follows this route, he will encounter (C) the world of real objects and (D) the sun. These levels correspond to the modes of awareness and levels of reality on the divided line depicted in Figure 4-2.

who had knowledge of the higher reality and returned back to the cave to free the others obviously represented Socrates (or any other person with the correct philosophical vision). He was misunderstood by the cave dwellers and thought to have gone mad because he was accustomed to living in the other world. Nevertheless, he felt an obligation to try to free the others, even at the cost of his own life.

Moral Theory

AGAINST RELATIVISM

As with much of his philosophy, Plato's discussion of morality is set in contrast to those of the Sophists, the antagonists of his beloved teacher, Socrates. Recall that the Sophists taught that we base our moral norms either on subjective, per-

sonal opinions or social conventions. However, if this is all there is to morality, then ethical values will be arbitrarily decided by whoever in society is the most persuasive. In the worst scenario, whoever in society is most powerful will determine its ethical values. Since, according to the Sophists, there are no higher standards of morality beyond convention, it would be impossible to evaluate or criticize the morality of a particular society. Hence, we could not find fault with the Nazi regime when they slaughtered multitudes of innocent men, women, and children, because this simply reflected the values and laws of their society at that particular time. Neither could we say that a humanitarian such as Mother Teresa, who cared for the poor and dying, was morally superior to Hitler. On the Sophist's view, we would have to say that these two people are morally equal in that they each sincerely pursued their own subjective moral code and both received the approval of their society.

Plato, of course, would point out that these conclusions indicate that something is deeply mistaken about moral relativism and subjectivism. Plato's general approach will be to maintain that ethics is just as objective a science as mathematics. In mathematics we explore the nonphysical Forms of Circularity, Triangularity, Equality, and so on. Similarly, in ethics we are concerned with such things as the Forms of Justice and the Good. This may seem like a very big leap. It seems relatively easy to arrive at and agree on the objective properties of a circle. However, even Plato would acknowledge that it is very difficult to get people to agree on a definition of moral goodness. Plato would respond, no doubt, that consensus is not a criterion of truth. The history of science makes clear that it is not unusual for the majority of people to be mistaken. Nevertheless, since mathematical and scientific issues in themselves do not impinge on our ethical choices, it is easier for people to perceive the truth in these areas. With morality, however, our bodily appetites, our irrational desires, and the shadow world of false values persistently cloud our vision and tempt us away from the truth. Therefore, we find less agreement about ethical issues, but this does not prove there are no right answers and wrong answers.

Plato persists in maintaining that if there are not objective, ethical Forms, then the Sophists are right and all moral terms are simply sounds and puffs of air that do not refer to anything real. In this case, human life would be comparable to being adrift in the middle of the ocean with no navigational maps, no compass, no guiding stars, no rudder, and no power. We would have no sense of direction in life and would be tossed about by the waves of our irrational desires and blown here and there by the arbitrary winds of power and persuasion in our society.

WHY BE MORAL?

A large part of Plato's moral theory revolves around the discussion of justice. For Plato, this was a very broad notion. It included a large part

of what we think of when we hear the word *justice*. Hence, it refers to a fair, decent, and correct ordering of society and its transactions. In this sense, we could say that the laws of a society, a judicial decision, or a business deal is just. But in Plato's philosophy the term also refers to the quality within a person who has a well-ordered soul. In this sense, a just person is the truly moral person. The parallel between the just (or well-ordered) individual and the just (or well-ordered) society is important to Plato. As we will see when we discuss his political philosophy, he believes that the principles of moral theory and of political theory are identical.

Justice receives Plato's fullest treatment in the *Republic*. Plato first gives a hearing to the voices of his skeptical and cynical peers, who question why we should even be concerned with justice. Accordingly, the question is raised, "Why be morally good?" In other words, what is the point of being a morally good person? Why should we prefer the just life over a life of pleasure and uncaring self-interest? To lay the groundwork for this discussion, Glaucon (one of the characters in the dialogue) sets out three categories of things that are good. First, some things are good for their own sake and not for their consequences. These would be simple pleasures, such as enjoying a sunset. Second, some things we value both for their own sake *and* for their consequences, such as knowledge and health. Third, some burdensome things we value *only* for their consequences. For example, no one enjoys going to the dentist, but the benefit of having healthy teeth is worth the pain. In which category should we place justice (or moral goodness)? Glaucon points out that most people would place it in the third category. It is "one of those things, tiresome and disagreeable in themselves, which we cannot avoid practicing for the sake of reward or a good reputation" (R 2.358a). Socrates, however, claims the just life falls into the second category. It is the highest sort of good, "a thing which anyone who is to gain happiness must value both for itself and for its results."

To make his point more forcefully, Glaucon tells the story of the magic ring. According to legend, a shepherd by the name of Gyges found a ring that gave him the magic power to become invisible at will. Glaucon asks whether anyone possessing such power would have the moral strength to resist the temptation to steal, kill, commit adultery, or engage in any immorality they desired, if they knew that they could never be caught or identified? To expand on this thought experiment, Glaucon then asks us to imagine two men. One is perfectly unjust or evil, and the other is perfectly just. However, the evil man (being very clever) manages to fool his society and maintains a spotless reputation while committing the worst crimes imaginable. In contrast, the society totally misunderstands the good man. Although he is perfectly just, his society wrongly inflicts him with an evil reputation and persecutes and torments him because of it. Under these circumstances, what would be the point of being just? Wouldn't it be better to be the evil man, who is admired and praised by his peers and receives all of society's rewards? We could expand on Glaucon's question and ask, "What if there were no afterlife or heaven to reward us for good behavior?" Don't these considerations make it clear that the only point of being a good person, the only value that justice has, is the good reputation and the external benefits it brings us (either in this life or the next)? Glaucon summarizes his speech by confronting Socrates with the following challenge:

> You must not be content merely to prove that justice is superior to injustice, but explain how one is good, the other evil, in virtue of the intrinsic effect each has on its possessor, whether gods or men see it or not. (R 2.367e)

Although these questions concerning the value of the just life are raised early in the *Republic*, Plato takes most of the book to provide an answer to Glaucon's challenge. To make clear why being a just person is a goal worth pursuing, Plato thinks it necessary to first give an account of human nature. In doing this, his approach to ethics is typically Greek. He does not begin by setting out a list of dos and don'ts. Instead, he examines what sort of creatures we are and from that extracts what moral goodness is and why it is life's most important pursuit.

MORALITY AND HUMAN NATURE

From his theory of Forms, it should be clear that the universe for Plato is not a chaotic hodgepodge of random objects and processes. Instead, it has a built-in, purposive, rational structure underlying it. According to Plato, we can understand anything in nature in terms of the Form that determines its function. To understand any type of thing, therefore, we must understand what constitutes its perfect end: what standard of excellence it is trying to fulfill. Hence, it would not be too far off the mark to say that for Plato, we derive moral principles from a correct understanding of human psychology.

For Plato, the essential core of the person is his or her *psyche*. This is usually translated as "soul." However, we must be careful not to read too much traditional religious content into that term. Whenever the word *soul* appears, it is best to think of it as referring to the "self." If we examine our own, inner experience, Plato says, we will find that the soul is not completely unified. We find inner conflicts and competing forces warring within us. This suggests that several types of elements or faculties are at work within the soul. Although Plato refers to the different "parts" of the soul, we should not think of these in the same way we think of the parts of an engine. Instead, we might think of them as different kinds of desires, or principles of action, or different types of psychological drives.

To illustrate these divisions, he asks us to imagine a thirsty man who has a desperate craving to drink, but refrains from doing so (perhaps because he knows the water is polluted). This shows that at least two conflicting forces are at work in a person. The first group of drives are the appetites or the appetitive part of the person. These are associated with our bodily needs and desires, such as the desire for food, drink, and sex. The appetites pull us in the direction of physical gratification and material acquisition. However, there is also the more reflective, rational part of the soul, which sometimes vetoes the urgings of the appetites. This is the voice of reason within us. This element also has desires, but these are rational desires. It is the source of the love of truth and the desire to understand. It might seem as though the struggle between these two forces is enough to explain human behavior. However, Plato finds a third element within the soul. This is the "spirited" part of us. The term *spirit* here has no religious connotations. It is used in the same sense that we talk of a spirited horse. This is the willful, dynamic, executive faculty within the soul. The spirited part expresses itself in anger, righteous indignation, ambition, courage, pride, or assertiveness. It is the source of the desire for honor, respect, reputation, and self-esteem. The spirit is associated with the passions or the emotions. It is distinct from the other two drives because we can be moved by anger or by moral fervor, when these are neither physiological drives nor the products of reflective reason. The spirit is a motive force, but it receives its direction from the other two faculties. It can follow the commands of either the appetites or the reason.

The appetites are the lowest and the most dangerous of our desires. They are the voice within us that says, "I want, I want," without regard for the consequences. For example, we may feel the desire for sexual gratification even though, under the circumstances, it would be harmful and irrational to follow through on this. However, if our reason is not in control, the spirit's desire for self-esteem and its pride may cause it to conspire with the appetites, leading us into an unfortunate situation. In contrast, my appetitive part may crave a gluttonous dessert, while my reason (the highest part of the soul) tells me this would not be good. In the midst of this struggle, a third voice within me may express disgust and anger with myself saying, "How can I be such a pig?" This is the spirited part, the intermediate element, reinforcing the pull of reason.

In the *Phaedrus*, Plato captures the dynamic structure of his psychology with a striking image. He presents the picture of a man driving a chariot with two horses (P 246a–b). The charioteer is the rational element of the soul, continually having to control the appetites and the spirited element. The one horse (the spirited element) is eager to obey. He is "a lover of glory, but with temperance and modesty; one that consorts with genuine renown, and needs no whip, being driven by the word of command alone." The other horse (the appetites) is eager to take control. He continually seeks to run wild and pull the chariot off its path into destruction. He is "crooked of frame, a massive jumble of a creature, . . . consorting with wantonness and vainglory; shaggy of ear, deaf, and hard to control with whip and goad" (P 253d–254e). Only when reason tightly controls the reins can the other two elements be led to pull the person in the appropriate direction.

With this brief account of human psychology in place, Plato can now begin to apply it to the issues of morality. For Plato, there were four primary moral virtues: wisdom, courage, temperance, and justice. Each finds its place within the different elements of the soul. If reason is in control of the person and guides the other parts of the soul, the person possesses the virtue of *wisdom*. Like a military commander or an orchestra director, reason has an understanding of the whole picture and helps the others play out their appropriate roles. Like a parent or a physician, reason knows what is genuinely good for its charges.

If the spirited part subordinates itself to the counsel of reason and applies its energy, ambition, and assertiveness toward the right goals, then the person manifests the virtue of *courage*. The healthy spirit holds fast to the commands of reason and ignores the pulls of pain and pleasure. With the virtue of courage, the spirited element finds its sense of glory only in doing what is right, it fears only what is genuinely fearful, and bravely confronts all enemies of truth and goodness. It does not waste its passions on petty quarrels but rises in anger only at what is morally base.

If the appetites control and moderate their desire for pleasure and subordinate themselves to the two higher elements, then the person has the virtue of *temperance* or self-control. Notice that although Plato tends to downplay the importance of the body, he does not think the ideal is an ascetic denial of the body's needs altogether. If a person, for example, was so obsessed with the desire to study the history of philosophy that she turned a deaf ear to her body's need for sleep or food, this would not be an example of wisdom. Temperance, then, does not mean complete denial of the body's needs and desires, but a sense of balance and self-mastery.

Finally, where does *justice* fit in? It is an overarching virtue that is present when all the other elements have achieved their correct balance within the person. The just person is one who possesses wisdom, courage, temperance and in whom each element plays its proper role and maintains its proper place. Late in the *Republic* Plato uses yet another dramatic analogy to make clear the value of a well-balanced or just soul. He imagines that inside each human is a smaller person who represents the voice of reason. There is also a lion (the spirited part) and a wild, many-headed beast (the appetites). To say that immorality pays and that there is no point in doing right is like saying,

> It pays to feed up and strengthen the composite beast and all that belongs to the lion, and to starve the man till he is so enfeebled that the other two can drag him whither they will. . . . On the other hand, to declare that justice pays is to assert that all our words and actions should tend towards giving the man within us complete mastery over the whole human creature, and letting him take the many-headed beast under his care and tame its wildness, like the gardener who trains his cherished plants while he checks the growth of weeds. He should enlist the lion as his ally, and, caring for all alike, should foster their growth by first reconciling them to one another and to himself. (R 9.588e–589b)

The Socrates of the dialogue adds that a good action "tends to subdue the brutish parts of our nature to the human—perhaps I should rather say to the divine in us." In contrast, evil actions "enslave our humanity to the savagery of the beast" (R 9.589c–d).

Although the single-minded pursuit of pleasure is the obsession of the appetites and must be put aside to seek justice, Plato believes that the highest sort of pleasure and happiness accompanies the attainment of moral goodness. The person in whom wisdom and justice find their home knows the physical pleasures and allows them their proper place. Such a person also knows the pleasures of honor and reputation and enjoys them to the proper degree. However, out of all the pleasures, "the sweetest will belong to that part of the soul whereby we gain understanding and knowledge, and the man in whom that part predominates will have the pleasantest life" (R 9.583a).

In the preceding passages, Plato, through the voice of Socrates, has made clear the nature of human psychology and the effects that justice and injustice have on our inner selves. Justice constitutes the health and well-being of the soul. Much like physical health, justice is a condition in which all the various elements of the person are balanced and in the right order. In contrast, wickedness is like a cancer of the soul. It is an inner abnormality, deformity, weakness, or a fatal disease that has taken over the person. A character in the dialogue sums up Plato's moral philosophy thus:

> People think that all the luxury and wealth and power in the world cannot make life worth living when the bodily constitution is going to rack and ruin; and are we to believe that, when the very principle whereby we live is deranged and corrupted, life will be worth living so long as a man can do as he will, and wills to do anything rather than to free himself from vice and wrongdoing and to win justice and virtue? (R 4.445a–b)

At the beginning, the question "Why be just or morally good?" seemed like a serious question. But after Socrates has laid out the options, it is like asking, "Why be in control of my life instead of being a slave? Why not be ravaged by the beasts and wild desires within me? Why be in the correct relationship to reality? Why be healthy instead of diseased?" When the question about the value of morality is asked in these ways, we can only reply as did Socrates, "It is a ridiculous question."

Political Theory

THE THREE DIVISIONS IN SOCIETY

The move from Plato's moral theory to his political theory is an easy one. In fact, the two topics are intertwined in the *Republic*. We have separated them only for ease of exposition. When Socrates runs into difficulties explaining the nature of the just life, he suggests they switch to a discussion of the just society since society is like an individual person "written large" (R 2.368d-e). In other words, the principles of psychology and political science are the same. The soul of the individual person is a miniature version of the structure of society and society could be viewed as the individual person projected on a large screen. However, the relationship between the two is deeper than that of simply having a parallel structure. Plato believes it is impossible to live the good life or to be a fulfilled individual apart from the state. Furthermore, a good society is only possible if the people in power are good and live by the light of philosophical reason. The good person and the good society depend on each other. This contrasts with Christian thought, where morality is often viewed as the solitary journey of the individual soul in relationship with God. Plato has a strong bias against individualism, unlike our modern age. There is no place in his society for hermits, rugged individualists, or people who march to the beat of a different drummer. For Plato, the state is like an organism in which each part finds its life in relationship to the whole. In the body it is impossible for an organ such as the heart to be healthy if poisons are circulating in the system or if the organ is severed from the rest of the body. Similarly, in human affairs, persons are organically related to each other and to the whole of society. Our fortunes rise and fall together.

For Plato, the most functional state is built around a division of labor. It is foolish for me to take the time to make my own shoes, because there are skilled workers who are much better at it than I. However, Plato expands this rather obvious point into a whole political philosophy that is highly critical of democracy. For him, politics is a science that should be left to the experts no less than with any craft, skill, or science. To elaborate on one of Plato's medical analogies, if you wanted to know whether you needed open-heart surgery, you would not put it to a democratic vote among your friends, your banker, or your automobile mechanic. Instead, you would seek the wisdom of

physicians who are experts on this matter. Similarly, when it comes to formulating the policies and laws that govern the state, the democratic majority represents those least likely to make an informed decision. If we are concerned with the health of the body, we yield to the advice of the experts. So, when we are concerned with the health of the state, we should similarly seek out those who have the necessary wisdom to govern. These experts must have a vision of the Good. They must know what constitutes true knowledge. Just as a navigator must understand the stars and be able to use them to guide a ship through the vast ocean, so our political rulers must be able to navigate the ship of state by means of a vision of the Forms and the Good. Who else would these political navigators be but those with philosophical wisdom?

> Unless either philosophers become kings in their countries or those who are now called kings and rulers come to be sufficiently inspired with a genuine desire for wisdom; unless that is to say, political power and philosophy meet together . . . there can be no rest from troubles . . . for states, nor yet, as I believe, for all mankind; nor can this commonwealth which we have imagined ever till then see the light of day and grow to its full stature. (R 5.473)

If justice in the individual soul is the balanced harmony of all the elements in the person, under the sovereignty of reason, then justice in the state will have the same structure. Corresponding to the three elements within the individual, therefore, there are three kinds of people within society. Each kind has its appropriate role to play within the state. The first kind of people are the *producers*. These provide the necessities of life and all its material and economic goods or services. This includes such groups as farmers, shoemakers, carpenters, and general laborers. It also includes shopkeepers, importers, and bankers. The second group is originally called the *guardians*. They are concerned with the welfare of society as a whole and protect it from both its external and internal enemies. Eventually, those trained to be guardians will be divided into two further groups based on their abilities. The one group is called the *auxiliaries*. They correspond to our police and military personnel, as well as to the other federal agents and administrators that support and enforce the policies of the rulers. The third and highest group retains the title of *guardians*, and its members are the ultimate rulers of the state. They are a select group, distinguished by their intelligence and philosophical wisdom. Their job is to establish the policies and laws within the society. Since the producers are concerned with material acquisition and physical comfort, they correspond to the appetitive part of the soul. The auxiliaries are those people who are ambitious, assertive, and desire honor. They manifest the spirited element of the soul. The guardians or rulers, of course, represent reason. The parallel structure of the individual and the state is now complete.

We will now make a more detailed examination of each role within society. It is tempting to suppose that the lowest class, the producers, correspond to the Marxist proletariat and suffer all the oppression and deprivation that we usually associate with the underclass. However, Plato's class structure defies all our usual notions of class divisions. Notice that the lower class in Plato's society includes not only the workers but merchants, physicians, businesspeople, and bankers as well. In other words, it includes those whom we would rank in the middle to upper classes in our society.

Ironically, the people in the lower class, for Plato, are afforded the most freedom and economic gain. They can live their lives as they wish, within the bounds of the law. They can marry whom they wish, can own property, and can acquire all manner of personal wealth and luxury, as long as society does not become unbalanced with too much wealth and too much poverty. Furthermore, the power and leadership roles in society are not apportioned in terms of family name, social origins, or gender. Plato thinks it entirely possible that the daughter of a mechanic will be blessed with the intelligence and aptitude to serve as a ruler. And the son of a ruler may turn out to be best suited to be a fisherman. Plato also recognizes that superior women are as equally qualified as their male counterparts to be rulers. This was quite radical for his time, because women were not very highly esteemed in Greek society

and were mainly relegated to domestic roles. However, Plato realized that intelligence and skill in ruling have nothing to do with gender. Thus, Plato's society is a meritocracy (a society based on merit alone). However, a social mobility is possible in his meritocracy that goes far beyond that of most societies that have ever existed. Nevertheless, just as the son of a superior flute player is likely to inherit natural musical abilities, so the offspring in each social class are likely to inherit the skills and abilities of their parents and thus play the same role within the state.

The lower class has the most freedom and physical comfort; the two higher classes (the auxiliaries and the guardians) live very regulated and austere lives. In the early years of life, the children of all classes are subjected to rigorous testing and observation and those with superior abilities and aptitudes are selected. Plato would have been delighted at the battery of intelligence tests and psychological diagnostic instruments our age has developed, since these sorts of instruments are crucial to his social planning.

Plato's *Republic* stands as one of the great classics in utopian literature. The idealism of his vision is inspiring, but most people would agree with Glaucon's complaint that such an ideal community exists nowhere on earth. To this Plato has Socrates reply,

> No . . . but perhaps there is a pattern set up in the heavens for one who desires to see it and, seeing it, to found one in himself. But whether it exists anywhere or ever will exist is no matter; for this is the only commonwealth in whose politics he can ever take part. (R 9.592)

THE DECLINE OF THE IDEAL STATE

Plato was well aware that this ideal society is a very fragile accomplishment. In fact, he calculated the forces that would cause it to fall apart. From the stage of an intellectual aristocracy (which was his ideal) the state could degenerate into a timocracy. This would occur if the rulers come to love honor and ambition rather than the good of society. Thus, the spirited element would take precedence over the rational part. Such rulers will be wary of intellectuals and will be more interested in the glories of war than in peace. The desire for honor could easily degenerate into a desire for wealth. The government would now become an oligarchy or plutocracy in which the wealthy few held the power. As the rulers became richer, the rest of society would become poorer, and the one unified country would now be divided into two groups with opposite interests. Once the passion for wealth is unleashed, then the self-discipline necessary for the ideal state will disintegrate. Finally the dissatisfaction of the powerless poor will reach a turning point, and the rulers will be overthrown and a democracy will result.

Plato has a very dismal view of democracy, for in such a state, "liberty and free speech are rife everywhere; anyone is allowed to do what he likes" (R 8.557b). Instead of the country being run by those who are most competent, a democratic public "will promote to honour anyone who merely call himself the people's friend" (R 8.558b). According to Plato, each of the various forms of government tends to shape its citizens after its own image. By making an idol out of equality and failing to recognize distinctions between people's abilities, a democratic government will encourage a personal stance toward life in which people will believe that "one appetite is as good as another and all must have their equal rights" (R 8.561c).

Plato believes that democracy is unstable, both as a political system and as an organizational principle of the soul, for if we treat every interest and desire equally, then there will be war between them for supremacy. As the different factions lobby for their interests, the ruler will give heed to whichever voice is the loudest and will gratify the masses at the expense of the rich. As the tensions mount, the people will rally around a leader who promises to champion their interests and will anoint him (or her) with power. But to consolidate his power, he will need to suppress all who might challenge it: the courageous, the proud, the intelligent, and the rich. Soon the state will degenerate into a despotism or a tyranny. In seeking to gratify their lust for money and pleasure, the people will have given themselves over to an un-principled ruler whose only goal is power. Similarly, the democratic individual who gives free reign to all his passions instead of ranking them from better to worse, will find himself the victim of one master passion. Democracy, both as a political ideal and personality type, will lead to political and psychological bondage.

Plato's Cosmology: Purpose and Chance

Just as a society cannot exist unless there is order, so, Plato believes, the universe could not exist without a principle of order governing it. In his *Philebus*, he refers to the regular motion of the heavenly bodies as evidence of a "wonderous regulating intelligence."[4] For this reason, Plato rejects the Atomists' theory that the world is solely the product of chance collisions of moving particles. But what is a more plausible account? He provides his answer in the *Timaeus*, a work that was enormously influential throughout later eras in history. Before setting out his theory, Plato acknowledges (as do physicists today) that it is extremely difficult to arrive at a consistent and precise account of the origins of the universe. The best we can do, he says, is to construct a highly probable theory or "likely story."

Plato starts from the premise that "everything that becomes or is created must of necessity be created by some cause" (Tm 28a). Since the universe is so vast and complex, its cause must be immeasurably powerful and intelligent. This supreme cause is referred to as God or the Demiurge (meaning "Craftsman"). However, unlike the Judeo-Christian account, Plato's God is not omnipotent and does not create the cosmos out of nothing.* Instead, he is like a human craftsman who creates an article out of pre-existing materials by following a blueprint. The raw material the Demiurge works with is completely formless and chaotic, while the "blueprint" consists of the eternal Forms. Like a

---

*For the ancient Greek philosophers, the notion that anything could come out of nothing was unintelligible.

sculptor shaping a mass of clay, the Demiurge imposes the Forms on the malleable matrix of spatial "stuff," which is called the Receptacle.[†] Why did the Demiurge desire to bring order out the chaos? Plato explains that

> He was good, and the good can never have any jealousy of anything. And being free from jealousy, he desired that all things should be as like himself as they could be. (Tm 29e–30a)

The Divine Craftsman's motive is like that of the philosopher whose love of the Forms motivates him or her to bring the Forms to bear on the body of government. Hence, philosophers imitate God by extending the order and excellence of their own souls into the world.[5]

Since the Demiurge imparts some of its nature into the universe, Plato speaks of the created universe as a "living creature." Because it is an organic whole and not a hodgepodge of matter in motion, the universe is harmonious and all its elements work together. Furthermore, it consists of a visible body and an invisible soul, accounting for both its material and purposeful nature. The cosmic soul mediates between the eternal realm of the Forms and the Demiurge, and the changing, perishing physical world. The Demiurge did not create every object in the world directly, but having sowed the seed, he allowed the creative, rational powers of the cosmic soul to carry on the task of creation.

A significant feature of this narrative is that Plato explains the universe in terms of a purposeful order that permeates it. An explanation in terms of a purposeful or a goal-directed order is known as a **teleological explanation**. If I ask "Why are you sitting there?" you do not answer the question by talking about the physiology of your bones and muscles that enable you to sit. Instead, I want to know your goal or purpose for being there. Similarly, Plato thinks that explaining the universe by simply referring to its material elements is insufficient.[6] The order in the world exhibits purpose that points to a mind behind it all.[†]

Those measures of beauty, goodness, and order found in the world are the result of the Forms and the Demiurge's activity. Plato explains the presence of disorder in the world by postulating an element of chance in the raw material from which the world is fashioned (the Receptacle). Plato calls this chaotic force "necessity" or the "variable cause" (Tm 47e,48a). For Plato, "necessity" is not related to logic, for it is the opposite of mind or rationality. Instead, it is a purposeless, random cause. Hence, while faulting the Atomists for ignoring the presence of purpose and intelligence in the cosmos, Plato did concede that some things just happen through blind chance. The world as we know it came about through a struggle or negotiation between the rational power of the Demiurge and the irrational, unruly nature of the raw materials. The mind of the Demiurge "persuaded necessity to bring the greater part of created things to perfection" and "through necessity made subject to reason, this universe was created" (Tm 48a).

The thesis that the material aspect of the world is basically irrational has three implications. First, matter resists the imposition of order, making the complete perfection of the physical universe a metaphysical impossibility, even for the God-like Demiurge. Second, this ingredient of chance or randomness in the physical world prevents us from making it fully intelligible or understanding it to the degree that we do mathematical objects. Third, since only beauty, goodness, and order come from the Forms, the intrinsic irrationality of matter and its continuous deviation from the Divine order is the source of all evil, both in humanity and nature.

Evaluation and Significance

Although almost every one of Plato's philosophical claims has been subjected to critical scrutiny,

---

[†]Scholars are divided as to whether Plato believes that the world began with an actual creative event or whether the creative production of the world is an ongoing eternal process.

[†]Following Plato's example, Aristotle developed a teleological (purposeful) account of the universe. Similarly, Thomas Aquinas (thirteenth century A.D.) used the teleological nature of the universe as an argument for God.

his theory of the Forms has received the most attention. Since this theory is central to his view of knowledge, ethics, and politics, it will be worthwhile to take a closer look. The theory is a testimony to Plato's greatness as a philosopher, for he anticipated most of the major objections to his account of the Forms. He discusses three significant problems in his dialogue titled the *Parmenides*.* The first problem concerns the question "Are there Forms of everything?" Plato has discussed the Forms of Beauty, Justice, Goodness, and other exalted concepts, but the Parmenides of the dialogue asks if there are Forms of hair, mud, filth, and disgusting things as well. Since these objects exist in the physical world, have definite properties, and can be discussed, it seems to follow that we understand them only because of the Forms they represent. Yet this admission would detract from the notion that the Forms represent ideals of perfection. Surely there can be no standards of excellence for disgusting objects. The second problem concerns the relationship between the Forms and particulars. How does the one Form of Humanity distribute itself over many particular individuals? Is the Form divided among the particulars like a birthday cake? Since a Form cannot be broken into smaller chunks, this answer will not do. Does the whole Form reside in each particular? This would deny the transcendence of the Forms that was so important to Plato. The Socrates of the dialogue replies that the sunlight is one, single light, yet it covers and illuminates everything without itself being diminished. Parmenides counters with a similar analogy of one sail spread over a number of people. He points out that, strictly speaking, only a fraction of the sail covers each person. Therefore, this analogy brings us back to the problematic position of each person participating in only a fraction of the Form of Humanity.

The third problem has been given the name "the Third Man Argument." According to Plato's philosophy, we identify Harry and Robert as both

males because they both participate in the same Form. But if the Form of Man is responsible for what is common between Harry, Robert, and all other men (the first level), then what accounts for their similarity to this universal Form of Man (the second level)? We would have to posit a Super-Form of Man (a Third Man) to explain what they have in common with the first Form. Obviously, this process would go on forever and so nothing ever gets explained.

Some have said that Plato's whole problem started when he made the realm of the Forms completely separate from the physical world of particulars. Once this dualism is in place, then it becomes hard to bridge the chasm between the world we live in and the transcendent world of Forms. Furthermore, by making the Forms so detached from the here and now, he seemed to downgrade the value of our individual, earthly existence. Individual things have value and meaning only in so far as they represent the universal, abstract Forms. To make matters worse, Plato's otherworldliness diminishes the value of the natural sciences. Science, as we think of it, studies physical nature. But to Plato, the physical aspect of the world is messy, changing, and unintelligible. Only when we contemplate the eternal Forms do we achieve knowledge. Plato's student, Aristotle, later took these problems as his agenda and tried to extract what was of value in his teacher's theory while avoiding its difficulties.

Despite some of the problems that Plato never resolved, his theory of the Forms turned out to be one of the most profound and far-reaching ideas in the history of thought. For this reason the philosopher and historian Alfred North Whitehead has said that "the safest general characterization of the European philosophical tradition is that it consists of a series of footnotes to Plato."[7] Although this may be somewhat of an overstatement, it is still true that the story of Western intellectual history is unintelligible without an understanding of Plato. Philosophers can be divided into two groups according to whether they find Plato's theory illuminating or an unfortunate mistake. In either case, philosophers through the centuries have inevitably found it necessary to come to terms with Plato's thought.

*The historical Parmenides never encountered Plato's theory. His character is used in this account as means of raising these issues with the character of Socrates.

Questions for Understanding

1. How does Plato argue against relativism?

2. What problems does Plato have with the view that knowledge is based on sense experience?

3. Why would Plato say that it is impossible to draw a circle?

4. Why is knowledge something more than simply having true beliefs?

5. Summarize Plato's requirements for genuine knowledge.

6. What are Universals or Forms according to Plato?

7. Why does he think there must be such Forms?

8. According to Plato, what is innate knowledge, and how do we acquire it?

9. Draw Plato's Divided Line. Explain the different modes of awareness and how they relate to the different objects of awareness.

10. What is the Good in Plato's system and what is its relationship to the world and knowledge?

11. Why does Plato believe the Forms are real and not simply ideas in our heads?

12. How does Plato explain change?

13. What is metaphysical dualism?

14. What are the various ways Plato explains the relationship between the Forms and particular things?

15. Explain what Plato means when he says there are degrees of knowledge.

16. Explain the various points Plato is making in the Allegory of the Cave.

17. What is moral relativism and why does Plato reject it?

18. What is Glaucon's view of the nature of morality?

19. What are the parts of the soul? How does each one function?

20. Given Plato's view of human psychology, what does this tell us about how to live well?

21. What is Socrates' and Plato's answer to the question "Why be moral?"

22. What are the three divisions in society, and how do they relate to Plato's theory of human nature?

23. What is the ideal society according to Plato?

24. What sorts of changes would cause a decline in the perfect society?

25. Why is Plato opposed to democracy?

26. What is the Demiurge in Plato's view of the universe? What is its function? How is it similar to and different from the Judeo-Christian view of God?

27. What is a teleological explanation?

28. What are some problems in Plato's theory of the Forms?

Questions for Reflection

1. Develop your own argument for or against Plato's thesis that the nature of Justice is objective and independent of what subjective notions we have of it. Furthermore, argue for or against his view that Justice is something real even though it is not physical.

2. Thinking about Plato's Allegory of the Cave, what are the shadows in our society? When have you had the experience of discovering that something you thought was important was really a shadow? What caused you to discover this?

3. Argue for or against Glaucon's view of morality.

4. Do you think Socrates and Plato give a satisfactory reason for being moral? Why?

5. Would you like to live in Plato's ideal society? Why or why not?

6. Would Plato be happy or unhappy with our current culture? Why?

7. In what ways is Plato's view of the world and human life similar to and different from traditional religious views with which you are familiar?

Notes

1. Unless indicated otherwise, references to Plato's works will be made in the text using the following abbreviations:

L   *Letters*, trans. L. A. Post, in *Collected Dialogues of Plato*, ed. Edith Hamilton and Huntington Cairns (New York: Bollingen Foundation, Pantheon Books, 1961). References will be made using the numbers of the letter and section.

P   *Phaedrus*, trans. R. Hackforth, in *Collected Dialogues of Plato*. References are made using the section numbers.

R   *The Republic of Plato*, trans. Francis MacDonald Cornford (London: Oxford University Press, 1941). References are made using the book and section numbers.

Th   *Theaetetus*, trans. F. M. Cornford, in *Collected Dialogues of Plato*. References are made using the section numbers.

Tm   *Timaeus*, trans. Benjamin Jowett, in *Collected Dialogues of Plato*. References are made using the section numbers.

2. Plato, *Meno* 98a, in *Five Dialogues: Euthyphro, Apology, Crito, Meno, Phaedo,* trans. G. M. A. Grube (Indianapolis: Hackett, 1981), 86.

3. Plato, *Meno* 80d, trans. W. K. C. Guthrie, in *Collected Dialogues of Plato,* ed. Edith Hamilton and Huntington Cairns (New York: Bollingen Foundation, Pantheon Books, 1961), 363.

4. Plato, *Philebus* 28d–e, trans. R. Hackforth, in *Collected Dialogues of Plato,* 1106.

5. Terence Irwin, *Classical Thought,* A History of Western Philosophy:1 (Oxford: Oxford University Press, 1989), 112.

6. *Phaedo,* 98c–e.

7. Alfred North Whitehead, *Process and Reality: An Essay in Cosmology* (New York: Harper Torchbooks, Harper & Brothers, 1957), 63.

5

Aristotle:
Understanding the
Natural World

Aristotle's Life: Biologist, Tutor, and Philosopher

After Sparta's defeat of Athens at the end of the Peloponnesian War in 404 B.C., the Greek city-states were gradually torn apart by continual conflict. As Greece became weaker and fragmented, the nearby empire of Macedonia became stronger until the Greek city-states were conquered by Philip of Macedon in 338. From Macedonia would later come the military genius of Alexander the Great (Philip's son), who would conquer the known world at that time. But this province would also produce the philosophical genius of Aristotle, whose ideas would conquer vast expanses of intellectual territory. Alexander's kingdom would eventually crumble, but in the twentieth century, after the passage of over twenty-three hundred years, Aristotle's ideas still maintain their hold on significant portions of the philosophical landscape.

Aristotle was born in 384 B.C. in the Macedonian town of Stagira. Following a long family tradition, Aristotle's father, Nicomachus, was a physician to Amyntus II, the king of Macedonia. It is not unlikely that the scientific, empirical flavor of Aristotle's philosophy, his attention to detail, and his skills at classifying and analyzing the features of nature were inspired by his father's profession. Around age eighteen, Aristotle sought out the best education offered in his day and became a student in Plato's Academy in Athens. He studied and taught there with Plato for twenty years until the latter's death around 348. Plato was succeeded by his nephew, Speusippos, a mathematician who single-mindedly pursued the mathematical side of Plato's teachings. Whether or not Aristotle was repelled by this new emphasis, we can only speculate. We do know anti-Macedonian feelings were emerging in Athens, making it an uncongenial atmosphere for Aristotle. Consequently, Aristotle left the Academy and Athens. He spent several years traveling around the Greek islands, doing research in marine biology. In 342 he was summoned to the Macedonian court by King Philip, who had been a prince in Aristotle's childhood. The philosopher was asked to become a tutor to thirteen-year-old Alexander, the royal heir. A few years later, Aristotle's student inherited the empire and realized his father's dream of extending its dominion to the boundaries of the known world. According to one story, Alexander instructed his troops to collect biological specimens and send them back to his former tutor while they were on military expeditions to the remote corners of the world.

In 335 Aristotle returned to Athens and founded his own school and research institute, which became a rival to the Academy. It was named the Lyceum because it was near the temple of the god Apollo Lyceus. For the next twelve years he directed the scientific research there and wrote most of his major works. The research in the Lyceum ranged over a wide variety of fields, including natural science and history. It contained an extensive library, a museum, and both live and preserved collections of plants and animals.

When Alexander the Great died in 323, a wave of anti-Macedonian rage swept through Athens. Aristotle feared that his associations with Alexander would put him in danger. Remembering the fate of Socrates, but feeling no need to be a martyr, Aristotle fled the city "lest the Athenians should sin twice against philosophy." He died the following year. We have a copy of his will that underscores his reputation for having a generous and affectionate nature. In it, he refers to his happy family life and provides for the future of his wife, children, and servants. He had married a woman named Herpyllis after the death of his first wife, Pythias. While expressing affection for Herpyllis, he requested to be buried next to Pythias.

Plato and Aristotle

Focusing on Aristotle provides an interesting case study of the way in which philosophical ideas develop. To understand his agenda, we need to understand the relationship between his vision of philosophy and that of his teacher, Plato. On the one hand, the impact of Plato on his most famous disciple could never be erased. Throughout his philosophical writings, Aristotle sought to give more coherent and satisfactory solutions to the problems his teacher addressed. Soon after his teacher's death, Aristotle praised him as a man "whom bad men have not even the right to praise, and who showed in his life and teachings how to

be happy and good at the same time."[1] On the other hand, Aristotle was a powerful, independent, and innovative thinker. He was not content simply to repeat the ideas of his beloved teacher. He cautiously modified some of them and vigorously refuted and rejected others. In his work on ethics, he tenderly expresses the necessity of following the truth even if it means painfully dismissing ideas introduced by Plato, his close friend:

> It would perhaps be thought to be better, indeed to be our duty, for the sake of maintaining the truth even to destroy what touches us closely, especially as we are philosophers or lovers of wisdom; for, while both are dear, piety requires us to honour truth above our friends. (NE 1.6)[2]

Initially, the most striking difference between the two thinkers seems to be their style and temperament. The sorts of words that are commonly used to describe Plato are *idealistic, inspiring, otherworldly, perfectionist.* In contrast, Aristotle is described as *realistic, scientific, this-worldly,* and *pragmatic.* Although some of these contrasts are based on differences in the content of their philosophies, many are responses to their writing style. However, due to a historical accident, the obvious stylistic differences in their publications are misleading. We know that Plato gave technical lectures to advanced philosophy students in the Academy. However, there is no written record of these. Instead, the only manuscripts of Plato we have are his dialogues, which were designed to make his philosophy popular among a lay audience. Although these rank as some of the greatest works in world literature, they give us only a one-sided view of Plato's style. In contrast, all we have of Aristotle's works are his technical writings. We are told Aristotle also wrote some very elegant dialogues, but these have not been preserved for us. Many of the works that endured were detailed lecture notes not intended for publication. Consequently, they lack the grace and literary flourish of Plato's conversational writings. Nevertheless, the reader who is willing to work through Aristotle's careful arguments will find that they contain, as the philosopher Schopenhauer said, a sort of "brilliant dryness."[3]

In this detail from Raphael's School of Athens, *the artist subtly depicts the philosophical differences between Plato and Aristotle. Plato is pointing upward to the transcendent world of Forms, while Aristotle is gesturing toward the here-and-now world of nature.*

Beyond these literary differences, there are a number of other more substantive differences between the two thinkers. It has been said that everyone is either a Platonist or an Aristotelian. Although we should not ignore their similarities, the two thinkers present us with different visions of the world and different convictions as to how it should be approached. Some people, because of their temperament or philosophical convictions, tend to be more sympathetic to Plato's speculative flights toward the ideal reality that transcends the mundane, here-and-now world. Others find Aristotle's down-to-earth approach—carefully cataloguing and analyzing the world as we experience it—to make more sense. The late-eighteenth-century poet Goethe described Plato's philosophy as a tongue of flame shooting up to heaven and

Aristotle's philosophy as a pyramid built on a broad, earthly base that rises systematically to its highest point. To see their differences, note that Plato often looks to mathematics as his model of knowledge. Mathematics deals with perfect, ideal entities such as circles, which can most fully be understood by reason and not through the senses. This model characterizes his approach to everything from art to politics. Aristotle, however, favored the science of biology. Biology involves reasoning about entities that are given to us in concrete experience. The world the biologist studies is a world that is constantly changing, and understanding these changes is an important part of the science. At some point, the biologist goes beyond the individual real specimens in her laboratory to formulate the universal characteristics, principles, and laws the specimens exemplify. Nevertheless, all universal knowledge arises out of and is used to make sense of the changing world of particulars.

Whether one takes mathematics or biology as the paradigm of knowledge will affect how one goes about doing philosophy. For this reason, Aristotle's method and conclusions differ greatly from Plato's. For example, Plato approaches political life by setting out a vision of the ideal society. Plato argues that anything less than this will be inferior. Consequently, he predicts the various stages of deterioration that will occur if there is any deviation from the perfect ideal. When confronted with the obvious complaint that it is unlikely this perfect state will ever exist, Plato has Socrates counter that it does not matter. We must still think in terms of perfection, he says. By way of contrast, Aristotle supported his political philosophy with a survey of some 158 constitutions of actually existing states. He arranged these in a series of general categories and examined which political structures work best in which circumstances. Although he concludes that some societies are clearly better than others, Aristotle never gives us one formula that all societies must follow. Both the similarities and the differences between Plato and his student indicate that Aristotle's philosophy was driven by the struggle to preserve what was of value in Plato's system while avoiding its shortcomings.

Theory of Knowledge: Finding Universals Within Particulars

ARISTOTLE'S APPEAL TO EXPERIENCE

We will begin our exploration into Aristotle's philosophy with his theory of knowledge. This starting point is appropriate, for Aristotle's all-consuming passion is to know and to understand the world in which he lived. Furthermore, he believes that such a project is intrinsic to being a member of the human species. He begins his *Metaphysics* by optimistically asserting that "All human beings by nature desire to know." He gives us a clue as to his basic orientation by claiming that the evidence that we desire to know is found in "the delight we take in our senses; for even apart from their usefulness they are loved for themselves." Hence, the source of knowledge is found in our immersion in sense experience. If we employ the correct method, we will rise from the level of sense data to theoretical or scientific knowledge. However, "science" is a much broader word for Aristotle than for us today, who associate it with laboratories filled with test tubes and spectrometers. For Aristotle, "science" means, quite simply, rational discourse. When we truly know something, we can say what it is and why it is the way it is. A person who knows the ultimate causes and principles governing things has wisdom.

Aristotle has quite a different view of science from Plato. For Plato, there could be no science of the physical things that our senses reveal because they are changing and too imperfect. Aristotle, however, says that knowledge begins with a study of particular things. Thus, he thinks it is a mistake to study an abstract quality in isolation from its concrete exemplifications. For example, "Musicalness cannot exist unless there is someone who is musical" (M 5.11). In other words, if we want to study "musicalness" we had better take a close look at musicians and what they do. Again, he says that a doctor does not attempt to cure the Form of Man but only individual men, such as Callias and Socrates (M 1.1). Plato urged his students to turn away from the realm of particulars,

but Aristotle says that someone who is full of theory but lacks experience of the relevant particulars is deficient in his or her knowledge. Knowledge, therefore, begins with experience of particular things. But this alone does not tell the whole story. Having knowledge is more than having sensations and more than simply being familiar with a collection of individual facts. The dog experiences the smells, the textures, and the tastes of things in its experience (such as its stash of bones), but does not have genuine knowledge. Science goes beyond knowledge of particular facts to show how these particular facts follow from more fundamental truths.

To understand how Aristotle conceives of science, we can contrast an artist's, a gardener's, and a scientist's interest in a tree. The artist revels in the individuality and particularity of the tree. She is fascinated with the play of colors in its leaves, the particular twists and turns of its limbs, and the unique textures of its bark. However, her acquaintance with this particular tree lacks the sort of generality necessary for scientific knowledge. The gardener has somewhat more knowledge, because he knows what fertilizers make trees flourish and how to prune them to increase their fruit. We could call this "recipe knowledge." It has the form "If you do this, then that will happen." He has a knowledge of what works, but doesn't fully understand why it works. Now, when the scientist tries to understand a tree, she is not interested in *this* particular tree as such. She wants a general understanding of trees in terms of their universal characteristics. To understand what is essential to being a tree, she mentally sifts out what is irrelevant and what is unique to this particular case. In Aristotle's terms, the scientist abstracts the essence of the tree from its accidental features. Furthermore, the scientist is not content to simply know what works. She wants to be able to account for how each fact fits into a system of facts and to understand the causes for each. For Aristotle, a scientific account shows that a particular fact could not be other than it is.

True scientific knowledge, then, is not a catalogue of facts. It inquires into the universal nature of things and finds the necessary connections among them. This requires a knowledge of the ultimate principles from which particular facts can be derived. This establishes what seems an extraordinarily high goal for science. Today's scientists are content with knowledge of probabilities. For Aristotle, however, the structure of true science is like that of geometry. It consists of necessary truths demonstrated from self-evident axioms and definitions that compose a complete deductive system.

LANGUAGE, THOUGHT, AND REALITY

One of Aristotle's fundamental convictions is that the structures of language, thought, and reality are the same. He never doubts that we do have knowledge and that the structures of human knowledge are congruent with the structures of reality. How else could our minds ever come to know or understand nature if there were not some sort of affinity between them? When we reason from one proposition to another proposition, we are not simply going from one mental item to another. Instead, we are going from one piece of information about the world to other facts that are true of the world. We need to add language to this harmonious picture. How could we even begin to speak about the world unless there is an affinity between language and reality? Thus the structure of language (in Aristotle's case, the Greek language) more or less divides reality at its joints. Language is important because knowledge does not consist of a mute, mystical insight but in the ability to discourse intelligently about the world. Language must have the same structure as thought, for how else could we put our thoughts into words?

THE ESSENTIAL CATEGORIES

Given this conviction, the task is now to uncover the basic structures of language, thought, and reality. According to Aristotle, the way we understand things is revealed by the sorts of assertions we can make about anything. These will reveal not only the categories of our thought and language but the categories of reality as well. In his most complete account, Aristotle gives us a list of ten categories.

For purposes of exposition, we can view them as ten kinds of questions we can ask about something (see Figure 5-1).

The first category of substance is unique among all the others that follow after it. Substances are individual things such as Socrates, Mount Olympus, Fido the dog, or the tree in my backyard. Substances have the characteristic that "they are the entities which underlie everything else, and . . . everything else is either predicated of them or present in them" (C 5). We can ask, "Where is Socrates?" "What is he like?" or "What is he doing?" The answers to the last two questions might be "Socrates is bald" and "Socrates is talking." Socrates is the subject that is the locus of many different properties and activities. However, the reverse is not the case. We could not say "Talking is Socrates." Furthermore, while Socrates would still exist whether or not he was bald or talking, baldness and talking cannot exist unless they are present in some subject or another. Hence, substances are defined by the role that they play in statements. They are the subject of assertions to which predicates (or the other nine categories) are applied. They are also distinguished by the role they play in reality. They have independent existence while the other categories can only exist insofar as they are present in some substance.

THE DISCOVERY OF LOGIC

To be more than a mere list of facts, science must employ reasoning. This is a process by which we acquire new information from information that we already have. However, for reasoning to be useful it must follow a procedure that guarantees that true information will always yield more true information and never a false conclusion. Aristotle was the first person to discover the rules of reasoning that we now call logic. His work on logic was so complete that very few modifications were made to it until the late nineteenth century.

Aristotle's logic concerned the ways in which we reason about the relationships between categories. We can make four kinds of assertions about the relationship between two categories. For example, we can say (1) "All students are poets,"

Questions	Typical Answers	Categories
1. What is it?	(a tree, a man)	Substance
2. How large is it?	(30 ft. or 6 ft. tall)	Quantity
3. What is it like?	(cone-bearing, wise)	Quality
4. How is it related?	(double, half, greater)	Relation
5. Where is it?	(in the Grove)	Place
6. When does (did) it exist?	(yesterday, today)	Time
7. What position is it in?	(leaning, sitting)	Position
8. What condition is it in?	(flowering, clothed)	State
9. What is it doing?	(growing, talking)	Action
10. How is it acted on?	(being burned, being arrested)	Passivity

FIGURE 5-1 Aristotle's ten categories

or (2) "No students are poets," or (3) "Some students are poets," or (4) "Some students are not poets." These different kinds of individual statements can be related together to form arguments. In an **argument**, the arguer claims that one set of statements, the premises, provide reasons for believing another statement, the conclusion. One of the most common forms of arguments, and the form that Aristotle analyzed, is the syllogism. A syllogism is an argument that is composed of two premises that lead to a conclusion. For example, we could argue that

All mothers are females.

Some parents are not females.

Therefore, some parents are not mothers.

This is a *valid* argument, which means that the conclusion necessarily follows from the premises. Thus, if the premises are true, the conclusion will always be true. Aristotle's great genius was in realizing that the validity of the reasoning does not depend on the content but on the structure of the argument. Thus he showed we could replace the category terms with symbols and the argument would still be valid. This was the first attempt in history to represent reasoning by means of symbols. Reduced to its skeletal structure, the preceding argument reads

All P are M.

Some S are not M.

Therefore, some S are not P.

In this argument, if you consistently substitute any other terms in place of the original ones and if the premises are true, this form of argument will always give you a true conclusion. However, Aristotle showed that some forms of reasoning are not valid. They do not reliably lead you from true information to a true conclusion. Consider this argument:

All mothers are parents.

Some parents are professors.

Therefore, some mothers are professors.

In this particular example, the premises are both true and the conclusion *happens* to be true. Nevertheless, the conclusion does not follow logically from the premises. This can be shown by substituting the word "fathers" for "professors." You will find that the premises are still true, but now the argument allows you to reason to a false conclusion. If this can occur, we say the argument is *invalid*. Just as the relationship between form and content is important in logic, so the relationship between form and content (or matter) plays an important role in Aristotle's metaphysics.

FIRST PRINCIPLES

Aristotle points out that not everything can be deductively demonstrated. If we insisted on demonstrating everything, we would end up in an infinite regress. So before we can deductively prove anything, we must start with premises or axioms that stand on their own two feet and do not depend on anything else. Aristotle calls these the "first principles." How do we arrive at these first premises for all knowledge? Are our first premises simply assumed by a sort of leap of faith? This would make them arbitrary and would not yield scientific and necessary knowledge. Then are the first principles innate, as Socrates and Plato thought? Again, Aristotle rejects this alternative because he finds it absurd to suppose that we possess detailed and certain knowledge from birth but are unaware of it.

Aristotle's answer is found in a twofold process of induction and intuition. Through induction we become acquainted with the universal and necessary features within the changing world of particulars. He says that sense experience leaves its traces within memory. Numerous sense perceptions of the same sort strengthen each other in memory, and a knowledge of the similar and universal qualities begins to emerge. Aristotle gives us this pictorial image of the process: "It is like a rout in battle stopped by first one man making a stand and then another, until the original formation has been restored" (PA 2.19). In other words, from an early age we are besieged with a booming, buzzing barrage of sensations. Initially, our minds are as confused as an army being overwhelmed in battle. Some of these sensations remain in memory, however, and the similar ones reinforce each other. An intelligible order begins to reveal itself as each universal takes its stand in the mind. Like soldiers holding their ground and then advancing to conquer new territory, the universals expand our understanding to greater and greater levels of generality. For example, we experience Tom, Dick, Susan, and Jane. We perceive their unique qualities, and we also experience their similarities. The mind can then extract the universal "human" from its particular examples. Through a similar process, we form the concepts of "dog," "lizard," "deer," and so forth. From this "stand" the mind advances to the universal of "animal" and eventually to the most fundamental universals that are found in all existing things whatsoever (such as substance, quality, relation, place).

Although it is clear how induction can enable us to make generalizations in this way, it is not clear how induction alone can give us necessary first principles. Here is where intuition comes in. Aristotle is convinced that the world consists of a rational order. Experience alone cannot demonstrate this order to us, but can acquaint us with it. However, only through a sort of intellectual intuition do we really "see" the universal and necessary truths that are the foundation of all genuine knowledge. For example, adding two apples and two apples, then two oranges and two oranges, may trigger the intellectual insight that $2 + 2 = 4$. This universal and necessary mathematical truth is not based on the changing world of apples and oranges. However, the concrete experiences provoked the intellectual intuition. For Aristotle, then, intuition is an additional step beyond the process of induction. Whereas Plato described the act of intuiting universals as a kind of "recollection" of knowledge already latent within the soul, the more empirical Aristotle refers to it as an act of "recognition." Hence, the mind has the power to recognize, or come to know for the first time, universal truths that are lurking within experience.

Two main classes of first principles are revealed in this process. There are the unique, fundamental principles and definitions of each particular science. Most of Aristotle's examples here are taken from mathematics with its self-evident axioms and definitions. However, he thinks that physics, medicine, ethics, and any other special science is likewise based on intuitively discovered and necessary principles. The second class of first principles are the laws of logic. These are fundamental to any sort of reasoning, no matter what its subject. The supreme principle among these is what is commonly called the "law of non-contradiction." It may be formulated as "A cannot be both B and Not-B." Others are the "law of excluded middle": "A must either be B or Not-B," and the "law of identity": "A is A." Notice that for Aristotle these principles describe both the laws of thought and the nature of reality itself, since he assumes that there will always be a correlation between the structure of rational thought and the structure of reality.

Metaphysics: Understanding the Here-and-Now World

CRITIQUE OF THE PLATONIC FORMS

The examination of the principles that are the common foundation for every science are what Aristotle called "first philosophy." The most complete discussion of this topic is in his book *Metaphysics*. We now use the term "metaphysics" to refer to the area of philosophy concerned with the nature of reality. However, this label is the result of a historical accident. A later editor of Aristotle's manuscripts did not know what to call a certain collection of monographs, so he labeled them as the writings that come after (*meta*) Aristotle's *Physics*.

To understand Aristotle's metaphysics, it is important to see how his approach differs from Plato's. Recall that Plato had a very severe dualism in which reality consisted of two worlds. The world of the Forms was nonphysical, eternal, unchanging, and known only by reason. The world of our everyday experience was material, temporal, constantly changing, and known through the senses. The first world, according to Plato, is what is ultimately real, whereas the world of our experience is like a collection of shadows. Aristotle has some very sharp criticisms of the Platonic Forms and tries to replace them with a radically revised theory of how universals and particulars are related.

Here are some of the main criticisms that Aristotle offers in his *Metaphysics* (M 1.9):

1. The Forms are useless. They have no explanatory power. Instead of explaining the natural world, Plato's theory creates a second world, thereby doubling the number of things that require explanation. Instead of bringing some unity to the multiplicity of things in experience, it complicates matters by introducing more multiplicity.

2. The Forms cannot explain change or the movement of things within our experience. "Above all one might discuss the question what on earth the Forms contribute to sensible things. . . . For they cause neither movement nor any change in them." In many passages, Plato presents change as a symp-

tom of the irrationality and imperfection of the physical world, and he was less interested in it than he was in what was eternal and permanent. For Aristotle, however, our lives are lived in a changing world, and we need to make some sense out of it. Hence, he complains that if the unchanging Forms are the basis for all explanation, then "the whole study of nature has been annihilated."

3. The Forms cannot be the essence or substance of things if they are separated from them.

4. It is not clear what it means for particulars to "participate" in the Forms. To say that the Forms are patterns and that particulars share in them "is to use empty words and poetical metaphors."

5. Also, Aristotle uses the Third Man Argument that was introduced in the chapter on Plato. If the relationship between two men is explained by means of the Form of Man, then do we need yet another Form to explain the similarity between the individual man and the Form of Man? If so, then this process would never end, for we would have Forms explaining Forms forever (M 1.9, 11.1).

For such reasons, Aristotle does not believe that the Platonic theory of Forms can be salvaged. Despite of his great respect for Plato, Aristotle harshly concludes, "The Forms we can dispense with, for they are mere sound without sense; and even if there are such things, they are not relevant to our discussion" (PA 1.22).

Despite Aristotle's rejection of the Platonic version of the Forms, we must not suppose that Aristotle does away with them altogether. With Plato, he still believes there are universal forms that are objective and that constitute the essences of things in the world. It is because of these forms that we are able to have knowledge. Furthermore, Aristotle agrees that the order in reality can only be explained by reference to the forms.*

---

*To avoid confusing Aristotle's concept of the forms with Plato's, we shall adopt the convention of capitalizing the word (*Form*) only when it refers to Plato's theory.

SUBSTANCE: THE KEY TO REALITY

Having dismissed Plato's extreme dualism, where does Aristotle locate the forms? To answer this question, he turns to the only reality we have—the natural world around us. For Plato's picture of *transcendent* Forms, Aristotle substitutes the notion of *immanent* forms. The forms can only be the cause and explanation of things if they are an intrinsic part of things. There is no abstract Form of "Tableness" apart from this world. There are only individual tables, each exhibiting the form that identifies something as a table. Hence, for Aristotle, the fundamental reality is the collection of substances we find in our everyday experience. We saw previously that substance was the key category in his account of propositions and thinking. Now he argues that it is the fundamental category in reality itself. The phrase "is bald, pot-bellied, and short" makes no sense until we supply the grammatical subject "Socrates." Similarly, baldness and the other qualities can have no existence apart from their inherence in some actually existing metaphysical substance such as a particular, individual person. Substances, then, are the fundamental unit of reality.

To understand any individual substance, I must understand two things about it. First, I must understand the individual's *whatness*. If I say, "What is that?" the answer might be "Socrates." But now if I say, "What is Socrates?" the answer might be "a rational animal," "a Greek," "a philosopher," "a short and bald man," and so on. This list would be a number of properties found in Socrates. But notice that these are all common or universal properties that also characterize other particulars. Although universal properties are important, they do not capture what is particular or unique about an individual substance. Socrates is a rational animal, but so are you; Socrates was a Greek, but so were Thales and Heraclitus. Particular substances, therefore, must be composed of more than just their universal features. How do we account for the particularity of particular things? To do this, we have to refer to their *this-ness*. Socrates is this particular Greek, standing there in his slovenly toga and occupying a specific

amount of space (the northeast corner of the marketplace of Athens) at a particular time (June 6, 420 B.C.). Even though there may be many bald, short, rational, Greek philosophers, Socrates is a unique exemplification of these properties.

FORM AND MATTER

These two aspects of individual substance can be captured by the notions of *form* and *matter*. The "whatness" of something refers to its form. Its "thisness" is its matter. The easiest way to see how these two features work together to constitute individual realities is to consider a simple object such as a coffee cup. We can answer the question "What is it?" because we recognize that the object has a particular form. In this case, it is an object that is cylindrical, about three inches in diameter, with a closed bottom and an open top, which is used to drink coffee. Even though many such objects are mass-produced with the same form, its matter lets us identify *this* cup as an individual reality of its own because it is this particular piece of formed ceramic sitting on my breakfast table.

This particular example may lead us to suppose that form and matter refer to physical shape and physical matter alone. However, certain subtleties in Aristotle's account must be understood. Broadly speaking, an object has the form it has because of a particular purpose or function it serves. The form constitutes an object's essence. The **essence** of something is the set of qualities that make it the sort of thing it is. Typically, the essence of a thing is what a dictionary definition attempts to describe. For example, the essence of a coffee cup is to hold coffee so that we can drink from it. Hence, even if an object had the physical shape of a cup but was made from soluble materials, it might be a decoration or an item in a practical joker's inventory, but it wouldn't really be a coffee cup. A coffee cup has an open top because its function is to serve beverages, whereas a juice bottle has a secure cap because its function is to store and transport beverages. Similarly, a legal brief has a particular form unique to it. However, in this case its form cannot be simply characterized by its physical characteristics. A rectangular sheet of paper with words on it physically characterizes the manuscript of a children's story as easily as it does a legal brief. Hence, the form of a legal document is better characterized by its style, its vocabulary, and its purpose. A manuscript for a children's story may look physically similar to the legal brief, but it will have a different literary form because it serves a different function. It will begin with "Once upon a time . . ." and will have a style that enlivens the imagination rather than a logical organization that establishes some abstruse legal conclusion.

Similarly, we must view matter in a broader way. Matter, as we have indicated, is the principle of individuation. It is what distinguishes the individual members of a class that share the same form. Matter may also be described as a collection of possibilities from which something else may be actualized. A pine board is an example of formed matter. But it can be stacked with other boards in a pile to become the matter for a bonfire. These same boards could be nailed together to form a bookcase. Although the boards are distinct substances in themselves, they can become the matter for a new kind of entity to be realized. Hence, if the same formed matter has a different form imposed on it, it will become a different kind of object. To use a more subtle example, an airplane disaster (which has its own "whatness" and "thisness") could itself become the matter for either a news report, a TV drama, a historical account, or a lawsuit. In each case, the same "matter" can be formed or organized in new ways to fulfill different functions. The flip side of this is that a form by itself does not give us a substantive object until it inheres in some sort of matter. The carpenter's diagram is not yet a bookcase. It suggests how the matter of lumber should be formed to produce a bookcase. Similarly, the general form of a TV drama is a mere abstraction without the matter of the characters and some sequence of events for its realization.

In summary, every individual substance is made up of two dimensions, its form (whatness) and its matter (thisness). We may discuss each dimension separately, but this is always an abstraction. They are not two parts of a substance the way that the legs and the seat are two parts of a stool.

We do not find bare matter to which form is added as an additional ingredient. However, one piece of formed matter can be the basis for a new object if it is reorganized by means of a different form.

POTENTIALITY AND ACTUALITY

The concepts of matter and form can be used to understand the reality of individual substances. However, this does not tell us the whole story. It is obvious that all earthly things (whether they are human artifacts or natural objects) come into being and undergo change or development. Let us take a particular individual substance—an acorn, for example. We could analyze the acorn as having its own, unique matter (this particular hunk of organic stuff nestled between two tufts of grass). We could also focus on its form (the qualities that make it like all other acorns). But according to Aristotle (and I think we would have to agree with him here), we do not fully understand what we have in our hands if this is all we know about it. Only when we understand its potential to become an oak tree do we know what it is.

Aristotle describes the stages that a changing, developing individual goes through as *potentiality* changes to *actuality*. Potentiality is associated with matter. The acorn on the ground is not a tree but it contains this possibility. In contrast, actuality is associated with form. The actual oak tree that results comes from the form guiding its process of development. In becoming first the sapling and then the tree, the acorn loses the form that originally made it an acorn. But part of what makes it an acorn is its capacity to take on these other forms that were potentially there. For this reason, the acorn cannot become a tomato. The tomato's form was not part of the acorn's potentiality. To understand the process of potentialities becoming actualities, we have to look more closely at Aristotle's theory of change.

UNDERSTANDING CHANGE

To understand a changing world, Aristotle says, we must understand the causes that operate in the world. According to Aristotle, four kinds of causes explain why a particular event happens or why something is the way it is. Since Aristotle uses the word *cause* in a much broader sense than we do today, these four causes may be best thought of as four different aspects that go into the explanation of any individual thing. The first thing we may want to know about something is (1) the *material cause* or its matter. For example, Aristotle says a hunk of bronze is the material cause of a statue. In the case of the oak, the material cause is the organic material of the acorn. Next, we need to know (2) the *efficient cause*. This is the origin of the process that produced the article in question. In the case of the statue, this would be the sculptor and his tools. For the tree, the action of moisture, the nurturing soil, and sunlight actualize the acorn's potential. Thus far, these two causes or modes of explanation seem roughly consistent with our modern scientific view of the world. We tend to think of nature as being made up of material objects being acted on by a set of forces.

For Aristotle, however, the most important part of the story is yet to be told. To explain something, we also need to know its (3) *formal cause*. This is the essence of the item, the form being actualized in its matter, that which makes it the sort of thing it is. Thus, when the sculptor begins his work, he has the form in mind as he works with the bronze. The form at work in the acorn causes it to grow into a tree and not a tulip. For Aristotle, the most important aspect of something was (4) *the final cause*. This is the end or purpose or function it is to fulfill. For an artificial object such as a statue, its purpose may be to depict the likeness of someone. A natural object such as an acorn is a growing entity that points toward its fulfillment in the tree that bears its own acorns.

We can imagine Aristotle's four-cause analysis being applied by an archeologist. Let's suppose that in one of her digs in South America, an archeologist runs across what seems to be some sort of implement. She will seek to know its material cause (silver), for this will tell her something about it. She will also want to know the efficient cause that produced it (Inca artisans). Next, she

might try to decide if it is a knife or a household decoration. This would be a search for the formal cause. Assuming that it is a knife, she then needs to figure out if it was used for religious rituals or hunting or cooking (its final cause). Only if she can answer these four kinds of Aristotelian questions has she fully understood the artifact.

The development of something from its beginnings to its final culmination is a process that involves several stages. The baby grows into the toddler and the toddler into the child on into the adolescent who then becomes an adult. At each stage, some potentiality is actualized (involving some or all of the four causes), but this then provides the potential for further stages to be actualized until the final end is realized. Each stage has its own matter and form. We may say that the 16-year-old is a model teenager. But though she has achieved excellence at this stage of her life, the form of the teenager will pass away and be replaced by the form of the adult. Thus, all change is the process of a particular matter successively being shaped by different forms until the final stage is reached.

TELEOLOGY

Aristotle's theories give us a picture of nature as a collection of dynamic processes all pointing to the fulfillment of various ends. This purposeful, goal-oriented structure that Aristotle attributes to the universe is called **teleology**. This comes from the Greek word *telos*, which means end or goal.* This does not mean that the acorn striving to grow into the oak is consciously trying to achieve that end. Nor, for Aristotle, does it mean that any other conscious intentions are at work in nature. Nevertheless, acorns grow into oaks, they do not become cabbages. The essence of each kind of substance includes its inner drive to behave or develop in a certain way. Aristotle uses the word *entelechy* to describe the end stage of a process,

---

*In the *Timaeus*, Plato used the notion of teleology to account for the origin and nature of the cosmos as a whole.

meaning the full actualization of a thing's form.[†] The entelechy of an acorn is the oak tree, for the oak does not go on to realize a further end other than to produce more acorns.

GOD: THE UNMOVED MOVER

Nature is a busy drama of restless, changing entities. Everywhere we look potentialities are being actualized, creating new potentialities, and every process is directed toward some end. What is the origin of all the activity of nature? Matter by itself, according to Aristotle, is merely a bundle of potentialities. It needs some other force to actualize its potential. We can imagine the universe with all the heavenly bodies suspended in space but completely motionless. They would have the potential to move but this potential must be actualized by something else. Hence, for Aristotle, motion is something that always requires an explanation. What he is looking for is not some temporally first cause that sets things moving, for he believed the universe and the motions of the heavenly bodies are eternal. For Aristotle, as for all the Greeks, the notion that the entire universe had an absolute beginning and was created out of nothing made no sense. Instead, the universe, for him, is like a flower that has eternally been moving to face the sun. Even if the flower had always existed, its eternal motion would require an eternal sun to continually sustain its life and motion.

If Aristotle is correct about what has been said thus far, then a very basic strand within the universe must account for the motion of everything else. However, this source of motion cannot itself be in motion, for then something else would have to sustain its motion. This would lead to an impossible infinite regress. Aristotle calls this fundamental cause the *Unmoved Mover*. There are several important points to understand about his Unmoved Mover. First, although it seems to be Aristotle's version of God, it is not a transcendent, anthropomorphic, personal God such as we find

in the Judeo-Christian tradition. Aristotle's God no more loves or performs acts of the will than does the law of gravity. To care for something is to have an emotional life, which makes you vulnerable to and affected by what you love. If the Unmoved Mover is the source of all motion, it cannot be emotionally affected by or moved by other things. Second, since the Unmoved Mover is not itself in motion, it cannot be an efficient cause. In other words, it cannot cause motion the way a batter does by hitting a ball. So how can it move other things? Aristotle's answer is that it operates as the final cause. It is the source of the teleology in the universe. In seeking to be fully complete, all things (unconsciously) desire to be like the Unmoved Mover. Different parts of nature strive for actuality in their own way. The plant seeks fulfillment when it works its way up through the ground. You and I attempt to know as much as possible and to realize all our potentialities. This drive toward actuality, which is present in every being, is like the power of love. You can be in love with someone and that love can affect everything you do. You try to improve yourself for the sake of the one you love or rearrange your schedule so that you can be near him or her. However, this does not mean that the one you love is similarly affected by you. The person may be completely unaware of your existence. Similarly, nature is moved by God, while he remains unmoved. Since all things in nature are moved by their innate love of God, Aristotle literally believes that "love makes the world go round"!

Finally, the Unmoved Mover must be the highest sort of reality. Everything else is full of potentiality that has not yet been realized. We are incomplete and always on the way, and thus our lives are never finished. But something that is a pure actuality does not need to change, for by its nature it is already complete. What then does the Unmoved Mover do? If it is the highest sort of reality, it must be engaged in the most valuable sort of activity. For Aristotle, this supreme activity is thought. Although the rest of nature blindly pursues its ends, human beings are capable of rational thought, making them the highest sorts of

---

[†]"Entelechy" translates the philosophically rich Greek word *entelecheia*—having (*echō*) its purpose (*telos*) within (*entos*).

creatures in nature. By extrapolation, the highest form of being in the universe must be one that is engaged in the highest form of rational thought. However, God cannot think about the particulars of the changing world, for this would introduce fragmentation and change into the heart of his being. Instead, the object of his thought must be undivided and eternal. "Therefore it must be of itself that the divine thought thinks (since it is the most excellent of things), and its thinking is a thinking on thinking" (M 12.9). The only analogy we can have of this singular, undivided intellectual vision would be that of a mathematician contemplating the whole of a mathematical proof instead of focusing on its individual steps. Aristotle's theology was influential throughout all antiquity, especially because of its impact on the Stoic and Neoplatonic philosophers. Furthermore, even though it may appear that this view of God is in tension with elements of the biblical tradition, it was very influential with the medieval theologians, particularly Thomas Aquinas.

Ethics: Keeping Things in Balance

Aristotle's most complete work on ethics is called the *Nicomachean Ethics* (which refers to the name of both his father and his son). It stands as one of the great classics of moral philosophy and is still influential. Aristotle does not pretend to offer us a radically novel ethical theory. He thought it would be absurd that no one in the history of the human race had ever discovered what it means to be morally good. We have abundant examples of good people who serve as models for the rest of us. Hence, we already have a sense of the character traits and moral principles that produce human excellence. This approach contributes to both the strengths and the weaknesses of Aristotle's moral theory. On the positive side, the whole of his ethical writings are characterized by a sort of down-to-earth, commonsense approach that captures the moral intuitions that we bring to philosophy. Yet adhering too closely to the moral wisdom of our society can blind us to the limitations and prejudices of our particular age and culture. Aristotle's acceptance of slavery and his

exclusion of women from political life are examples. Therefore, people who are sympathetic to Aristotle's overall perspective must separate his universal insights from what is culturally relative.

In Aristotle's view, ethics constitutes a body of objective knowledge. In this sense it is a science of correct conduct that guides us toward the goal of achieving human excellence. Aristotle agreed with Plato on this point. Both believed that for an individual in a particular set of circumstances there is a morally correct way of acting. Since morality is a matter of knowing, internalizing, and applying objective principles, it is possible to be mistaken in our moral opinions and objectively delinquent in our behavior. Plato had a very extreme interpretation of this point, for he believed that ethical principles were like mathematical principles. Aristotle, however, did not think that ethical theory can be as exact a science as mathematics. When we begin applying universal principles to the conduct of concrete human beings, we run into all the ambiguities and fine shades of gray that characterize the human situation. For this reason, he starts out the *Nicomachean Ethics* by explaining,

> Our discussion will be adequate if it has as much clearness as the subject-matter admits of, for precision is not to be sought for alike in all discussions, any more than in all the products of the crafts . . . for it is the mark of an educated man to look for precision in each class of things just so far as the nature of the subject admits. (NE 1.3)

HAPPINESS

Aristotle begins his book on ethics by observing that all human action aims at some end. Now some ends are merely instrumental. We pursue them only so that we can achieve other goals. For example, a student may stay up late studying for a statistics exam. She does this to pass the course, and she aims at this end to complete an accounting degree. This goal has value because it enables her to get a good job, and this has value because it enables her to earn money, and so on, and so on. However, this string of instrumental goals cannot go on forever or there would be no point to the whole process. All intermediate goals must ultimately aim at some final good we desire for its own sake. The most important task in life, then, is to determine what this chief and final good might be.

The answer is easy enough: the final goal of all human activity is *happiness*. The Greek term Aristotle uses is *eudaimonia*. This should not be confused with pleasure but is best thought of as meaning "well-being" or "living well" or "having a life worth living." You can ask about everything else someone does, "Why are you doing that?" But the question "Why are you trying to achieve happiness?" is absurd and cannot be given an answer because happiness is the final goal of all that we do and requires no further justification. Aristotle recognizes, however, that this does not get us very far, for there are many different opinions on this topic. Different people associate living well with pleasure, wealth, honor, and a wide variety of things. Accordingly, Aristotle admits that "to say that happiness is the chief good seems a platitude and a clearer account of what it is is still desired" (NE 1.7).

As we saw in his metaphysics, the purpose or function of something constitutes its real nature. Moreover, this will constitute its virtue or the standard of its excellence as well. The good carpenter is one who fulfills the purpose of carpentry, which is construction. The good eye is one that fulfills its function of seeing. Accordingly, becoming a good human being or finding personal fulfillment (which are basically the same for Aristotle), means fulfilling the end of being human. What can this be? It must be something unique and special to human beings that we do not share in common with other creatures. For this reason, Aristotle cautions that we will go astray if we equate happiness with pleasure. People who do that are "preferring a life suitable to beasts" instead of what would be the appropriate fulfillment for human beings (NE 1.5). Toward the end of his book, he concludes,

> *Happiness, therefore, does not lie in amusement; it would, indeed, be strange if the end were amusement, and one were to take trouble and suffer hardship all one's life in order to amuse oneself. For, in a word,*

> *everything that we choose we choose for the sake of something else—except happiness, which is an end. Now to exert oneself and work for the sake of amusement seems silly and utterly childish. (NE 10.6)*

Having said that pleasure does not equal happiness, Aristotle points out that a minimal amount of pleasure is an ingredient in the good life. "Those who say that the victim on the rack or the man who falls into great misfortunes is happy if he is good, are, whether they mean to or not, talking nonsense" (NE 7.13). The same is true of all other "external goods." The lack of such resources as friends, health, and sufficient material support take the luster from happiness. Finally, while pleasure is not the goal of human life, it accompanies the life that is morally excellent.

> *The lovers of what is noble find pleasant the things that are by nature pleasant; and virtuous actions are such, so that these are pleasant for such men as well as in their own nature. Their life, therefore, has no further need of pleasure as a sort of adventitious charm, but has its pleasure in itself. (NE 1.8)*

We now come back to the question "What is the purpose of human life?" Aristotle answers this question in one of the most central passages of his *Ethics*: "We state the function of man to be a certain kind of life, and this to be an activity or actions of the soul implying a rational principle, and the function of a good man to be the good and noble performance of these" (NE 1.7). Several points in this passage need to be emphasized. First, we do not *give* ourselves a purpose. The end of human life is something that is *given to us* by nature and makes up the essence of our humanity. It distinguishes the kinds of beings we are from rocks, plants, beasts, and computers. Second, this passage emphasizes that the purpose of human life is found in a sort of performance or activity that exhibits excellence. Happiness is not a passive state we achieve, but it characterizes what we do and how we do it. Aristotle adds the qualification "in a complete life." As he explains, "One swallow does not make a summer, nor does one day; and so too one day, or a short time, does not make a man blessed and happy" (NE 1.7). Just as one winning game does not make an athlete a champion, so one noble act or one happy moment does not make a person's life excellent.

Third, the preceding description of the purpose of human life also stresses that it entails a life lived according to a certain plan or strategy that is furnished by reason. Thus, the good life involves both thinking and doing. This is because we are rational beings, as well as beings that feel, desire, and act. Hence, the road to happiness involves two dimensions. You must rationally judge what are the right principles to follow, and your appetites, feelings, and emotions must be disciplined to follow those rules. This requires two kinds of human excellence. These are *intellectual virtue* (or excellence of intelligence) and *moral virtue* (or excellence of character). A good life cannot be had if either of these is neglected.

Under the heading of intellectual virtue, the two main categories are philosophic wisdom and practical wisdom. Philosophic wisdom is purely theoretical and is achieved by understanding the unchanging structure of reality. Practical wisdom is the intellectual virtue required to be moral, for it is the rational understanding of how to conduct one's daily life. Aristotle points out, however, that something more is needed besides intellectual excellence. "For we are inquiring not in order to know what virtue is, but in order to become good, since otherwise our inquiry would have been of no use" (NE 2.2). What is needed is moral virtue or the ability to balance one's desires and emotions.

Aristotle begins by first discussing moral virtue. For us, this might be the whole of ethics, but for Aristotle it is just one ingredient in the good life. He describes virtue (or human excellence) as

> *a state of character concerned with choice, lying in a mean, i.e., the mean relative to us, this being determined by a rational principle, and by that principle by which the man of practical wisdom would determine it.* (NE 2.6)

Each term in this definition is analyzed in the sections that follow.

VIRTUE IS A STATE OF CHARACTER

First, he speaks of virtue as "a state of character." By this he means that a morally good person is not simply one who performs morally right actions but one who has developed a habit or disposition to do what is right. We can imagine someone who tells the truth on his income tax form—but only after he struggles with the temptation to cheat. By contrast, the truly moral person is one who tells the truth readily, happily, and without such a struggle. Hence, a well-formed character manifests itself not only in what we do but in our motives, our desires, our likes and dislikes. For this reason, Aristotle says that a good person "delights in virtuous actions and is vexed at vicious ones, as a musical man enjoys beautiful tunes but is pained at bad ones" (NE 9.9).

Although the intellectual virtues can be acquired by being taught, the moral virtues can only be acquired through practice, much as we acquire a skill. Thus, developing a moral character is more like learning how to play the piano or drive a car than it is like learning history. Aristotle criticizes philosophers (he may have been thinking of Socrates here) who think that being moral is simply a matter of knowing the good. He says that such theorists are like "patients who listen attentively to their doctors, but do none of the things they are ordered to do. As the latter will not be made well in body by such a course of treatment, the former will not be made well in soul by such a course of philosophy" (NE 2.4).

If moral virtue is a matter of *knowing how* to make moral decisions and not just *knowing that* certain things are true, then "we become just by doing just acts, temperate, by doing temperate acts, brave by doing brave acts" (NE 2.1). At first this may seem like a vicious circle. How can we do just acts unless we are already just? The answer is that when we learn a new skill, whether it is piano playing or being a moral person, we receive instructions from a parent or a teacher. They tell us what to do and we model our behavior after theirs. Eventually, through a process of repetition, the external actions become more or less effortless and are internalized in the form of dispositions. In the case of piano playing, the mature musician does not need the teacher to place her fingers where they are to go. She looks at the music and instantly responds. In the case of morally mature people, their parents do not have to remind them to tell the truth, for they do so by habit.

VIRTUE IS CONCERNED WITH CHOICE

Aristotle stresses that being moral involves choice of a certain kind. For example, suppose I swerve my car when driving down the street because I am testing out my new tires, but while doing so I unknowingly avoid hitting a small child. My avoiding the child was good, but it was by accident. In another case, suppose I take care of an aged aunt only because I hope to inherit her fortune. Again, this is a good action, but it is done for a despicable reason. In neither case can I be praised for being a virtuous person, for being moral involves knowing what is good and choosing it for its own sake.

Furthermore, for an action to be a genuine choice and thus capable of moral praise or blame, the action must be voluntary. Aristotle clarifies the notion of voluntary action and moral responsibility by looking at cases in which an action is not voluntary. He thinks that there are two classes of involuntary action or actions for which we are not morally responsible. These are all actions that are done under compulsion or out of ignorance. When an action is done under compulsion, the action originates in some external force operating on me. For example, if I slip on a rug or am pushed and break your favorite vase, I am not blameworthy for this because I did not choose to act as I did. However, there are some gray areas. Let's suppose I am forced to do an immoral act, because my family is being threatened with torture. Aristotle calls cases like this "mixed" cases. On the one hand, I voluntarily moved my own body to perform the act. On the other hand, because I was acting out of fear, it was an action I preferred not to do and my moral responsibility is diminished.

When am I acting out of ignorance? Aristotle says that I am not free of blame simply because I am ignorant of what is right or wrong. To say, "I didn't know that murder is wrong," does not relieve me of blame. However, if I am ignorant of certain relevant facts through no fault of my own, I am excused. Suppose that in good faith I offer someone what I think is water, not realizing his enemy has poisoned it. Here, my action is unfortunate but not blameworthy. However, there are limits here. In some cases my ignorance is the result of my own negligence. For example, I should check to see if a gun is loaded before I play with it, and a physician should check for possible allergic reactions before prescribing a medicine.

To further refine the notion of excusable ignorance, Aristotle makes a distinction between "acting *in* ignorance" and "acting *by reason of* ignorance." If I stab someone while drunk or in a blind rage, I may genuinely not realize what I was doing. However, although I am acting in ignorance, the ignorance was self-inflicted because I allowed myself to become drunk or never developed the character trait of self-control. When I act by reason of ignorance, there is something that, regrettably, I did not know, but for which I cannot be blamed.

VIRTUE AND THE MEAN

Next, Aristotle says that virtue is choice "lying in a mean." This became known as his famous "doctrine of the mean." The "mean" referred to here is the intermediate position between two extremes or vices. He observes that moral virtue is "concerned with passions and actions, in which excess is a form of failure, and so is defect, while the intermediate is praised and is a form of success" (NE 2.6). In other words, the virtuous person is one who finds the correct balance or the mean between the extremes. This emphasis on moderation was not new in Aristotle, for it had been a standard Greek ideal going back to Homer and the poets. Nevertheless, Aristotle gives it his own distinctive formulation.

The notion of virtue being a mean can best be explained by looking at a few examples based on

Activity	Vice (excess)	Virtue (mean)	Vice (deficit)
Confidence in Facing Danger	Rashness	Courage	Cowardice
Enjoying Pleasure	Self-indulgence	Temperance	Being puritanical
Giving of Money	Vulgarity	Generosity	Stinginess
Truth Telling About Oneself	Boastfulness	Self-honesty	Self-deprecation

FIGURE 5-2 Aristotle's analysis of virtue as the mean between extremes

Aristotle's discussion. For each kind of activity, there is a correct character trait that is the balance between the extremes of too much and too little (see Figure 5-2).

Aristotle points out that this analysis in terms of the mean does not apply to all feelings and actions. For example, we would not want to say that a good person is one who does not commit too much cruelty, nor too little cruelty, but just the right amount. Obviously, some feelings and actions are by their nature simply evil, and no amount of moderation will make them good. Examples he provides are feelings such as spite, shamelessness, and envy, and actions such as adultery, theft, and murder (NE 2.6).

UNIVERSAL PRINCIPLES AND RELATIVE APPLICATIONS

Fourth, Aristotle has said that virtue entails finding the "mean relative to us." Hence, the mean will not be the same for every individual under all circumstances. The genius of Aristotle's ethics is his recognition that universal and objective principles have relative applications for different people and within different circumstances. To use a nonmoral example, everyone ought to follow the general rule "Eat nutritious and well-balanced meals." Even though this principle applies equally to all persons, the specific diet it dictates for a 250-pound football player will differ from that of a 110-pound clerk. Notice that Aristotle is definitely not saying that the principles governing action are simply a matter of subjective opinion. I may feel that my new fad diet is good for me when it is actually robbing my body of essential nutrients and doing more harm than good. In the case of a moral virtue such as courage, we may praise the courage of a young child who overcomes his terror of the water and sticks his face in the water. It would not be an act of courage for a professional lifeguard to do this. Similarly, a widow who gives a dollar to charity when this is a substantial portion of her living expenses is exhibiting the virtue of generosity. However, if she inherits a million dollars, then giving a dollar under these circumstances would be exhibiting the vice of stinginess.

THE MEAN DETERMINED BY PRACTICAL WISDOM

Obviously, the mean is not identical to a mathematical average. If giving all my money to a charity is excessive and giving none is stingy, it does not follow that giving away half of my life savings is the correct amount to give. Even if we know the correct moral principles, how do we know what is right to do in a specific case? Aristotle can only say that it is "determined by a rational principle, and by that principle by which the man of practical wisdom would determine it" (NE 2.6). It is at this point that moral virtue links up with the intellectual virtue of practical wisdom. A person who has moral virtue will know which goals are the right ones for human life (the balance among her various desires and emotions). But she also needs practical wisdom to know how to achieve those goals. This involves the intellectual activity of deliberating correctly. Aristotle offers very little else in the way of guidance except to say that practical wisdom "is concerned not only with universals but with particulars, which become familiar from experience" (NE 6.8). Hence, though practical wisdom is an intellectual virtue, the person who has learned how to make decisions from practical experience is most likely to exemplify this form of wisdom.

In summary, the morally good person is one who carefully follows reason, desires to do the right thing, has a well-formed character, knows the proper goals in human life, can estimate how to achieve those goals in practice, and probably the one who has the most experience in making tough, moral decisions. Being ethical is more like learning how to keep one's balance on a bicycle than like calculating mathematical results. When we first learn how to ride the bicycle, we make a number of mistakes and fall down. Eventually, however, we can feel the correct point of balance. You cannot give someone a formula for doing this; he or she must learn it from experience. As Aristotle says,

> Both fear and confidence and appetite and anger and pity and in general pleasure and pain may be felt both too much and too little, and in both cases not well; but to feel them at the right times, with reference to the right objects, towards the right people, with the right motive, and in the right way, is what is both intermediate and best, and this is characteristic of virtue. (NE 2.6)

THE BEST FORM OF LIFE

Aristotle has argued that happiness is achieved by living in accordance with our nature, by fulfilling what it means to be human. But since human nature is multidimensional, it is reasonable to assume that the highest and most satisfying form of happiness is linked to what is the very best within us. There is no question, Aristotle believes, that the activity of contemplation fits this description. Aristotle lists several reasons for this conclusion. First, reason is that part of us that most fully expresses our humanity. Second, we can engage in reason continuously, in the midst of life's other engagements. Third, rational contemplation is a self-sufficient activity, for we can engage in it on our own. Apart from life's basic necessities, we do not need other people, equipment, or anything external for this activity. Fourth, it is the one activity we engage in for its own sake and not for the tangible results it brings. Finally, contemplation imitates the activity of God, the Unmoved Mover.

Evaluation and Significance

In the period of philosophy following Aristotle, many philosophers abandoned his metaphysics for the materialism of the Epicureans and Stoics and the otherworldliness of the Neoplatonists. Nevertheless, he was rediscovered in the Middle Ages, where his authority was so respected he was referred to simply as "the Philosopher." Because his system served as the foundation for the science, philosophy, and theology of the medieval thinkers, the early modern philosophers and scientists attacked his thought as being responsible for all the intellectual ills of the past. A system that views the changes in nature as the result of substances striving to fulfill their final ends will not pay close attention to the material and efficient causes that are so important to modern science. Consequently, the modern period came about when Aristotle's authority was abandoned and new ways of conceiving nature emerged. Not until the nineteenth and twentieth centuries did interest revive in a modernized Aristotelianism.

Some of the criticisms of Aristotle's system will be discussed when we examine the rise of modern science. Yet even his critics cannot detract from his extraordinary accomplishments. Among other things, he gave birth to the science of logic and did his job so well that no major modifications to his work were made for more than two thousand years. His was the first systematic work on ethics and is still a prominent theory in ethics today. Western culture would not have been the same without him. The Christian doctrines developed in the Middle Ages were expressed in Aristotelian categories. Many passages in Dante, Chaucer, Shakespeare, and Milton presume a knowledge of Aristotle's conception of the universe. Furthermore, his influence on traditional literary criticism has been formidable. However, it would be wrong to consider him a dusty museum piece, notable because of his influence over thinkers long dead. His ideas do not retain the supreme authority over intellectual life they once enjoyed, but they are still alive and well in many regions of contemporary philosophical thought.

Questions for Understanding

1. What are some differences between Plato's and Aristotle's style of doing philosophy?

2. According to Aristotle, what is the relationship between language, thought, and reality? What considerations might count in favor of his view and what count against it?

3. How do Aristotle's categories serve to explain both thought and reality? Do you think his view is plausible? Are there any changes, additions, or deletions you would make to his list of categories?

4. What is the relation between form and content in Aristotle's logic? How does he go on to use this distinction in describing reality?

5. What are first principles? How do we arrive at them? What role do they play in knowledge?

6. Why does Aristotle reject Plato's view of the Forms? How is Aristotle's view of form similar to and different from Plato's view?

7. What is Aristotle's view of substance? How does this result in a different view of reality than Plato's?

8. What does Aristotle mean by potentiality and actuality? What role do they play in his view of the world?

9. How does he use the notions of form and matter to explain the nature of things?

10. What are the four kinds of causes? Why does Aristotle think that we can never understand something completely without them?

11. What is teleology? What are some examples Aristotle could use to demonstrate that it is at work in nature?

12. What is the Unmoved Mover? Why does Aristotle believe in it? How is it similar to and different from traditional notions of God with which you are familiar?

13. Why does Aristotle distinguish happiness and pleasure?

14. Given that happiness is the goal of human life, how does Aristotle think that this is best achieved?

15. What does Aristotle mean by virtue? What are the two kinds of virtue?

16. How is moral virtue acquired? Can it be taught? What are its various dimensions?

17. What is the doctrine of the mean? What role does it play in deciding what to do and what sort of persons we should be?

18. What is practical wisdom?

19. In the final analysis, what is the best form of life according to Aristotle?

Questions for Reflection

1. Plato and Aristotle give two different visions of the nature of reality and how to approach our lives. Which one do you think is the most plausible? Why?

2. Construct your own examples to illustrate Aristotle's view that everything is made up of form and matter.

3. Use Aristotle's notions of potentiality and actuality and his theory of the four causes to describe the general outline of your own life from infancy to your present stage.

4. Many would say that modern science has reduced Aristotle's four causes to just two: material causes and efficient causes. How might Aristotle argue that our explanations are insufficient without the other two causes?

5. Aristotle argues that everything has an essence, a form, or a general nature and, hence, that everything in the world has a natural purpose. Do you agree with this? Do you think it is true of human beings? What would be the implications of accepting or rejecting this thesis with respect to human beings?

6. In what ways is moral virtue an objective quality and in what ways is it relative to each individual and his or her circumstances?

7. List examples of people in our contemporary culture who you consider to be excellent role models. To what degree do they fit Aristotle's model of a virtuous person? Do you agree with his description of what human life should be? In what ways might his account be criticized?

8. If you were a parent (perhaps you are) and an Aristotelian, what concrete means would you use to train your child to be an excellent human being?

9. Aristotle thinks that moderation is the key to the virtuous life. Do you think this is true? Can you think of any good people, people who made society better, who were more extreme than moderate? What would Aristotle say about these cases?

10. Aristotle believes that the life of contemplation is the best life. What are his reasons for saying this? Explain why you agree or disagree with his conclusion.

Notes

1. Quoted in Frederick Copleston, *A History of Philosophy*, vol. 1, pt. 2 (Garden City, NY: Image Books, Doubleday, 1962), 9.

2. All quotations from Aristotle's works are from *The Basic Works of Aristotle*, ed. Richard McKeon (New York: Random House, 1941). References to specific works will use the following abbreviations:

   C   *Categories*, trans. E. M. Edghill. (References are to chapter number.)

   M   *Metaphysics*, trans. W. D. Ross. (References are to book and chapter numbers.)

   NE   *Nicomachean Ethics*, trans. W. D. Ross. (References are to book and chapter numbers.)

   PA   *Posterior Analytics*, trans. G. R. G. Mure. (References are to book and chapter numbers.)

3. Arthur Schopenhauer, *The World as Will and Idea*, trans. R. B. Haldane and J. Kemp (London: Routledge & Kegan Paul, 1883), 2:21.

6

Classical Philosophy
After Aristotle

The Transition to Hellenistic and Roman Philosophy

The deaths of Alexander the Great in 323 B.C. and of Aristotle in 322 B.C. mark the end of the Hellenic period, an era in which Greek civilization was primarily self-contained. These dates also mark the beginning of the Hellenistic (that is, "quasi-Greek") period during which Greek civilization blended with other cultures, especially those of Egypt and the Near East. This was followed by the Roman period, which began when the Romans conquered the Hellenistic states during the second and first centuries B.C. Although the Romans triumphed militarily, the Hellenistic tradition triumphed culturally. Recognizing the richness of the philosophy, literature, and art of the region, the Romans absorbed its culture and passed it on to western Europe. The Roman period finally came to an end around the middle of the sixth century A.D. with the collapse of the empire.

To understand the philosophies that emerged during the Hellenistic period, we have to view them against the background of the overwhelming social changes taking place at this time. The

first factor that influenced the philosophies of this period was the dramatic change in the political life of Greece. The wars between the Greek city-states had left them exhausted, both physically and spiritually. The result was that the small, comfortable, democratic communities of Greece were now caught up into a succession of military empires. To the Greek citizen, these events were overwhelming, and it seemed that history was beyond human control. To citizens living in the time of Socrates, Plato, and Aristotle, participation in one's city-state offered opportunities for personal fulfillment. However, when the Greek states lost their independence, people felt alienated from the distant and powerful government. Their proud sense of civic duty gradually changed into a grudging compliance with the laws of the empire. A second factor shaping the philosophy of this period was the fact that the social conditions Socrates reacted against still remained. There were no integrating values to produce social cohesion. The old institutions had failed, and popular religion was declining. The gods of the city-state seemed impotent, and blind fate seemed to be in charge.

These factors tended to produce an individual-istic, practical approach to philosophy. The philosophies of this age competed in offering solutions to the problems of living. There was little interest in theoretical concerns for their own sake. Instead, people wanted to know, What is most worthwhile in life? What is left to strive for? What do I need to know to best shape my life? They were searching for some form of escape from the dismal events of the day and were longing for personal peace and rest for their weary, alienated souls.

Although the Hellenistic philosophers dealt with metaphysical issues, they were interested primarily in practical, ethical concerns. For them, theoretical knowledge only had value if it gave them some insight into how to make their individual lives more liveable. Hence, many of the philosophical concerns of traditional Greek philosophy went by the wayside. We find some bursts of originality in this period, but the philosophers were mainly content to piece together any ideas of their predecessors that seemed to work. Seven philosophical movements were prominent in this period. Because they met deep-seated human needs, many of them became very popular and lasted a long time. The first two movements will only be mentioned briefly here. First, there were the Academics who carried on Plato's school. After Plato's death the school strayed far from the vision of its founder. In its middle period it even fell into the hands of the Skeptics. Second, there were the Peripatetics (this was the name of Aristotle's school). They were primarily devoted to empirical observation and science, but lacked some of the integrating vision of Aristotle.

The next four schools were very popular. These were Cynicism, Epicureanism, Stoicism, and Skepticism. These four philosophies have left their impact on our ordinary language: *cynical*, *epicurean*, *stoical*, and *skeptical* describe different types of people or particular stances toward life. Neoplatonism, the final and seventh movement, was a religious mysticism. It offered escape from the burdens of this world by means of religious enlightenment. We will now discuss each of these last five philosophies in turn.

Cynicism

The movement known as Cynicism actually began in the Socratic era, but the Cynics are important to this time period for their influence on the Stoics. The founding of the movement can be traced to Antisthenes (about 445–365 B.C.), who started out as a student of the Sophist Gorgias but later became a devoted disciple of Socrates. He considered himself the true spiritual heir of Socratic teaching, which made him a rival of Plato.

Cynicism is more of a stance toward life than a carefully worked-out philosophy. The Cynics' main interest was the opposition of nature and convention, a theme they borrowed from the Sophists. The Cynics glorified doing what is natural and repudiating all of society's conventions, claiming they were artificial and tyrannical. They taught that happiness is found in virtue and that virtue is attained by setting oneself free from all earthly possessions and pleasures. The Cynic Antisthenes said that he would rather fall victim to madness than to desire. The key to life is to stick with what is natural—namely, to cherish only your native mental and spiritual possessions—for all else is worthless. External and physical possessions such as wealth, reputation, freedom, and pleasure are not of value, nor are poverty, shame, loss of freedom, illness, and death thought evil. They taught that there is one God, who is best served by practicing virtue. Organized religion, with its temples, priests, prayers, rituals, and fantastic stories was vigorously condemned as a human invention. The Cynics' commitment to otherworldliness and freedom from fleeting desires was a model for the Stoics and, later, the Christians.

The Cynics made every effort to unsettle the conventional values of a society they thought corrupt and artificial, including carrying on their sexual and biological functions in public. They were insulting in their manners and squalid in appearance, wearing their trademark tattered poncho and leather pouch. Traveling from town to town, they preached in the streets, usually condemning the folly of the human race. The most famous and outlandish Cynic was Diogenes of

Sinope (412 to 323 B.C.). He called himself the dog and admired the animals for their ability to stick with the bare essentials.* The stories about Diogenes abound. It is said he once roamed around at noonday with a lantern, announcing that he was looking for an honest man. Supposedly Alexander the Great was charmed by him. A well-known story relates that when Alexander made his grand entrance into Corinth, he came on Diogenes sunning himself on the street. Moved by Diogenes' miserable condition, the ruler asked him if he could grant him any royal favors, to which the Cynic replied, "Stand out of my light." Such stories reflect the contemporary meaning of cynicism. However, the Cynics' more extreme behaviors should not be allowed to eclipse the highly spiritual and admirable ethical concerns at the core of their outlook.

Although Diogenes was a contemporary of Aristotle, he had the spirit of the Hellenistic age. Diogenes lacked the optimism and contentment with his society that we find in Aristotle. Instead, a world weariness and a longing for escape through resignation, independence, and the pursuit of personal virtue characterized the philosophies of this era. His disciple Crates passed on the best features of Cynicism to the Stoics. They carried on the Cynics' concern for virtue, independence from worldly cares, and liberation from the narrow confines of one's culture while leaving behind the latter's more abusive characteristics.

Epicureanism

Epicurus (341–270 B.C.) was born seven years after Plato's death. By the time he had reached his mid-thirties, he had achieved fame for the philosophy and the way of life that he taught. He purchased a garden at the edge of Athens where he created a very close-knit philosophical commune. The Garden (as the school was called) attracted many followers and was open to all people, the

---

*The name Cynic means "canine" and may have been a term of abuse by opponents, or it may have referred to Diogenes' self-proclaimed nickname. Another theory is that the name comes from the Cynosarges, a place where Antisthenes taught.

community being made up of both men and women, and included children, slaves, soldiers, and courtesans as well as prominent citizens. Epicurus was noted for his warm affection for his followers, who in turn were deeply devoted to him. After his death, his followers at the Garden gladly carried out the request in his will that they hold a monthly feast in his memory and yearly celebrate his birthday. Epicureanism proved a very attractive philosophy, and with missionary zeal its adherents made so many converts that the philosophy rapidly permeated the Greek-speaking world. The successors of Epicurus made very few changes to his doctrines, because the philosophy was taught by means of a catechism (a form of memorized teachings common among religious groups). Even though his writings took up over three hundred scrolls, only three letters and several fragments have survived.

EPICUREAN METAPHYSICS

For Epicurus, the whole point of philosophy is to heal the soul and enable us to live a happy life. He is accordingly disdainful of theoretical speculations, whether in philosophy or the sciences, unless they serve practical human needs. He is reported to have said,

> Empty is the argument of the philosopher by which no human disease is healed; for just as there is no benefit in medicine if it does not drive out bodily diseases, so there is no benefit in philosophy if it does not drive out the disease of the soul. (I&G 66)[1]

The condition of the soul he hopes to cure is the psychological turmoil that robs us of a happy life. This sense of unrest is generated by false beliefs about what is true and valuable in life. Consequently, he intended his metaphysics to serve as an antidote to what troubles us. The first thing we need to realize, according to Epicurus, is that reality is made up of an infinite number of atoms continually moving in an infinite void. With his atomistic predecessor Democritus, he believed that these atoms vary in size and shape. However, he differed with Democritus on one crucial point. Since atoms are material, Epicurus concluded that they each must have weight. It follows from this, he reasoned, that their natural motion is to move downward through infinite space like cosmic rain. However, as they fall, some atoms randomly swerve to the side. This spontaneous deviation from their paths causes the atoms to collide and combine into groups. This accounts for the changing collections of large-scale objects such as rocks, trees, stars, and people.

If we start with material atoms as the fundamental reality, what implications for human life follow? Clearly, we must be collections of atoms in motion. The soul, or the seat of all our thoughts, emotions, and values, is really a material entity made up of very fine atoms collected together in the body. However, because the atoms can spontaneously deviate from their mechanically determined paths, the Epicureans believed that not everything is determined or predictable. Therefore, they concluded, there is some room in a materialistic universe for free will after all.

ETHICS AND PLEASURE

If the purpose of metaphysics is to provide us with a guiding vision for life, what sort of ethical theory could be developed out of an atomistic materialism? Certainly there could be no place in this universe for any nonphysical values such as Plato described. All values must be based on the way in which atoms impinge on our sense organs and create experiences of pleasure and pain. Epicurus believed that it was simply a psychological fact that the pursuit of pleasure motivates all human action. This claim is called **psychological hedonism**. As he puts it, "pleasure is the starting-point and goal of living blessedly"(LM, I&G 24). Every action you perform can be explained in terms of the pursuit of either physical or psychological pleasure. What other explanation could there be, Epicurus asks, but that you do things because you want to do them, and you want to do them because they make life more pleasant?

If this is the correct theory about human behavior, then any ethical advice about what we ought to do must be based on it. Accordingly, Epicurean philosophy identifies the notions of good and evil with pleasure and pain. Most people would say that pleasure is good. However, the Epicurean claim is that *only* pleasure is good. This position is called **ethical hedonism**. Thus, for Epicurus, the pursuit of pleasure both describes human behavior (psychological hedonism) and prescribes what is ultimately of value in human life (ethical hedonism). All moral philosophies say, "Pursue the good and avoid evil." According to Epicureanism, however, this translates into "Pursue pleasure (good) and avoid pain (evil)." If we stress the first part of the formula ("pursue pleasure") it leads to imprudent hedonism. Epicurus, however, thought the good life would be one that achieved repose, tranquillity, or quietude. Hence, the goal of wisdom is *ataraxia* or freedom from care. For this reason, he stressed the last part of the formula ("avoid pain"). If this is the overriding concern, then clearly not every pleasure is worthy of being pursued. The physical pleasures of promiscuous sex, rich foods, and strong drink are only momentary pleasures and tend to bring some form of pain in their wake (disease, emotional turmoil, poor health, hangovers). Only mental pleasures and friendship are enduring and produce tranquillity.

In a letter to a correspondent named Menoeceus, Epicurus catalogues the kinds of desires available to us:

> One must reckon that of desires some are natural, some groundless; and of the natural desires some are necessary and some merely natural; and of the necessary, some are necessary for happiness and some for freeing the body from troubles and some for life itself. (LM, I&G 24)

We may picture the desires structured as in Figure 6-1. Examples of each of these desires are as follows:

- Groundless (not rooted in nature)
  —Fame, material luxuries (jewelry, designer clothes)
- Natural, but unnecessary
  —Sex, delicious foods
- Natural and necessary
  —For happiness: wisdom, friendship

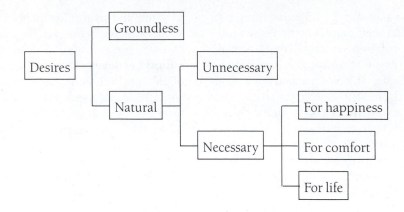

FIGURE 6-1 Epicurus's classification of desires

—For comfort: adequate clothing

—For life: water, food

It should be clear from what has been said, that Epicurus has gotten bad press. The label *epicurean* is often associated with the philosophy "Eat, drink, and be merry." Obviously, however, his ethics could not be further away from this vision of life. Epicurus says that the following characterizes the life of the happy person:

Prudence

Self-sufficiency

Sober reasoning

Honor

Justice

Wisdom

Health of the body

Peace of mind

Plain food

Accordingly, the disciples of the Garden lived very frugal and austere lives and placed a great emphasis on friendship as the supreme form of pleasure. Although the Epicureans lived very virtuous lives, it is important to realize that they did not consider moral virtue to be a matter of excellence, something to be pursued for its own sake. In the final analysis, virtue is a means to the end of individual pleasure. Epicurus says, "One must honour the noble, and the virtues and things like that, *if* they produce pleasure. But if they do not, one must bid them goodbye" (I&G 50).

EPICUREAN SOCIAL PHILOSOPHY

In the individualistic tenor of Epicurus's ideas, there is little social philosophy. He advises that the civil laws are based on human conventions and expediency and should be obeyed only because this will make our lives more peaceful. However, he cautioned people against involvement in politics, for this can only burden us with responsibilities, create enemies, and lead to personal unrest. Accordingly, Epicurus says that the wise must "free themselves from the prison of . . . politics" (I&G 31). He summed up his social philosophy in these words: "The purest security is that which comes from a quiet life and withdrawal from the many" (I&G 27).

RELIGION AND DEATH

One disease of the soul Epicurus seeks to heal is the fear produced by superstitious myths concerning the gods and our fate after death. Consistent with his belief that immaterial substance is unintelligible, Epicurus asserts that the gods have material bodies. Nevertheless, they are immortal, for their bodies consist of a different sort of atoms from the rest of nature. The point of the Epicurean teaching about the gods is to assure us that they are too aloof and preoccupied with their own pleasure to bother themselves with the problems of this world or to cause trouble for us. Ironically, the gods themselves seem to be adherents of the Epicurean philosophy:

> They spend their time in such a manner that nothing can be conceived which is more blessed or better supplied with all kinds of good things. For a god is idle, is entangled with no serious preoccupations, undertakes no toilsome labour, but simply rejoices in his own wisdom and virtue, being certain that he will always be in the midst of pleasures which are both supreme and eternal. (I&G 41)

If the gods are too peaceful to be capable of either gratitude or anger we do not have to worry about appeasing them or being punished by them. When we understand this, we can live our lives as autonomously and serenely as the gods.

Even if we don't have to worry about the gods, doesn't the fear of death still haunt us, robbing us of all our hard-won tranquillity? Again Epicureanism offers us peace of mind with the following argument: if we exist, then death does not; and if death exists, then we do not. In either case we will never literally experience death, for death is simply the moment when the soul atoms disperse into the air with our last breath and our ability to experience pain or anguish ceases. Epicurus gives the following advice in a letter:

> Get used to believing that death is nothing to us. For all good and bad consists in sense-experience, and death is the privation of sense-experience. Hence, a correct knowledge of the fact that death is nothing to us makes the mortality of life a matter of contentment, not by adding a limitless time [to life] but by removing the longing for immortality. (LM, I&G 23)

THE SIGNIFICANCE
OF THE EPICUREANS

Although the Epicureans lived an admirable lifestyle, they considered that virtue was valuable only for its egoistic consequences. We are to be virtuous because it makes life more pleasant and is to our advantage. One should be just only to avoid the consequences of one's evil actions being exposed. However, what if someone decides that the discomfort of social rebuke pales in comparison to the pleasures of being greedy and unfair? It would be difficult for an Epicurean to say that such a decision was morally wrong if it genuinely did maximize pleasure.

The tensions in Epicurean moral philosophy become apparent when we look at Epicurus's attitude toward friendship. Consistent with his principles, he says that "friendship comes to be because of its utility" and continually links it with the pleasure it brings us (I&G 35). But such passages make the Epicurean sound like a scheming, calculating, self-serving opportunist who makes friends and uses them for the pleasure they make possible. However, as with so many philosophers, the character of Epicurus was better than the ethical principles he espoused. By all accounts he showed kindness and generosity toward others that went beyond any personal payoff these actions may have brought. We are told that "Epicurus assembled . . . large congregations of friends which were bound together by a shared feeling of the deepest love" (I&G 47). He even says that friendship may require that you sacrifice your life for a friend. The problem is that the Epicurean ethics of pleasure clearly is an egoistic hedonism. This view implies that my friendships are valuable only for what pleasure *I* get out of them. In contrast, Epicurus says that "every friendship is worth choosing for its own sake" (I&G 30). This would imply that other things besides pleasure (such as friendship) are intrinsically valuable. If we embrace this doctrine, we must abandon the fundamental thesis of hedonism.

In conclusion, the individualism and withdrawal that lie at the heart of Epicureanism characterized the Hellenistic period. By way of contrast, the elaborate social philosophies of Plato and Aristotle indicate that they thought the good life was to be found in involvement in political life and in the attempt to make the state better. The Hellenistic philosophers, however, despaired over the possibility of meaningful involvement in society beyond one's intimate circle of friends. Clearly, Epicureanism met the needs of the age, for it spread very rapidly and lasted as an organized movement until the fourth century A.D. Although it no longer exists in this form, it is not hard to find people today whose lifestyles consciously or unconsciously follow the Epicurean ideals.

Stoicism

Stoicism developed about the same time that Epicurus founded his school. The Stoic philosophy developed into a formidable rival that competed with the hedonism of Epicurus for the minds of the Greek and Roman populace. The popularity and influence of these two systems indicate that they touched on real needs in their culture even though they provided different answers to the problems. We find them prevalent even in the Christian era, in the account of the Apostle Paul speaking to both groups in Athens (Acts 17).

Stoicism was founded by a philosopher named Zeno (who lived about 336 to 264 B.C.).* He journeyed from his native city of Citium (located in Cyprus) to Athens, where he founded a school. Zeno lectured on a porch or open colonnade. Accordingly, the name of the school comes from the Greek word *stoa*, which means "porch." He attracted many followers in Greece and Rome. He was widely admired for his moral earnestness, and the Athenians gave him official honors.

We will not be able to cover all the facets of Stoic thought, because they made contributions in so many different fields. For example, they developed a detailed empiricist philosophy of knowledge. Furthermore, the Stoics made a number of original contributions in the discipline of logic. They developed a logic of propositions that anticipated modern propositional logic and that went beyond the logic of categories that Aristotle had formulated. Building on their system, they founded our traditional science of grammar. However, it was their metaphysics and the ethical theory based on

it that made them famous. To introduce their ideas in these last two fields, let's briefly compare and contrast the Stoics with the Epicureans.

COMPARISON OF EPICUREANISM AND STOICISM

The Epicureans and the Stoics had a great deal in common: (1) they built enormously popular philosophies, yet they still attempted to provide rational justifications for their beliefs; (2) they were both concerned with logic and physics, but emphasized the relevance of these fields to practical ethics; (3) both were materialistic in their metaphysics and empiricists in their epistemology; and finally (4) both advised us to act according to nature (by "nature," referring to both the cosmos and human nature). However, in the details of this latter point their positions diverged, because they had different conceptions of the cosmos and human nature. For the Epicureans, the universe was mechanistic and governed by blind chance. For the Stoics, however, the universe was purposeful and governed by a benevolent, divine plan. According to the Epicureans, humans are basically pleasure-seeking organisms whose highest good is to pursue pleasure. Thus virtue has value only if it helps us achieve this end. For the Stoics, character, virtue, self-discipline, and the fulfillment of duty have value in themselves. Their ethical outlook was influenced by Socrates' life and death and by his confidence that no real harm can come to a person whose life is based on virtue and eternal values. The Epicureans built their social philosophy on enlightened self-interest and expressed disdain for involvement in larger social concerns. Accordingly, the attention they gave to social virtues such as justice was motivated by individualistic, prudential concerns. The Stoics, however, taught that we should subordinate our selfish interests to fulfillment of more universal ends and developed a social philosophy emphasizing that all humanity constitutes one great community or family.

STOIC METAPHYSICS

Like the Epicureans, the Stoics embraced materialistic monism or the claim that all reality is material.

---

*This Zeno should not be confused with the pupil of Parmenides who proposed the famous paradoxes.

*The philosophy of Stoicism received its name from the Stoa
(meaning porch) where its founder Zeno lectured.*

However, unlike their rivals they did not believe
there was any room for chance in the scheme of
things. The realm of matter obviously includes the
crasser sorts of stuff that make up things such as
rocks and wood. However, when they came to discuss God and the human soul, as well as all the
forms and forces operating in the world, they consistently concluded that these entities were also material. These sorts of beings are made up of very fine
matter. Accordingly, they frequently used *pneuma*
(the word for breath or wind) to describe these very
subtle but still material realities.

As opposed to the Epicureans' universe of material particles governed by blind chance, the Stoics' universe was teleological (purposeful) and
permeated by the divine. The Stoics used multiple
names such as Zeus, God, Nature, Order, Universal Reason, Fate, Destiny, and Providence as
interchangeable terms to refer to the same, funda-

mental reality. Unlike the impersonal or uncaring
gods of Aristotle and Epicurus, the Stoic divinity
is benevolent and just. He guides all things by his
wisdom to realize the perfect, most beautiful, and
good outcome. Although there is an aspect of God
that is transcendent, he also diffuses himself
throughout the world and assumes its form.
Showing their indebtedness to Heraclitus, the Stoics taught that God is the Logos, or the rational
principle pervading everything. He is immanent
in the world as its creative and guiding force.
Again drawing on Heraclitus, they said that the
Logos takes the form of an all-permeating cosmic
fire. The fiery vapor manifests itself in the flaming
spheres in the heavens, in the warmth and vitality
of plants and animals, and as rational thought in
the soul of humans. Although the world is material, it is a continuum, like a field of force, or a dif-
fused vapor, instead of the discrete particles of the

Epicureans. Thus, the world is one, living, divine body, and the Logos is its soul and reason. Little sparks of the divine fire, the *logoi*, are dispersed throughout the world like seeds to guide the growth and development of each thing.

But this God is not a free personality or free creator, for the process of nature flows from his substance with a rigid necessity. Hence, the Stoics believed there was no chance or contingency in the universe. Everything in the world is determined down to the smallest detail, and events could not be any other way than they are. However, because this logical determinism is an expression of a benevolent, divine providence, it is not cold, blind, and impersonal. Instead, it nurtures and fulfills our deepest human needs.

Human beings are sparks of the divine fire. Hence each individual is a microcosm or a miniature version of the universe. Our individual reason is identical with the universal world reason. This is why our finite minds can know the cosmos. After death, our souls endure until the end of the world, when they return to God along with everything else. At this point the Stoics disagreed among themselves. Cleanthes (around 331–232 B.C.) hypothesized that the afterlife applied to all souls, whereas Chrysippus (around 280–207 B.C.) claimed it was attained only by the virtuous souls.

An obvious problem arises for any philosophy that claims every detail of the world serves a benevolent, divinely ordered purpose. How does one reconcile this belief with the problem of evil? Sometimes the Stoics blamed human wickedness. However, corrupt human choices can only explain such evils as crimes and wars; they cannot account for natural evils such as disease, earthquakes, and famines. To this problem the Stoics offered two kinds of solutions. The first answer was to assert that if we could see the cosmos as a whole, we would see that the world really is perfect, beautiful, and good. Some things appear evil only because of our limited perspective. For example, if we focused narrowly on the dark shadows in a painting and did not see the lighter colors, we would not appreciate the beauty of the painting. The second answer claimed that some evils are the necessary means for realizing the good. For example, bitter medicine may produce health. Painful exercise may produce a muscular body. The Stoics pointed out that the existence of evil is essential to the production of virtue. Without vice and suffering to struggle against, there could not be courage, patience, or fortitude. In the final analysis, no matter how severe physical evil may be, it cannot affect the human character, which alone has intrinsic value.

ETHICS AND RESIGNATION

The Stoics agreed with Aristotle that the highest good for human beings is a life in accord with reason. Happiness is found in living a rationally self-determined life. The Stoics' ethics is tied in with their metaphysics, for the goal in life is to make one's mind a microcosm of the order in the universe. But how do I achieve rational control over my life? The first answer is, I must be free from all passion. If my emotions control me, then I am their victim and am not living a rationally self-determined life. The second answer is to tie my happiness only to what I can control. The search for such things as fame, wealth, pleasure, or the love of another person puts external events in control of my happiness. Furthermore, if every event in the universe is determined, then I cannot change the inevitable. The one thing I can control is my attitude toward life. I must welcome every event as the expression of God's will and as an essential part of the harmonious, beautiful scheme of things. In submitting my will to the will of the universe, I do not spend my life thrashing against the irresistible tide of necessity, but serenely go with the flow. If my happiness is based on the pursuit of virtue and an inner serenity, then I am in charge of my life:

> *And this very thing constitutes the virtue of the happy man and the smooth current of life, when all actions promote the harmony of the spirit dwelling in the individual man with the will of him who orders the universe. (S 112)*[2]

Zeno and Chrysippus used the following illustration:

Suppose a dog to be tied to a wagon. If he wishes to follow, the wagon pulls him and he follows, so that his own power and necessity unite. But if he does not wish to follow, he will be compelled to anyhow. The same is the case with mankind also. Even if they do not wish to follow, they will be absolutely forced to enter into the fated event. (S 109–110)

Epictetus (around A.D. 50–138) made the same point, saying, "Ask not that events should happen as you will, but let your will be that events should happen as they do, and you shall have peace" (S 135). Underscoring this sentiment, he quotes a prayer written by Cleanthes:

Conduct me, Zeus, and thou, O Destiny,
Wherever your decrees have fixed my lot.
I follow cheerfully, and, did I not,
Wicked and wretched, I must follow still.[3]

According to the Stoics, you and I are free as long as we act on basis of logical thought. Otherwise, we will be governed by our impulses like the brutes. Plato and Aristotle had a low view of the emotions but thought they were acceptable if they could be moderated and controlled by reason. The Stoics, however, thought that moral evil was the result of our passions and sought to eliminate them altogether. According to Chrysippus there are basically four kinds of emotions, each based on a false judgment:

Emotion	Object of the Mistaken Judgment
Pleasure	A present good
Desire	A future good
Grief	A present evil
Fear	A future evil

However, if all things that happen are inevitable and part of the beautiful plan of the universe, then it is irrational to be aroused by these emotions. To experience these sorts of emotions toward the events in my life is as irrational as regretting the necessary order of the multiplication tables or either desiring or fearing a change in them.

Because they disdained the emotions, the Stoic ideal of life was "apathy." This term should not be understood as listlessness but rather as the freedom from passion or the refusal to be upset by anything that happens. Even today we still say, "Be stoical" or "Be philosophical," when we are advising people to be content with what life brings their way. These slang expressions testify to how deeply the Stoics have influenced our cultural traditions. Consistent with their philosophy, the Stoics taught that death is not an evil and was not to be feared. It is a natural and inevitable part of being human. The Stoics were even willing to hasten its arrival when appropriate, finding no shame in an honorable suicide. The story is told that when Zeno tripped and injured his foot, he took this as a sign from God that his life had reached its appointed end. So he dutifully killed himself.

Initially, the Stoics did not acknowledge any degrees of virtue or vice. One was either perfectly virtuous or, like the rest of humanity, a fool and a reprobate. However, the later Stoics were more flexible and tried to broaden the appeal of their philosophy by acknowledging that some people were neither perfectly virtuous nor entirely bad, but were on their way to being wise. This tendency to make concessions was also illustrated by their modification of the doctrine concerning "indifferents." An indifferent is any external thing that does not affect the moral virtue or the happiness of the wise person. The list of indifferents would include health, pleasure, beauty, wealth, as well as disease, pain, ugliness, and poverty. But if these are all neutral, why choose health over sickness? The Stoics compromised with common sense by saying that while these things do not contribute to nor detract from our happiness, some indifferents can be classified as "preferences" or "advantages." It is permissible to pursue them as long as we do not pin our happiness to them.

STOIC SOCIAL PHILOSOPHY

Some may find the Stoics' view of the world to be quaint but antiquated. However, their social philosophy turned out to be an enduring and important contribution to the foundations of Western civilization. It is significant that many of the Stoics before the Christian era were from outside

Greece. By the time Stoicism developed, Athens had lost its role as the hub of culture. This led to a more international perspective and avoided some of the Athenian provincialism that pervaded Plato's and Aristotle's political theories. When Zeno was asked what his city was, he replied that he was "a citizen of the cosmos." The Cynics' emphasis on rising above the narrow conventions of one's society had an influence here. The Stoics taught that each individual is part of the larger whole of humanity and must be concerned with more than one's narrow self-interest. Their metaphysics implied that all rational beings, even slaves and foreigners, had a spark of the divine fire. Their metaphor of the fatherhood of God suggested that we are his children and the entire human race is one great family. Hence, gender, wealth, race, or social class ceased to have significance in the Stoic social philosophy. Whereas the Epicureans withdrew from politics, the Stoics emphasized our civic duties. It is our job to make society image the rationally ordered universe and reflect the justice and benevolence of God.

THE ROMAN STOICS

The Romans are noted for their innovations in engineering and politics but less so for their philosophies. They were content to borrow their philosophical conceptions from the work done by the Greeks. The Stoic philosophy was particularly appealing to them because of its notion that all people belong to one universal community, governed by one standard of justice—exactly the kind of universal state the Romans were trying to develop. For a time, it became the semiofficial philosophy of the Roman political establishment. Although a few Romans were suspicious of philosophy, the Stoics' emphasis on resignation made them popular with the established order. It is not a philosophy that encourages activists or revolutionaries. The Romans helped popularize Stoicism by downplaying its more severe elements and developing its practical aspects. To make it more coherent with the Roman context, they emphasized the virtues associated with civic duty more than the ideal of apathy. The universal ap-

peal of Stoicism is illustrated by the fact that its Roman phase attracted first a Roman lawyer (Cicero), then one of Nero's prime ministers (Seneca), as well as one of Nero's slaves (Epictetus), and even a Roman emperor (Marcus Aurelius Antoninus).*

An important contribution of the Roman Stoics was their application of the Stoic notion of natural law to Roman legal theory. All proponents of the **natural law theory** in ethics believe that nature is not only ruled by physical laws but that it is permeated by a moral order as well. This unwritten natural law is a moral code that applies to all people no matter what their culture. Thus, Cicero distinguished two kinds of laws. First, some laws are merely local, human inventions. Second, the natural moral order constitutes a universal law. All of us are subject to this second law by virtue of the fact that we all share in the divine reason. It is "the law above the law," and our human civil codes are valid and just only if they conform to the natural law. The opening paragraph of the American Declaration of Independence indicates the lasting influence of this theory, stating that people have inalienable rights "to which the laws of nature and of nature's God entitle them."

The Romans also developed the Stoic ethics of duty. Before Stoicism, Greek ethical theory placed very little emphasis on the notion of duty. Generally, even the most exalted, altruistic ethical advice was intimately tied up with one's own self-interest and the pursuit of the good life. The Stoics, however, gave duty and obligation a new importance. They taught that we must do some things simply because they are right. This emphasis is eloquently captured in Marcus Aurelius's comment: "Have I done something for the general interest? Well then I have had my reward."[4] Although he was a Roman emperor, his Stoicism extended his sense of loyalty far beyond the Roman Empire to embrace the whole human population: "But my nature is rational and social; and my city and country, so far as I am Antoninus, is Rome,

*Their dates are: Cicero (106–43 B.C.), Seneca (c. 4 B.C.–A.D. 65), Epictetus (c. A.D. 50–138), Marcus Aurelius (A.D. 121–180).

but so far as I am a man, it is the world."[5] Marcus Aurelius was the last great teacher of Stoicism, for it lost its hold on people as Christianity came into prominence. However, its voice was not completely silenced—many of its doctrines found their way into Christian thought.

THE SIGNIFICANCE OF THE STOICS

One of the most significant by-products of the Stoic philosophy was that it brought into focus the problem of freedom and determinism. Its critics claim that a fundamental incoherence lies at the heart of this philosophy. If the universe is determined down to the last detail, how can humans be free? If everything that happens is necessary and good, then how can any human actions or thoughts be bad? Yet the Stoics believed we are free and advise us that we can make good choices and bad choices, that we can harbor appropriate attitudes and wrong attitudes. However, given the deterministic Stoic metaphysics, it is hard to understand why human attitudes are not a part of the necessary order of nature and therefore beyond our control. It would be unfair to criticize the Stoics for not resolving this issue in their time, for it remains one of the most controversial problems in philosophy today.

Others have criticized Stoicism because of its ideal of apathy. Critics say that it purchases tranquillity at the expense of our normal and appropriate human emotions. If a child is suffering, the Stoics would say it is our duty to do what we can to alleviate her pain. However, if we are not successful, we should not feel grief or pity, because everything that happens is as it was meant to be. Seneca says that pity is not a virtue but "a mental defect." Expounding on this, he says,

> Pity is the sorrow of the mind brought about by the sight of the distress or sadness caused by the ills of others which it believes come undeservedly. But no sorrow befalls the wise man. (S 128)

For this reason Bertrand Russell says that there is "a certain coldness in the Stoic conception of virtue. Not only bad passions are condemned, but all passions."[6]

Stoicism had a continuous history of about five hundred years. Even while it declined as a philosophical movement, the Christian tradition was taking up many of its ideals. The Stoic outlook comforted the Christians, who were suffering persecution and trying to endure a cruel and corrupt government. Both the Stoics and the Christians felt the freedom that comes from a serene detachment, because they realized that the pains of this world were but insignificant specks on the face of eternity and even the worst of evils would find some purpose in the beautiful tapestry of cosmic history that God is weaving. As with the Epicureans, some people today live out the Stoic ideal, whether or not they call it by that name.

Skepticism

The Skeptics looked with scornful amusement at the quarrels between their contemporaries the Epicureans and the Stoics. The latter two philosophies were merely the latest additions to the long parade of human opinions. The Skeptics complained that both their rivals assumed what they had no basis for assuming: the competence of human reason to know reality. The Skeptics found no basis for such an extravagant claim. The term "skeptic" comes from the Greek *skeptikos*, which means "inquirers." The Skeptics prided themselves on their ability to inquire into the foundations of our beliefs as well as on having the honesty to face the fact that there are no foundations.

Skeptical thought had been around since the early Greeks and was a prominent part of the Sophists' teachings. However, in the Hellenistic period, it received a new burst of energy from Pyrrho of Elis (360–270 B.C.). By at least the first century B.C., Pyrrhonism became a synonym for Skepticism. Pyrrho never wrote anything, but we have accounts of his views from other writers in his tradition. Pyrrho declared that sense experience cannot give us knowledge. To do so, our sense data must agree with their objects. But if we can never get outside of sensation, how could we ever know this? Furthermore, rational argument cannot give us knowledge either, because for every argument there is a counterargument and the two opposing positions cancel each other out.

Because problems arise with all our sources of knowledge, the Skeptics concluded that we cannot know the real nature of things. Hence, all we can confidently talk about are appearances. You can say, "The honey *appears* to me to be sweet" but not "The honey *is* sweet." The prudent approach is always to suspend judgment and assume nothing at all. The same advice holds for moral judgments. We cannot know anything for sure, so stop striving for absolute moral truth, they said. Consequently, a serene apathy and indifference characterize the wise person. What you do not know, you do not have to worry about. The Skeptics favored a social conservativism. Since we cannot know what is good or bad in itself, we might as well leave such judgments to the consensus of law and tradition.

ACADEMIC SKEPTICISM

The power of the Skeptical movement is signaled by the fact that its seeds took root within Plato's Academy. Arcesilaus (roughly, 316–242 B.C.) headed the Academy about the time when Zeno was inaugurating Stoicism. Arcesilaus was influential in turning the Academy toward Skepticism, a course that it would take for about two hundred years. His leadership was passed on to Carneades (who lived about 214–129 B.C.). Carneades was considered one of the most brilliant philosophers of his century. The Academic Skeptics complained that the Academy had lost the Socratic spirit of inquiry and had settled into a comfortable dogmatism. This may seem a strange turn for the Academics to take, since Plato himself was confident we could know the Forms and fought against the skepticism of the Sophists. However, the Academic Skeptics selectively chose those elements from the Platonic tradition that they liked. For example, they emphasized that Socrates said he knew nothing and that the Socratic dialogues always ended without establishing any definite conclusions. The Skeptics used Plato's skeptical arguments against the senses and noted that in

the *Timaeus* he said that physics is merely a "likely story."[7]

The Skeptics never tired of attacking the "dogmatism" of both the Epicureans and the Stoics. They both based knowledge on the senses, which the Skeptics argued can only give us appearances. However, the Stoics thought that some sense impressions were so indubitable the mind could not help but assent to them. The Skeptics had an easy job demonstrating that in dreams and hallucinations, we are presented with false images that are also convincing. In a wholesale fashion, the Skeptics undercut any search for a criterion of truth, for any principle we can come up with will itself need justification; that is, it will need a criterion for determining that it should be our guiding principle. They did not make the mistake of dogmatically asserting that nothing can be known. Instead, they merely asserted that we *appear* to be without knowledge. Thus, with admirable consistency, they suspended judgment on whether, in the final analysis, Skepticism is true.

In 156–155 B.C. Carneades represented Athens as an ambassador to Rome along with a Stoic and an Aristotelian. In between doing business, they gave public lectures. This was the first exposure the Romans had to philosophy, and Carneades' speeches attracted the most interest. On the first day he argued in favor of justice and eloquently commended its practice to the Romans. The next day, he argued the opposite position, using equally brilliant rhetoric to downgrade justice. This two-faced arguing was a favorite method of the Skeptics for undermining those who thought we have reasons for any positive opinion.

The Stoics vigorously attacked these views. They claimed that a consistent Skepticism would lead to the suspension of not only judgment but of all activity, paralyzing human life. Carneades tried to respond to these attacks by modifying the Skeptical thesis and arguing that even though we do not have certainty, we can have probability, which is all we need for meaningful action. Reportedly, Carneades said that "the wise man will employ whatever apparently plausible presentations he meets with, provided there is nothing which opposes its plausibility, and thus will every plan of life be governed" (I&G 171). This compromise won him the disdain of both the Stoics and the later Pyrrhonic purists within his own tradition.

THE REVIVAL OF PYRRHONIAN SKEPTICISM

The purists among the Skeptics believed that the Academic Skeptics had taken a wrong turn because they were not skeptical enough. For example, the purists complained that the notion of probability was suspect, for the ability to distinguish the probable from the improbable requires a good deal of knowledge. These more strict Skeptics called themselves "Pyrrhonists" in honor of the movement's founder. The members of this group delighted in formalizing Skepticism in terms of various groups of principles. For example, Agrippa claimed that Skepticism rests on five pillars: (1) *Disagreement*—on any issue, not everyone will agree. (2) *Infinite regress*—to resolve disagreements, we must find reasons for our conclusions, but these reasons need justification, so then we need justifications for our justifications, and so on, and so on. (3) *Relativity*—things are perceived differently in different circumstances. (4) *Hypothesis*—if we try to solve the regress problem by taking some statement as an axiom or an indubitable starting point, anyone can come along and say its contrary is self-evident. Hence, the starting point of every proof is groundless and arbitrary. (5) *Circular reasoning*—all arguments that avoid the first four problems will end up, in one way or another, assuming what we are trying to prove. Later Skeptics reduced the whole arsenal of arguments to two simple theses: nothing is self-evident, and nothing can be proved. As with all the philosophies of this time, the Skeptics' tightly reasoned arguments had one goal: personal peace. If we cannot know anything, then we cease to worry about whether or not we have the truth. We are free of the struggle to distinguish truth from falsehood and good from bad. We can just accept what appears to be the case and what our customs and laws tell us to do. This

was expressed well by Sextus Empiricus, a physician who lived about the turn of the third century A.D.: "Therefore, he who suspends judgment about everything which is subject to opinion reaps a harvest of the most complete happiness" (I&G 238).

THE SIGNIFICANCE OF SKEPTICISM

As a close-knit movement, Skepticism died out in the third century A.D. The Skeptics could not answer the objection that it makes no sense to offer arguments unless we have some data to serve as the starting point of our reasoning. But this implies that at least we do have reasons to believe our premises are true. However, although they had no positive conclusions to offer, the Skeptics did contribute to philosophy. Skepticism of all varieties makes philosophy self-critical and keeps it honest and free of dogmatism. Furthermore, they set the agenda for later philosophers. Their successors had to either accept their arguments and live with the consequences or come up with an epistemology that survived all skeptical attacks. Thus, they inspired a good deal of work in epistemology. For example, St. Augustine wrote *Against the Academics* to lay the Skeptics' arguments to rest. In the beginning of the modern period, philosophers revived skeptical arguments and used them either as a foil for their own philosophies or as a weapon against their opponents. Descartes used skeptical doubt as a method for finding which beliefs were certain beyond all question. Berkeley sought to avoid skeptical conclusions by claiming that there was no reality beyond the appearances. Some religious philosophers found it a helpful critique of the pretensions of human reason, claiming that since reason cannot answer our questions, we are driven to faith and revelation. Worth mentioning here are Erasmus, Pascal, Montaigne, and Bayle. In the seventeenth century, the legacy of Skepticism seemed to have had some effect on the rise of modern science. If we cannot know the real essences of things, philosophers said, then we should not let ourselves be distracted by abstruse metaphysical perplexities. Instead, we should be content with an empirical study of the world of appearances.

By the time of its decline, Skepticism had not offered peace but only confusion. Traditional certitudes and the gods of Mount Olympus were no longer credible, but Skepticism offered nothing positive in return. Simply following religious and social traditions without conviction as some Skeptics urged, did not seem satisfactory. People in this age sought for something to cling to and, for many, faith filled this longing. Consequently, various religious philosophies based on Asian thought became popular. Eventually, Christianity emerged as a powerful cultural force, providing its own answers to the needs of the time.

Plotinus and Neoplatonism

When we reach the last vestiges of Greek thought in the Christian era, we find that a full circle has been made. Greek philosophy ends where it began—in religion. The conditions that caused this development are understandable. The third century A.D. represented the most dismal period in Roman history. Emperors rose to power by bribing the army, and assassination was the most common way to remove those in power. The Roman army was weakened by corruption and discord, and the barbarians chipped away at the territories in the north and the east. War and disease decimated the population, while corruption, exorbitant taxes, and diminished resources threw the empire into financial chaos.

In response to these depressing events, people felt a thirst for a better world and some sort of hope that they could pin to eternity far above the chaotic events of human history. People longed not simply for the Greek vision of the good life, but for a decidedly religious notion of salvation, to be found in a mystical absorption into God. Some found the answer in a revival of Platonic otherworldliness. Hence, there arose not just a Platonic philosophy of religion, but a genuinely religious philosophy. This new, religious Platonism (or Neoplatonism as it later came to be called) drew from all the nonmaterialistic and re-

ligious doctrines of earlier systems. Its sources were primarily Pythagorean, Aristotelian, Stoic, and, of course, Platonic.

The founder of Neoplatonism was Plotinus (A.D. 205–270). Raised in a provincial town in Egypt, he journeyed in his late twenties to Alexandria to study philosophy. Alexandria was a cosmopolitan city where Greek culture from the West and mystery religions from the East mixed freely. He sought out Ammonius Saccas, a famous teacher, and spent time under his instruction.* When Plotinus was forty, his journeys brought him to Rome, where he opened a school. He developed a large following that included several physicians, a poet, several women, and many members of the Senate. He even found favor with the Emperor Gallienus and his wife. Plotinus gained a reputation as a spiritual counselor and, although numerous people frequented him for advice, he never turned anyone away. Although continually in weak health, he had a powerful but gentle and affectionate spirit. We are told he never would reveal his birthday, because he did not want it celebrated. Instead, he invited friends to celebrations on the birthdays of Socrates and Plato. Although he never married, he took orphaned children into his house and became their guardian. After his death, his manuscripts were edited by his faithful disciple Porphyry. Porphyry divided them into six groups of nine called the *Enneads.*†

THE ONE

For Plotinus, those things that have the most reality are those with the most unity. Accordingly, the highest being is what he calls "the One." It is wholly transcendent, beyond all thought and being, and incomprehensible. To think about or describe it would be possible only if we could attribute properties to it. But to have distinguishable properties would mean that it was composed of parts. Thus, the source of all properties is be-

*Ammonius is said to have been raised as a Christian but later reverted to Greek religion.
†From the Greek word *ennea*, meaning "nine."

yond any of them and totally without any sort of plurality. It is engaged in neither thought, willing, nor any other conscious activity, for all these imply some sort of duality. Plotinus uses numerous names to refer to the One, such as God, the Good, First Existent, the Absolute, the Infinite, and the Father.

Although it does not consciously act, the being of the One is so full that it overflows and all things emanate from it, while the One itself remains the same. Plotinus borrows the metaphor of the sun from Plato to illustrate this. The sun sheds its light on all things but remains undiminished in the process. Similarly, an object may have its image reproduced in a mirror while being unaffected by this duplication. Thus, the One is like an eternal sun producing eternal light. However, this does not result from a conscious decision to create, for the world proceeds from the One by necessity.

INTELLECT

The first emanation from the One is *Nous*, which can be translated as Intellect, Intellectual Principle, Divine Mind, or Spirit. It is eternal and free of all imperfection. As with the One, Intellect is indivisible in the sense that it cannot be dissolved into parts. Yet, unlike the One, it has distinguishable aspects. These aspects are the knower and the objects of its knowledge. The Intellect intuits two objects: the One and itself. In knowing itself, it knows that it contains the whole of the Platonic Forms. However, it does not know them one after another but intuits the whole collection in one, eternal and unified vision. At this point, Plotinus goes on to differ from Plato, for he claims that there are not only Forms of universals but also Forms of individuals. Hence, there is not only a Form of Humanity, but a Form of Socrates as well. Thus, each individual is given an eternal value and status in the Divine Mind.

SOUL

Eternally emanating from Intellect is a third reality called Soul. It, too, is eternal and nonphysical. It functions as the mediator between the spiritual

realm and the world of the senses and makes the cosmos like one, living organism. According to Plotinus, Soul has two aspects. The higher part looks to Intellect and remains untouched by what is beneath it, while the lower part descends to generate the sensible world and replicate its own vision of the Forms within it. However, it no more consciously wills to create the world than the magnet wills to radiate its magnetic field and order the iron filings around it. Because it is the principle of life, growth, order, and movement in the universe, Plotinus says that it can be identified with Nature. The world of physical beings it generates corresponds to all the possible forms of Being contained in Intellect.

Individual human souls are aspects of the World Soul. Plotinus says our souls are like the light from the sun, which shines into each individual house. Each house seems to have its own light but all of it is really the manifestation of one sun (E 4.3.4).[8] Human souls duplicate the structure of the World Soul in that the higher element within us belongs to the realm of Intellect and the lower element is involved with the body. Our souls existed prior to their union with the body, which occurs through a sort of descent from the realm of the spirit. The soul survives the death of the body and is reincarnated, but does not retain its memories.

THE MATERIAL WORLD

So far, we have three primary realities, a hierarchical trinity made up of the One, Intellect, and Soul. However, the Soul is always restless and desires to exercise its powers. Hence, from the Soul comes the final emanation, which is the realm of matter. However, the production of the material realm is not a creative act that happens at some point in time. As with all the higher emanations, the generation of the realm of matter is a necessary and eternal process. This final emanation, however, cannot be considered a fourth kind of reality, for Plotinus believes that matter is nonbeing. His metaphor of the sun helps clarify this point. The sun sends forth rays of light. But the further they get from their source, the dimmer they become, until the light diminishes into total darkness. Similarly, the One radiates being and goodness, but just as darkness is a privation of light, so matter is a privation of all that is real and good.

Following the Platonic model, Plotinus says that what goodness or intelligibility physical objects have is attributed to the dim reflections of the intelligible world that we see in them. But the mixture is never a happy combination, for matter corrupts everything that it touches. So, even though matter receives illumination from Soul, it "darkens the illumination, the light from that source, by mixture with itself, and weakens it" (E 1.8.14).

THE PROBLEM OF EVIL

Not surprisingly, passages in Plotinus suggest that matter is the source of evil. These passages taken by themselves would underscore Plotinus's otherworldliness and lead to a devaluing of the physical. There are even suggestions that the production of the physical world was a tragic mistake (E 1, 1.8.5–6). But he adds confusion to this pessimistic view of matter by also giving us an optimistic outlook on the physical world. First, he argues that since the physical realm is the last stage in the long chain of necessary emanations from the source of all goodness, it must share in the goodness of its source. This process creates all the possible degrees of being, graded from the more perfect to the less perfect. This produces the greatest amount of variety and thus results in the richest sort of world (E 4.8.6). Second, Plotinus argues that anything short of God necessarily falls short of his perfect goodness. Thus, to have a world at all means that some imperfections will exist (E 3.2.5). The world has as much goodness as any material realm could possibly attain, for "what other fairer image of the intelligible world could there be?" (E 2.9.4). Third, the cosmos is like a beautiful painting or a well-written play. Each part has its appropriate role to play in the whole. But if we focus exclusively on only one part, we will miss this. The worst parts of the universe can be used by God to serve the good, even though the reasons for them cannot be discerned by us (E 2.3.18). Even the moral wickedness of those around us serves to get our attention and gives us a greater appreciation for the beauty of virtue (E 3.2.5).

THE WAY OF ASCENT

In his more negative passages, Plotinus frequently talks of the descent of the human soul into the body as a "fall" into the inferior and lower part of the universe. The cause of this is our audacity and desire to be autonomous (E 5.1.1). Agreeing with Plato, he says that the more we focus on our bodies, the senses, and our own individuality, the more we are caught, buried in a cave, ignorantly engaged with our own chains, and alienated from the Whole. The soul is naturally made to fly in the spiritual realm but it becomes distracted, causing it to fall to earth and abandon its wings (E 4.8.4). Yet, at the same time, we are never completely lost, because despite this fall we remain metaphysically a part of the higher realm (E 4.8.8). Evil, then, is not a reality that pulls us down. It is our own willfulness that turns us away from the Good. Evil does not exist for the perfect soul that always turns toward the intellect. Only those souls blinded by their passions and seduced by the material world are affected by the darkness and privation of evil (E 1.8.4).

Plotinus did not develop his philosophy simply to obtain metaphysical knowledge for its own sake, but to show the way to salvation. We can find freedom from our chains and peace for our restless souls if we stay aloof from the body, ignore its seductive songs, and focus on the spirit. Salvation is achieved by traveling through several stages. First, we must purify ourselves through intellectual and moral discipline. Like Plato, Plotinus thought that learning to see the forms in particulars would point us in the right direction. For example, seeing beauty in ourselves and in the things and people around us will leave us nostalgic for the true source of all beauty that we have abandoned. As Plotinus puts it so beautifully,

> Go back into yourself and look; and if you do not yet see yourself beautiful, then, just as someone making a statue which has to be beautiful cuts away here and polishes there and makes one part smooth and clears another till he has given his statue a beautiful face, so you too must cut away excess and straighten the crooked and clear the dark and make it bright, and never stop "working on your statue" till the divine glory of virtue shines out on you. (E 1.6.9)

The next stage is to engage in philosophical dialectic, in which we more fully come to understand the eternal intelligible world. The final stage is a mystical and ecstatic union with God. This experience is beyond all language and discursive thought. Plotinus's description of this experience is eloquent and moving:

> When we do look to [the One], then we are at our goal and at rest . . . as we truly dance our god-inspired dance around him.
>
> And in this dance the soul sees the spring of life, the spring of intellect, the principle of being, the cause of good, the root of the soul; . . . There the soul takes its rest and is outside evils because it has run up into a place which is clear of evils. . . . And if anyone does not know this experience, let him think of it in terms of our loves here below, and what it is like to attain what one is most in love with, and that these earthly loves are mortal and harmful and loves only of images, and that they change because it was not what is really and truly loved nor our good nor what we seek. But there is our true love, with whom also we can be united. . . . There one can see both him and oneself as it is right to see: the self glorified, full of intelligible light—but rather itself pure light—weightless, floating free, having become—but rather, being—a god.[9]

We can achieve this experience in isolated moments within this life. According to Porphyry, Plotinus was united to God in this way on four occasions during the six years they were friends. However, we always suffer from the hinderance of the body. The good news is that we look to a future state in which this union is permanent and continuous. The goal of Plotinus's philosophy was summed up in his last words as he lay dying, "Try to bring back the god in you to the divine in the All!"[10]

THE SIGNIFICANCE OF NEOPLATONISM

The movement of Neoplatonism continued on more than three and a half centuries after the death of Plotinus. The school in Rome seems to have come under the direction of Porphyry (whose life is dated about A.D. 232–305). Furthermore, there were schools in Syria, Asia Minor, Athens, and Alexandria that followed this philosophy. In Athens, it was introduced into Plato's Academy by Plutarch in the latter half of the fourth century and was carried forward and developed there by his successor Proclus.*

Plotinus never said much about Christianity, although he does criticize the pseudo-Christian Gnostics for suggesting that Plato's grasp of ultimate reality was incomplete. However, his disciple Porphyry and other Neoplatonists were decidedly anti-Christian. Nevertheless, Neoplatonism was attractive to a number of Christian thinkers and became very important in shaping the form that Christianity took in the Middle Ages. Origen (about A.D. 185–254), an early Church theologian, was a student of Plotinus's teacher Ammonius. Following the pattern of Plotinus, Origen arranged the three persons of the Holy Trinity in a hierarchy and suggested that through sin, pre-existent human souls "descended" into bodies.† St. Augustine based his Christian philosophy on Plotinus's interpretation of Plato's philosophy. Augustine said that with only a few changes in their doctrines, the Platonic philosophers such as Plotinus would become Christians. Boethius (A.D. 480–525), a Roman Christian influenced by Neoplatonism, translated one of Porphyry's books on Aristotle into Latin. Around A.D. 500 emerged a work that was claimed to have been written by Dionysius, one of the Apostle Paul's converts. However, it was really written by a Neoplatonist in the sixth century. Because the medieval theologians did not know it was a forgery, it was very influential in introducing Neoplatonic themes into theology and in fueling Christian mysticism. The official presence of Greek philosophy and Neoplatonism in the West came to an end in A.D. 529 when the Christian Emperor Justinian closed all the pagan schools of philosophy in Athens. However, because of the influence of Neoplatonism on Christian thought, a seed was

---

*Plutarch of Athens is not the same person as the famous biographer of the same name who lived in the first century.

†Later, Origen's view of the Trinity was condemned as heretical, for the official position was that the three persons were coequal.

planted that would allow Greek philosophy to remain alive in the West.

Questions for Understanding

1. What were some of the social conditions that influenced the change in philosophy after Aristotle?

2. What were some characteristics the various Hellenistic philosophies held in common?

3. In what ways was the philosophy of the Cynics in ancient Greece similar to or different from the meaning of the word "cynicism" as we use it today?

4. How did the Epicureans account for free will in a materialistic universe?

5. In what ways is the Epicureans' ethical theory based on their metaphysics?

6. What is the difference between psychological hedonism and ethical hedonism?

7. Contrary to popular conceptions, the Epicureans' philosophy did not say we should live a life of unrestrained pleasure. How so?

8. In what ways did the Epicureans distinguish between different sorts of desires? Which desires ought we to pursue?

9. Why did the Epicureans not say much about social philosophy?

10. What was the Epicurean view of religion?

11. Why should we not fear death, according to the Epicureans?

12. In spite of their differences, in what ways were the Epicurean and the Stoic philosophies similar?

13. What differences were there between Epicurean and Stoic metaphysics? How did this lead to differences in their ethics?

14. According to the Stoics, what is the relation between God and nature?

15. How did the Stoics reconcile their view of God with our experience of evil?

16. What did the Stoics mean and what did they not mean when they said that the ideal of life is "apathy"?

17. Since the Stoics preached the value of resignation, why would they prefer health over sickness?

18. What were the Stoics' contributions to social philosophy?

19. Why was Stoicism attractive to the Romans? What contributions did the Roman Stoics make to legal, social, and ethical philosophy?

20. Why were the Skeptics disdainful of both Epicureanism and Stoicism?

21. What were the various forms of Hellenistic Skepticism? How did they differ?

22. What did the Skeptics mean by "suspending judgment"? Why did they believe that this was the key to a happy life?

23. According to Agrippa, what are the five pillars of Skepticism?

24. In what ways is Neoplatonism related to the thought of Plato?

25. What roles do the notions of the One, Intellect, and Soul play in Neoplatonic metaphysics?

26. Why does Plotinus use the sun as his metaphor of what is fundamentally real?

27. How do the Neoplatonists address the problem of evil?

28. What is the "way of ascent" in Plotinus's philosophy?

Questions for Reflection

1. Consider the five philosophies of Cynicism, Epicureanism, Stoicism, Skepticism, and Neoplatonism. For each philosophy in turn, imagine that you were a dedicated follower of that philosophy. How would you approach life differently under each philosophy? How would it affect your career, your relationships, your involvement in society, your conception of yourself and life's meaning?

2. Each of these philosophies claimed to offer practical guidance for life. Which one do you think is most plausible and satisfying?

3. Of all the Greek philosophies, Stoicism was one of the most attractive ones to the early Christians. Why do you suppose this is so?

4. While you may not agree with all the teachings of the various philosophies discussed in this chapter, for each one, list what you consider to be its positive contributions.

5. For each of the five philosophies discussed in this chapter, explain what you believe is its greatest shortcoming.

Notes

1. Quotations from the Epicurean tradition and the Skeptics are taken from *Hellenistic Philosophy: Introductory Readings*, trans. and ed. Brad Inwood and L. P. Gerson (Indianapolis: Hackett, 1988). References are cited in the text using the abbreviation "I&G" and the page numbers of this collection. The abbreviation "LM" is used to indicate quotations from Epicurus's well-anthologized *Letter to Menoeceus*.

2. Quotations from the Stoics that are cited in the text are taken from Greek and Roman Philosophy after Aristotle, ed. Jason L. Saunders (New York: The Free Press, 1966). References to this book use the abbreviation "S" and refer to the page numbers of this anthology.

3. Cleanthes, quoted by Epictetus in *The Enchiridion*, 52, trans. Thomas Wentworth Higginson, in *Epictetus: Discourses and Enchiridion* (Roslyn, NY: The Classics Club, Walter J. Black, 1944), 352.

4. Marcus Aurelius, *Meditations* 9.4, in *The Stoic and Epicurean Philosophers*, ed. Whitney J. Oates (New York: Modern Library, Random House, 1940), 571.

5. Marcus Aurelius, 6.44, in Oates, 533.

6. Bertrand Russell, *A History of Western Philosophy* (New York: Clarion, Simon & Schuster, 1945), 255.

7. Plato, *Timaeus* 29c–d.

8. Quotations from Plotinus's *Enneads* are taken from *Plotinus*, trans. A. H. Armstrong, 7 vols. (Cambridge, MA: Harvard University Press, 1966–1988). This work is referenced in the text using the abbreviation "E." The number following this stands for both the volume number of the translation and the number of the Ennead. The last two numbers refer to the treatise and section numbers of Plotinus's work.

9. Plotinus, *Enneads*, vol. 7, Ennead 6, chap. 9, 8–9.

10. Quoted by Porphyry in *On the Life of Plotinus and the Order of His Books*, 2, in *Plotinus*, vol. 1.

GLOSSARY

This Glossary contains key philosophical terms set in bold type in all four series volumes. The chapter where the term is first introduced, as well as those where it plays a central role, appear in parentheses. "Introduction chapter" refers to the Introduction of the one-volume work.

Aesthetics (or esthetics)—An area of philosophy that pursues questions concerning art, including the nature and role of art, the standards for evaluating art, and the nature of beauty. (Introduction chapter)

Agnosticism—With respect to a particular issue, the claim that nothing can be known, one way or another, because the evidence is thought to be insufficient to provide us with any knowledge. Hence, the agnostic argues that we must suspend judgment on the issue. Typically, agnosticism refers to the position that the existence of God can neither be affirmed nor denied. (Chap. 21)

Altruism—The claim that people either are or ought to be motivated to serve the interests of others. The opposite of **egoism**. (Chap. 24)

Analytic judgment—A knowledge claim expressed by an **analytic statement**. (Chap. 22)

Analytic philosophy—A twentieth-century movement in philosophy, particularly strong in America and Britain, that approaches philosophical problems primarily through an analysis of language. Also called *linguistic philosophy*. (Chap. 32)

Analytic statement—A statement in which the predicate is contained within the subject (its truth is based on the meaning and relationship of its terms) and its denial results in a logical contradiction, e.g., "All mothers are parents." Contrasted with synthetic statements. (Chaps. 22, 32)

Antinomy—A pair of seemingly reasonable conclusions that flatly contradict each other and hence cannot both be true. Kant used antinomies to argue that reason contradicts itself when it reaches beyond its proper limits in attempting to answer traditional metaphysical questions about the nature of reality. (Chap. 22)

A posteriori—A type of knowledge, statement, or concept whose content and truth are derived from experience. For example, "Water freezes at 32°F" is an *a posteriori* truth. Contrasted with **a priori**. (Chaps. 13, 22)

Appearance—The way in which something presents itself to the senses which is different from how it is in reality. For example, a straight stick in water appears to be bent, even though it really is not. (Chaps. 2, 3, 6, 22, 23)

A priori—A type of knowledge, statement, or concept whose content and truth can be known prior to or independently of experience. For example, some philosophers believe that "two plus two equals four" and "every event has a cause" are *a priori* truths which cannot be proven by experience. Contrasted with **a posteriori**. (Chaps. 13, 22)

Argument—An attempt to establish the truth of a statement (the conclusion) by showing that it follows from, or is supported by, the truth of one or more other statements (the premises). (Introduction chapter, Chap. 5)

Atomism—A metaphysical position originating with the ancient Greeks that claims that reality is made up of numerous, indivisible particles of matter moving in a void. (Chap. 2)

Autonomy—Being one's own authority or rule giver, as opposed to being subject to external authority. In Kant's ethics this is an essential condition for rational morality. (Chap. 22)

Categorical imperative—According to Kant, a command that is binding on all rational persons at all times, which generates universal moral laws. It commands us to always act in such a way that we could rationally wish that everyone followed the principle governing that action. Contrasted with hypothetical imperatives, in which the command applies only under certain conditions. (Chap. 22)

Cogent argument—An **inductive argument** that is (a) inductively strong and (b) has all true premises. (Introduction chapter)

Cognition—Knowledge or the act of knowing.

Cognitive meaning—The informative content of a statement that asserts a claim that may be either true or false. The cognitive meaning of a statement is sometimes contrasted with its emotive meaning, or the emotional attitude it expresses or evokes. (Chap. 32)

Coherence theory of truth—The theory that a true assertion or belief is one that coheres with our entire system of interconnected and mutually supporting beliefs. (Chap. 24)

Compatibilism—The theory that human beings are *both* determined and free as long as their actions proceed from their own, inner choices and are not compelled by an external cause. (Chap. 17)

Conceptualism—The claim that **universals** are mental concepts obtained by abstracting the common qualities appearing in similar particular objects. See **Nominalism** and **Realism**. (Chap. 10)

Consequentialism—See **Teleological ethics**.

Contingent—A contingent event is one that is not logically necessary, for whether it occurs or not is dependent on other events. Similarly, a contingent statement is one whose truth is not logically necessary. It may be denied without asserting a contradiction. (Chaps. 12, 13, 16, 17)

Correspondence theory of truth—The theory that a true assertion or belief is one that corresponds with the fact or state of affairs in reality to which it refers. (Chaps. 27, 33)

Cosmological argument—An argument for the existence of God based on the claim that the universe requires a cause for its existence. (Chap. 11)

Deduction—The form of reasoning we use when we attempt to argue from the truth of one proposition or set of propositions to a conclusion that necessarily follows from those propositions. (Introduction chapter)

Deductively valid—See **Valid**.

Deism—A religious outlook, based on reason, that acknowledges the existence of God and his creation of the world, but denies that God intervenes in the world either in the form of miracles or revelation. Deists argue that the divinely ordered natural laws and reason make both nature and humanity self-sufficient. (Chap. 19)

Deontological ethics—From the Greek word *deon*, meaning "duty" or "obligation." Deontological ethics defines the moral rightness or wrongness of an act in terms of the intrinsic value of the act. According to this theory, our duty to perform an action (or to refrain from doing it) is based on the nature of the act itself and not on its consequences. Kant was a leading proponent of this theory. Contrasted with **teleological ethics**. (Chap. 22)

Determinism—The metaphysical position that claims every event (including human actions) follows necessarily from previous events. (Chaps. 14, 17, 30)

Dialectic—(1) For Socrates, a conversational method for progressing toward the truth, by continually examining proposed answers to a question, repeatedly replacing inadequate answers with more refined and adequate ones. (2) For Plato, it was the philosophical method of rising above particulars and hypotheses to achieve the highest form of knowledge. (3) For Hegel, it is a historical process in which both thought and reality develop as oppositions and tensions are resolved at a higher stage. (4) Marx adopted Hegel's historical dialectic, but changed it into the conflict and development of material forces. (Chaps. 3, 4, 24, 25)

Dogmatism—Asserting a position without providing adequate reasons for its truth.

Dualism—A theory that asserts that there are two irreducible realities, such as mind and body, spirit and matter, or good and evil. (Chaps. 2, 4, 15)

Egoism—(1) Psychological egoism is a descriptive theory that claims people always pursue what they perceive to be their own best interests. (2) Ethical egoism is a prescriptive theory that claims people *ought* to always act according to their own best interests. The opposite of **altruism**. (3) In both of the preceding types of egoism, egoistic **hedonism** identifies pleasure with one's best interests. (Chaps. 6, 14, 27, 28)

Empirical—Related to sense experience.

Empiricism—The theory that knowledge is obtained solely from sense experience. (Chaps. 2, 13, 19, 20, 21, 28, 32)

Epicureanism—A version of **hedonism**, based on the philosophy of Epicurus (341–271 B.C.), which claims that (1) only pleasure is intrinsically good and (2) all pleasures are not to be desired equally, the more prudent and sedate pleasures being the ones that lead to true happiness. (Chap. 6)

Epistemology—An area of philosophy that pursues questions concerning truth and knowledge. (Introduction chapter)

Essence—The defining characteristic of something. That property or set of properties without which it would not be the sort of thing that it is. (Chaps. 5, 11)

Ethical egoism—See **Egoism**.

Ethical hedonism—See **Hedonism**.

Ethics—An area of philosophy that reasons about morality, particularly the meaning and justification of claims concerning right or wrong actions, obligation, moral rules, rights, virtue, the good life, and the possibility of objective morality. (Introduction chapter)

Existentialism—A nineteenth- and twentieth-century philosophy that focuses on the nature and meaning of human existence as understood from the subjective standpoint of the subject. Repudiating the notion of a fixed human nature, existentialists claim that we are continually creating the self. They stress the priority of subjective choosing over objective reasoning, concrete experience over intellectual abstractions, individuality over mass culture, human freedom over determinism, and authentic living over inauthenticity. (Chaps. 23, 26, 27, 29, 33)

Feminism—A movement within philosophy and other disciplines that (1) stresses the role of gender in shaping the patterns of thought, society, and history, (2) focuses on the ways in which women have been assigned roles throughout history that excluded them from the intellectual and political realms, and (3) strives to produce a society that recognizes women and men as both different and equal. (Chap. 34)

Forms—According to Plato, the Forms are the ultimate realities and objects of genuine knowledge. Forms are nonphysical, eternal, known only through reason, and impart intelligibility and reality to things in the physical world that imitate them. For example, Plato believes all circular things (rings, hoops, wreathes) are imperfect representations of the Form of Circularity. (Chap. 4)

Hedonism—The position that claims pleasure is the only thing that has intrinsic value. (1) Psychological hedonism claims that it is a psychological fact that people always strive to pursue pleasure and avoid pain. (2) Ethical hedonism claims that pleasure is what people *ought* to pursue. (Chaps. 2, 6, 14, 28)

Historicism—The theory that everything human is affected by the processes of history, such that any idea cannot be understood apart from its historical context and is valid only for a particular time, place, and community. (Chaps. 23, 24)

Idea—(1) In general, any object of thought. (2) For Plato, Ideas were another term for the **Forms** (e.g., the Idea of Justice, the Idea of Circularity). (3) For Descartes and Locke an idea was any mental content, which could include sensations (redness, sweetness, heat) or the mind's mental states (doubting, imagining, believing). (4) For Berkeley, ideas and the minds that contained them were the whole of reality. (5) For Hume, an idea was a copy of an original sensation (called an *impression*) that was recalled in memory or the imagination. (Chaps. 4, 15, 19, 20, 22)

Idealism—The theory that reality is ultimately mental or of the nature of a mind. Idealism characterizes the philosophies of Leibniz, Berkeley, and Hegel. Contrasted with **materialism** and contemporary forms of **realism**. (Chaps. 17, 20, 23, 24)

Indeterminism—The theory that some events in the world (particularly human choices) are not the necessary result of previous causes, because these events are either random or the products of free will. (Chap. 30)

Induction—The form of reasoning we use when we argue from what is true of one set of facts to what is probably true of further facts of the same kind. An inductive argument either concludes something about a new case, based on what was true of similar cases, or it arrives at a generalization concerning all cases similar to those that have been observed. (Introduction chapter, Chap. 21)

Inductively strong argument—A successful inductive argument in which the premises, if true, would make the conclusion highly probable. (Introduction chapter)

Innate ideas or knowledge—Mental contents that are inborn or part of the natural content of the human mind and not derived from experience. Their existence is defended by most rationalists and attacked by empiricists. (Chaps. 3, 4, 15, 17, 19)

Intellectualism—The theory that the intellect is prior to or superior to the will. Accordingly, it is claimed that the intellect or reason perceives that certain ends or goals are desirable and then directs the will to achieve them. Theological intellectualism claims that God's intellect first knows that certain actions are either intrinsically good or evil and then he wills that they should be done or avoided. The opposite of **voluntarism**. (Chap. 10)

Intuition—(1) Knowledge that is directly and immediately known by the mind, rather than being the product of reasoning or inference; or (2) the object of such knowledge. According to Kant, humans can have only sensory intuitions. (Chap. 22, 31)

Linguistic philosophy—See **Analytic philosophy**.

Logical atomism—The philosophy of Russell and the early Wittgenstein, which claimed that the structure of language and reality are the same, since language is reducible to elementary units corresponding to the fundamental units that compose the world of facts. (Chap. 32)

Logical positivism—A twentieth-century version of **empiricism** and a version of **analytic philosophy**, which states that (1) logical and mathematical statements are logically necessary statements (**tautologies**) that do not provide information about the world and (2) factual statements are meaningful only if they are capable of being verified in sense experience (**verifiability principle**). (Chap. 32)

Logos—A particularly rich Greek term that has a large number of related meanings: speech, discourse, word, explanation, reason, order. It is the source of many English words such as "logic," "logo," "biology," "psychology." Heraclitus believed that *logos* was the rational principle that permeated all things. The Stoics identified it with God, Providence, Nature, or Fate. Christian writers identified it with God or Christ. (Chaps. 2, 6, 7)

Marxism—The philosophy based on the writings of Karl Marx, which asserts that (1) reality is material, (2) history follows a dialectical pattern controlled by economic forces, (3) each era of history is characterized by conflict between opposing economic classes, (4) history is a **dialectic** in which each economic stage produces its own contradictions, giving way to its successor, and (5) the present stage of capitalism will be overcome by socialism, leading to the final stage of pure communism in which class conflict will be abolished. (Chap. 25)

Materialism—The metaphysical position that claims matter is the only reality. Also called *material monism*. (Chaps. 2, 14, 25)

Material monism—See **Materialism**.

Metaphysical dualism—See **Dualism**.

Metaphysics—An area of philosophy that pursues questions about the nature of reality. (Introduction chapter)

Monism—Any metaphysical position that asserts that there is only one kind of reality. **Materialism** claims that matter is the only reality, while **idealism** claims that it is mental. (Chap. 2)

Monotheism—The belief that there is only one God.

Moral relativism—See **Relativism**.

Naive realism—The belief that the properties we perceive objects to have are the properties that they really do have in the external world. (Chap. 20)

Naturalism—The metaphysical position that claims that physical nature encompasses everything that is real and that all of reality can be completely explained by the natural sciences. (Chap. 33)

Naturalistic fallacy—The fallacy of attempting to derive ethical claims (what we ought to do) from factual claims (what is the case). (Chap. 32)

Natural law—In ethics, the claim that there is an objective moral law, transcending human conventions, which may be discerned by examining human nature. (Chaps. 3, 6, 10, 11)

Natural theology—A discipline within philosophy that attempts to prove conclusions about God based on our natural reason and experience without appealing to revelation. (Chap. 11)

Nihilism—From the Latin word for nothing; the belief that there is no knowledge or truth and, particularly, that nothing has any genuine value, meaning, or purpose. (Chap. 27)

Nominalism—The claim that there are no real, independently existing **universals** and that uni-

versal terms refer only to collections of particular things. See **Conceptualism**, **Realism**. (Chaps. 10, 12, 14, 20)

Noumena—Things as they really are in themselves, as opposed to how they appear in experience. Kant claimed that the noumena were unknowable. They are the opposite of **appearances** or **phenomena**. (Chaps. 22, 23)

Occasionalism—The claim that there is no causal relationship between mental events and physical events, but that certain mental events always seem to occur simultaneously with certain physical events only because the occurrence of one is the occasion on which God produces the other. (Chap. 15)

Ockham's razor—The principle that our explanations should always be as simple as possible, avoiding the postulation of unnecessary entities. Named after William of Ockham (c. 1270–1350), whose formulation of this principle was very influential, particularly in scientific methodology. (Chap. 12)

Ontological argument—An argument for the existence of God based on the concept of God's perfection and unsurpassable greatness. The argument was defended by Anselm, Descartes, Spinoza, and Leibniz and attacked by Kant, among others. (Chaps. 10, 15, 16, 22)

Ontology—The study of the generic features of being, as opposed to the study of the particular things that exist. Ontology is concerned with questions such as "What is most fundamentally real?" "What does it mean to exist?" and "What is the structure of reality?" Some writers virtually identify ontology and **metaphysics**, while others view it as a subdivision of metaphysics. Other philosophers, such as Heidegger and Sartre, distinguish their ontology from metaphysics in order to avoid the latter's association with questions about God, substance, and the origin of the universe. (Chap. 33)

Panentheism—The belief that God's being includes that of the world but is not limited to it. (Chap. 31)

Panpsychism—A form of **idealism** that maintains that all of reality consists of multiple centers of experience, such as minds or souls, who have various degrees of awareness. Leibniz called them "monads," and Whitehead referred to them as "actual occasions." (Chaps. 17, 31)

Pantheism—The belief that God and the world are identical. (Chap. 16)

Parallelism—The claim that there is no direct causal relationship between mental and physical events, but that the two series run parallel to each other. Essentially the same as Leibniz's **pre-established harmony** doctrine. (Chap. 15)

Phenomena—Things as they appear within experience, in contrast to how they are in reality. Kant said that this is all that we could know about the world. They are the opposite of **noumena**. (Chaps. 22, 23)

Phenomenalism—The doctrine that all statements about material objects can be completely analyzed into statements about sense data without making reference to any reality external to sensation. This position is the contrary of **representative realism**. (Chap. 20)

Phenomenology—The attempt to describe the structure and contents of consciousness in a way that is free of presuppositions and that does not go beyond what appears to consciousness. Versions were set out by Hegel, Husserl, and Heidegger. (Chaps. 24, 33)

Pluralism—The metaphysical position that claims that there are many kinds of reality. (Chap. 2)

Positivism—The view that all knowledge claims must be limited to observable facts, that only science provides genuine knowledge, and that the role of philosophy is to apply the findings of the sciences to problems of human conduct and social organization. Positivism rejects all metaphysical claims and any inquiry not reducible to scientific method. Advocated by Auguste Comte and John Stuart Mill. The movement was a predecessor of **logical positivism**. (Chap. 28)

Postmodernism—A movement that arose in the late twentieth century, that was influenced by Nietzsche and Heidegger and that embraces **relativism** and **historicism**. Postmodernists seek to unmask what they consider to be the pretensions of reason and the illusions of metaphysics. They repudiate the Enlightenment ideal of seeking for objective, rational truth and they replace the no-tion of one, true picture of reality with that of multiple, ongoing interpretations. Postmodernism has been particularly influential in literary studies. (Chap. 34)

Pragmatism—A philosophy that stresses the intimate relationship between thought and action. Pragmatists claim, for example, that the meaning of a concept is identical to the practical effects of the object of our conception. Likewise, a true belief is defined as one that will effectively guide action in the long run. (Chap. 30)

Pre-established harmony—The doctrine that events in the world, particularly the activities of the mind and body, do not causally interact, but have been arranged by God from the beginning of time to work in unison like two independent clocks that keep the same time. Leibniz was its most important proponent. (Chap. 17)

Primary qualities—Those qualities of an object that may be represented mathematically such as size, shape, number, quantity, motion, and location. According to Galileo and the early modern philosophers, such as Descartes and Locke, primary qualities represent the world as it really is. Contrasted with **secondary qualities**. (Chaps. 13, 15, 19)

Psychological egoism—See **Egoism**.

Psychological hedonism—See **Hedonism**.

Rationalism—The theory that at least some knowledge is obtained by the mind independently of experience. (Chaps. 2, 4, 13, 15, 16, 17)

Realism—(1) In its contemporary usage, the thesis that reality exists independently of our consciousness of it, in contrast to **idealism**. (2) In ancient and medieval thought: (a) Platonic or extreme realism refers to the claim that **universals** have an objective, independent existence apart from the minds that know them or the individuals that exemplify them; (b) moderate realism claims that universals are abstracted by the mind from objective features of individuals, but that they do not have any reality apart from minds or individuals. (This is sometimes called Aristotelian realism or equated with **conceptualism**.) All medieval versions of realism are in opposition to **nominalism**. (Chap. 10, 32)

Relativism—(1) In epistemology, the claim that there is no absolute knowledge, because different individuals, cultures, or historical periods have different opinions on the truth and all opinions are equally valid. (2) Likewise, in ethics, the claim that there are no objective moral truths, for all moral judgments are said to be relative to the knowing subject and equally correct. (Chaps. 3, 4)

Representative realism—The epistemological claim that the mind is directly acquainted only with its own ideas, but that these ideas are caused by and represent objects external to the mind. (Chap. 19)

Scholasticism—The dominant philosophy of the medieval period in which logic was used to demonstrate the harmony of philosophy and the authoritative writings of the religious tradition. (Chap. 10)

Secondary qualities—According to the early modern philosophers, these are the subjective sensations (colors, tastes, odors, sounds, temperature) produced within us by the **primary qualities** of an object. (Chaps. 13, 15, 19)

Sense data—A term used to refer to the particular, individual impressions received in sensation, such as particular colors, tastes, sounds, odors, and textures. Reference to sense data need not presuppose anything about their cause. (Chap. 32)

Skepticism—The claim that it is impossible to know anything to be absolutely true. (Chaps. 2, 3, 6, 21)

Social contract theory—The theory that the justification of government is based on an explicit or implicit agreement made by individuals among themselves or with a sovereign power (Hobbes, Locke, and Rousseau). (Chaps. 3, 14, 19)

Solipsism—The view that nothing can be known apart from my self and the contents of my conscious experience, usually leading to the conclusion that "only I exist." Finding solipsism to be implausible, philosophers such as Descartes were motivated to find demonstrations of the external world or other minds. (Chaps. 15, 20)

Sophists—A group of educators in fifth-century Athens who taught the skills of rhetoric and argumentation, usually to prepare people for political careers. Most of the Sophists were advocates of **skepticism** and **relativism**. (Chap. 3)

Sound argument—A deductive argument that is (1) **valid** and (2) has all true premises. (Introduction chapter)

Stoicism—The view that we will find happiness only if we resign ourselves to accept whatever may happen in life. Historically, this view was based on the belief that the universe is fulfilling the benevolent purposes of divine providence and that every event is inevitable. (Chap. 6)

Substance—A fundamental and independently existing reality that supports or underlies the various qualities or properties we perceive. Various philosophers who believe in substances disagree over how many kinds there are and what sorts of things qualify as substances. The concept was particularly important in the philosophies of the Pre-Socratics, Aristotle, Descartes, Spinoza, Leibniz, and Locke. (Chaps. 2, 5, 15, 16, 17, 19, 21, 22)

Synthetic judgment—A knowledge claim expressed by a **synthetic statement**. (Chap. 22)

Synthetic statement—A statement in which the predicate adds information to the subject that is not logically contained within it and in which its denial (even if false) does not result in a logical contradiction, e.g., "All mothers are under fifty feet tall" is a synthetic statement. Contrasted with **analytic statements**. (Chap. 22)

Tautology—A statement that is true because of its logical form; e.g., "X is identical to X." (Chap. 32)

Teleological argument—An argument for the existence of God based on the evidence of purpose and design in the world; e.g., Aquinas's fifth argument for God. (Chap. 11)

Teleological ethics—Any ethical theory that defines moral rightness or wrongness in terms of the desirability or undesirability of an action's consequences. Contrasted with **deontological ethics**. (Chaps. 11, 22, 28)

Teleological explanation—An explanation of an event or thing in terms of the end, goal, or purpose it tends to achieve. (Chaps. 4, 13)

Teleology (or teleological)—From the Greek word *telos*, meaning "purpose" or "end." A teleological metaphysics claims that nature exhibits purpose; i.e., events in the world are directed to the fulfillment of some goal. (Chaps. 4, 5, 11)

Theism—The belief that there is one God, who transcends the world.

Things-in-themselves—According to Kant, the contents of reality as they are, independent of the mind's apprehension of them. Identical to the **noumena**. (Chap. 22)

Transcendental—Refers to conditions within the knower which makes knowledge or action possible. Kant's critical philosophy tried to set out the transcendental conditions that enable us to be knowers and agents. (Chap. 22)

Universal—(1) Any general term or concept that refers to a number of particular things that are members of the same group; e.g., "human" is a universal that applies to each member of the human race. Since the time of Plato, there has been a controversy as to whether universals exist in reality, or whether they are mere concepts or words. See **Conceptualism**, **Nominalism**, and **Realism**. (Chap. 4, 10) (2) As an adjective, it designates that which applies to all persons, at all times, in all circumstances, e.g., universal truths, universal moral rules. (Chap. 4, 22)

Utilitarianism—A theory of ethics and a political philosophy built around the claim that a good action is one that creates the greatest amount of good for the greatest number over any other alternative action. (Chap. 28)

Valid argument—A successful deductive argument whose form is such that if the premises are true, the conclusion necessarily must be true. (Introduction chapter)

Verifiability principle—The criterion of meaning developed by the **logical positivists** stating that (1) a factual statement has **cognitive meaning** only if sense experience can provide evidence of its truth and (2) the experiences that would demonstrate its truth are identical to its meaning. (Chap. 32, 34)

Voluntarism—The theory that the will is prior to or superior to the intellect or reason. Accordingly, reason is viewed as merely an instrument for achieving the ends or goals that the will voluntarily chooses. Theological voluntarism claims that God declares an action to be morally good or evil solely on the basis of his free choice, for he is not compelled to do so because of any intrinsic property in the action itself. The opposite of **intellectualism**. (Chap. 10, 12)

INDEX